Sarah Harman is a PhD candidate at Brunel University's Screen Media Research Centre and has presented papers at international multidisciplinary conferences on the subject of femininity and film. She is assistant editor of *Intensities: The Journal of Cult Media*, and contributing co-editor of a special issue of the journal *Sexualities* on *Fifty Shades of Grey*. Her research interests include feminism, gender, adaptations, film, television and pornography.

Wickham Clayton is an independent scholar, having earned his PhD in Film and TV Studies at Roehampton University. His thesis focuses on formalism and the aesthetic rendering of perspective in the *Friday the 13th* film franchise. Wickham's ongoing research involves formalist analyses of a wide range of film texts, recently focusing on adaptations and authorship. He has been a Film Studies tutor and lecturer in both the USA and the UK for over a decade, is a published film critic, and has given presentations to the public with the aim of raising public awareness of Film Studies.

screening
TWILIGHT

Critical Approaches to a Cinematic Phenomenon

EDITED BY

Wickham Clayton and Sarah Harman

I.B. TAURIS

LONDON · NEW YORK

Published in 2014 by I.B.Tauris & Co. Ltd
6 Salem Road, London W2 4BU
175 Fifth Avenue, New York NY 10010
www.ibtauris.com

Distributed in the United States and Canada
Exclusively by Palgrave Macmillan
175 Fifth Avenue, New York NY 10010

The right of Wickham Clayton and Sarah Harman to be identified as the editors of this work has been asserted by them in accordance with the Copyright, Designs and Patents Act 1988.

ISBN: 978 1 78076 665 2 (HB)
         978 1 78076 666 9 (PB)
eISBN: 978 0 85772 360 4

A full CIP record for this book is available from the British Library
A full CIP record is available from the Library of Congress

Library of Congress catalog card: available

Printed and bound in Great Britain by T. J. International, Padstow, Cornwall.

Wickham would like to dedicate this book to his son, who, as he writes this, continues to grow at an alarming rate...

CONTENTS

ACKNOWLEDGEMENTS

The editors wish to thank the following people:

Milly Williamson, Leon Hunt, Stacey Abbott, Deborah Mutch, Mariah Larsson, Ann Steiner, Johnny Walker, Laura Mee, Ian Conrich, Rob Dew, Ken Gelder, Nina Auerbach, Lorna Jowett, Philippa Brewster, Clarissa Smith, Dan Taylor, Kerry Underhill, Steve Duckworth, Alex Dymock, Lisa Downing, Paul Sutton, Michael Chanan, Todd Berliner, Michael Ahmed, Gareth James, all of our contributors and anyone else we may have neglectfully omitted. It would also be remiss not to thank Stephenie Meyer, Summit/Lionsgate and everyone involved in bringing *The Twilight Saga* to our (perhaps reluctant) screens.

FOREWORD

Natalie Wilson

Author of *Seduced by Twilight:*
The Allure and Contradictory Messages of the Popular Saga

Much like the hard-won battle to justify cultural studies in the academy, let alone university courses focusing on popular culture, the analysis of *Twilight*, whether by fans or academics, has been mocked as lightweight, frivolous and unimportant. Mocked, in short, in the same way females and femininity have historically been mocked. Indeed, the criticism of the saga and surrounding franchise often relies on the same sort of gendered lens that not only constructs females as rabid, hysterical consumers, but also as silly fangirls.[1] Yet, like its pulpy romance predecessors, the *Twilight* franchise is being taken seriously by various academics, resulting in a growing field of what I like to call Twi-scholarship. Just as Janice Radway's *Reading the Romance* and Angela McRobbie's *Feminism and Youth Culture* helped to solidify the notion that academics need to take the popular seriously, so too are emerging monographs and collections justifying scholarly attention to *Twilight*.

As this scholarship reveals, much like the *Harry Potter* scholarship that preceded it, just because something is popular does not mean it is undeserving of critical, serious intention. Indeed, popularity is a reason to take a cultural phenomenon seriously, although it is still often used as an excuse for dismissal. This dismissive attitude towards the popular seems all the more likely when a cultural phenomenon is coded as 'feminine' – whether due to content or to fan-base. We need look no further than the varying reactions to *The Hunger Games* versus *Twilight* as example. As with the *Harry Potter* franchise, *The Hunger Games* was coded as a 'cross-gender' saga, appealing to male and female alike. *Twilight*, on the other hand, has been widely interpreted as a female cultural trend. As such, it has been attacked in much the same way as other supposedly 'female-only' genres like 'chick flicks', Harlequin romance and soap operas. This has been true not only of the books, but also of the films, perhaps even more so.

This surely partly explains the attempts to make the movie adaptations appeal to a wider audience – especially after the first film, directed by Catherine Hardwicke, received much ribbing despite its commercial success. Subsequent adaptations tried to 'gender neutralise' the saga via focusing more on action, special effects and derring-do, and, I would say non-coincidentally, all employed male rather than female directors. The present study focuses in particular on this transformation of the saga from page to screen, analysing issues such as audience reception and expectation, mainstream criticism and responses, the generic film traditions of horror, romance and the supernatural, and *Twilight*'s place within the vampire film canon.

The regular derision of the films, the chapters herein argue, must be examined not only via cultural studies, feminist analysis and film theory, but also with attention to genre and generic conventions, race studies, queer theory and psychoanalysis. Offering rigorous analytical dissection of the films, the essays that follow extend the existing work on *Twilight*, focusing on the franchise's creation of a film phenomenon that has, thus far, raked in over a billion dollars. This focus adds to existing work on the saga, most of which features analysis of the books and surrounding fandom rather than the film adaptations. Asking what the films leave out, what they add, what they assume about their audiences, and how they depict and question gender, sexuality, class, race, identity formation and so on, the following interrogations reveal that all of us, academics or not, can benefit from critically engaging with these highly popular yet often maligned films.

Not only does the collection prompt consideration of film versus book, but also of how film as a medium incites different reactions and experiences, different opportunities for fan engagement, and different prospects for adapting and re-visioning the saga. Viewing and 'reading' a film, this collection reminds us, is a much different experience to reading and analysing a book. While books draw us in through words alone, films rely on framing, depth of focus, scene design, camera angle and movement. Part of entering the cinema, or even popping in a DVD, is agreeing to enter into a visual text where, unlike with reading, the images, the sound, even the emotions, are largely chosen for us. In short, films are less open to interpretation than books as they are not 'adapted' in our mind's eye, but via screenwriters, producers, directors and so on. This is not to say that films do not allow for varied and multiple readings, but they do indeed leave less up to the viewer – from how the character looks to what facial expression she/he displays in a given scene. The larger-than-life images, the special effects and the emotionally tugging scores seem more able to sub-consciously affect us as viewers, to draw us in and to semi-mute the more conscious, analytical part of our brains (buttered popcorn surely helps with this too). Additionally, film's ability to create very real-seeming worlds results in a suspension of disbelief wherein we often accept, rather than question, the vari-ous identity constructions films offer. This is not to say that film viewers auto-matically agree with the underlying ideological constructs of any given movie, but films – more so than literary texts – ask us to accept a particular version of whatever story they tell.

As a medium, film tends not to highlight its fictionality (as literary texts, through metafiction, intertextuality and other devices often do). Instead, films present their created worlds in as 'real' a way as possible. Yet, as bell hooks argues in *Reel to Real*, 'Giving audiences what is real is precisely what movies do not do.'[2] Instead, they 'give the reimagined, reinvented version of the real'.[3] However, as films also allow for a closer, more vivid, and multi-sensory proxim-ity to the text, viewers are lured to 'submit' to the filmic text. Often inciting deep loyalty, the emotional responses evoked by film are more immediate and transient, and thus also often less analysed, both by viewers and by critics. As hooks characterises it, movies provide a shared experience that requires a certain amount of submission. She writes, 'It is that moment of submission, of overt or covert seduction that fascinates me as a critic.'[4] I find her use of the term 'seduction' here fascinating, not least as it is one of the concepts I chose to frame my own monograph, *Seduced by Twilight*, around. The suggestion that texts actively seduce us is a fascinating one, begging questions of how and why they do so, how willing and compliant we are in such seductions, and if and to what extent we can resist, reframe or re-envision the seducing power of texts.

The chapters that follow examine these and many other questions, speaking in particular to hooks' notion that 'Movies remain the perfect vehicle for the introduction of certain ritual rites of passage that come to stand for the quintes-sential experience of border crossing'.[5] Such 'border crossing' allows for, as the following articles intimate, crossing over not only into different worlds, but also for crossing of generic conventions, of gender and sexuality norms, of the lines between film, fiction, fan fiction and slash. Our identities and ideas about the world, especially in our film-saturated society, are certainly profoundly shaped and constructed through watching films. When a film saga is viewed multiple times, or when the experience is heightened by breathlessly awaited, sold-out midnight premieres, star-studded events, author/celebrity prize give-aways and 'making-of' books, movies are even more likely to imprint ideas and expectations about the world on viewers. What imprints is the *Twilight* saga leaving on viewers? How is it 'border crossing' into culture, shape-shifting into other texts and cultural phenomena?

As Constance Penley notes in *Feminism and Film Theory*, 'contemporary film theory ... has been notable for an anti-establishment iconoclasm and theoretical force.'[6] The works herein are no exception. While some of them expand upon existing *Twilight* criticism, such as analysing the fairytale framework of the saga, interrogating the Gothic elements of the narrative, and reading the series through psychoanalytic, post-colonial and/or feminist frameworks, all of the chapters offer original, thought-provoking and lucid arguments that open up the field of *Twilight* scholarship, particularly in relation to its filmic iterations.[7] The timing of a movie-based focus is particularly relevant given that the 'stars' of *Twilight* continue to be featured on the big screen, as in Kristen Stewart's lead in *Snow White and the Huntsman* (2012; dir. Rupert Sanders), Robert Pattinson's starring role as a debonair lover in *Bel Ami* (2012; dir. Nick Ormerod), and Taylor Lautner's action-packed roles in *Tracers* (2014; dir. Daniel Benmayor) and *Abduction* (2011; dir. John Singleton). The career trajectories of these three actors, none of them 'big stars' before *Twilight*, will tell us much about the staying power not only of the actors themselves, but also of fans' dedication to these 'real-life' versions of Bella, Edward and Jacob. *Snow White and the Huntsman* seemed to deliberately beckon *Twilight* fans via its depiction of Kristen Stewart as a Snow White/Bella hybrid complete with cliff-jumping and lip-chewing. Meanwhile, *Fifty Shades of Grey*, which started as *Twilight*-inspired fanfic, is now dominating bestseller lists and already has a lucrative multi-film deal.

For how long and to what extent the *Twilight* phenomenon will 'border cross' over into other books, films and fan events is anyone's guess. However, if the chapters that follow are any indication, this sparkly-vampire cultural zeitgeist will live on long after the midnight premiere of the fifth and final film instalment – and not only in the hearts of fans, but also in the pages of academic collections such as this one.

Notes

1. See, for example, Melissa A. Click, *'Rabid', 'Obsessed', and 'Frenzied': Understanding Twilight Fangirls and the Gendered Politics of Fandom*, FlowTV, Department of Radio, Television, and Film at the University of Texas at Austin, December 2009, http://flowtv.

org/2009/12/rabid-obsessed-and-frenzied-understanding-twilight-fangirls-and-the-gendered-politics-of-fandom-melissa-click-university-of-missouri/ (accessed 11 August 2010).

2. bell hooks, *Reel to Real: Race, Sex, and Class at the Movies* (Routledge: New York, 1996), p. 1.

3. Ibid.

4. Ibid., p. 3.

5. Ibid., p. 2.

6. Constance Penley, *Feminism and Film Theory* (Routledge: New York, 1988), p. 3.

7. For collections and monographs that offer such readings, see: Giselle Liza Anatol (ed.), *Bringing Light to Twilight: Perspectives on a Pop Culture Phenomenon* (Basingstoke: Palgrave Macmillan, 2011); Natalie Wilson and Maggie Parke (eds), *Theorizing Twilight: Critical Essays on What's at Stake in a Post-Vampire World* (Jefferson, NC: McFarland & Co., 2011); Melissa A. Click, Jennifer Stevens Aubrey and Elizabeth Behm-Morawitz (eds), *Bitten by Twilight: Youth Culture, Media and the Vampire Franchise* (New York: Peter Lang, 2010); Rebecca Housel and J. Jeremy Wisnewski (eds), *Twilight and Philosophy: Vampires, Vegetarians, and the Pursuit of Immortality* (New Jersey: John Wiley & Sons, 2009); Nancy Ruth Reagin, *Twilight and History* (New Jersey: John Wiley & Sons, 2010); Amy M. Clarke and Marijane Osborn, *The Twilight Mystique: Critical Essays on the Novels and Films* (Jefferson, NC: McFarland & Co., 2010); Natalie Wilson, *Seduced by Twilight: The Allure and Contradictory Messages of the Popular Saga* (Jefferson, NC: McFarland & Co., 2011); and Tanya Erzen, *Fanpire: The Twilight Saga and the Women Who Love It* (Boston: Beacon Press, 2012).

INTRODUCTION

Whether you love it or hate it, *The Twilight Saga* is a billion-dollar (and count-ing) cinematic phenomenon. Yet the film series is often criticised, derided and dismissed, even within academic circles as well as in the press. This reception – not unlike that seemingly experienced by fans – reveals that an examination of the films in their cultural, generic, socio-political and cine-historic position-ing is key to understanding their importance; and attempting to unpack what might lie at the root of their dismissal by oppositional film fans and academics alike. Whatever the case may be, the success of the franchise, and the resulting cultural phenomenon, makes it not only a fruitful topic for discussion, but such an examination is imperative to the understanding of contemporary society.

Neither is *The Twilight Saga* self-contained within the industry. Its tre-mendous success has seen the cultural adoption, and hence filmic production/adaptation and even success of similar properties. Considering the extremely recent success of *The Hunger Games* (2012, dir. Gary Ross), which earned $152.5 million in the US alone on its initial budget of $78 million,[1] and the current well-publicised plans to adapt *Twilight* fan-fic novel *Fifty Shades of Grey* (2011) into a film, the potency of *The Twilight Saga*'s success is palpable. While it would be crass to link all of these franchises to literary female-targeted sources, particularly as *The Hunger Games* (2008) and its two sequel novels (*Catching Fire* (2009) and *Mockingjay* (2010)) contain, seemingly intentionally, elements that attempt to appeal to readers of a wide range of gender identities, it is difficult to ignore the similarities of appeal to a primarily female demographic, often female young adults, from the position of an industrial consumer-driven mar-keting sensibility. The interest in these texts, including the continued success of *The Twilight Saga*[2], demonstrates that the franchise has influenced, and con-tinues to influence, high-profile mainstream major-studio filmmaking invest-ments and schedules, making an examination into *Twilight* a significant and timely endeavour.

The aim of this book, then, is to give *Twilight* the rightful academic attention and consideration that *The Twilight Saga*, as a body of artistic works (regardless of evaluative considerations of 'good' or 'bad'), a product for consumption
and a cultural artefact, demands. In doing so, these collected chapters seek not
necessarily to celebrate or justify the saga as *objet d'art*, as might be expected,
but instead offer up these film texts as worthy of academic critique. We wish
to redress the imbalance of recent cinematic studies favouring obscure cult
oddities and question: what is it that makes these films so successful; can they
really be 'devoid of worth' and yet so popular; can we rethink the films as being
more than simply straight-to-screen adaptations of Stephenie Meyer's 'vision';
and how might they reinforce, or perhaps challenge dominant ideologies, genre
conventions and notions of 'the fan', particularly when reread by a viewer with
his or her own vision?

This collection approaches *The Twilight Saga* from a wide range of method-
ologies in order to give a comprehensive understanding of this cultural phenomenon. Utilising relevant research of vampire film trends by writers such
as Stacey Abbott, Melissa Click, Ken Gelder and Milly Williamson aids the
understanding of *The Twilight Saga*'s context and contribution within this sub-
generic tradition. Work on fandom and reception by researchers such as Matt
Hills, Brigid Cherry and Sarah Thornton contribute an understanding of the
cultural practices built around the viewing of these films. Theorists on film
aesthetics and genre such as Todd Berliner, Mikel Koven, Alain Silver and
James Ursini contribute an understanding of how these films work in terms of
narrative and form and function, as well as creating and playing upon viewer
expectation. By building upon work on socio-political and psychoanalytic theory, such as work by Sheila Jeffreys, Tison Pugh, Shannon Sullivan and Robin
Wood, our contributors explain the films within the cultural context in which
they appear. This is just a small sample of the work that the writers in this collection draw upon to create an understanding of *The Twilight Saga*'s significance
within cinema and society.

These are the questions that lead us to explore why these films have elicited
such vehement responses, both positive and negative, and as a result, help us to
understand the social, cultural and artistic structures that strike such a powerful chord with both audiences and critics alike.

Our first section, *Mute Monsters and Vocal {Fan/} Critics: Genre and Reception*,
addresses this criticism of *The Twilight Saga*, ranging from individual responses
found both on amateur and professional websites and within ourselves, to the
critical reception in mainstream publications, including the press. In the first
chapter, 'Guilty Pleasures: *Twilight,* Snark and Ironic Fandom,' Francesca Haig

'outs' herself as a *Twilight* fan and explores the uncomfortable relationship she holds with this position. 'A colleague and I arranged to see the newly released film *The Twilight Saga: Eclipse* (2010, dir. David Slade) [and] we referred to this as "the excursion of shame",' she writes, later recounting her lending of a book copy to a student, who insisted it be left inside a brown paper bag so that no one else would know. Haig goes on to explore this unique tendency in audience reception and criticism, observing the implications of the avid consumption of these texts by viewers who concurrently deride the quality and merit of the films. Mark Jancovich contributes the following chapter, ' "Cue the Shrieking Virgins?": The Critical Reception of *The Twilight Saga*', analysing critics' derision of the series, exposing a simultaneous trend of demonising the texts and viewers that enjoy them. Through generalised assumptions, from gendered to sexualised, Jancovich adeptly explicates the discourses which aim to marginalise the films and their fans. By addressing this area of criticism, Jancovich recognises the constructs of this problematic rhetoric, and calls for a more open and objective approach to addressing not only these films, but similar cultural phenomena.

Nia Edwards-Behi's ' "Flicks for Chicks (and Chicks with Dicks) Who Can't Take Serious Horror": The Generic Misrecognition of *The Twilight Saga*' further argues that these vehement critical attacks on the franchise can be traced to its tenuous generic categorisation, the negative reaction thus resulting from the deviation from this false expectation. Furthermore, she introduces the pivotal role of gender, exploring its role in these genre debates and in the connected demonisation of *The Twilight Saga*'s fans. Sarah Harman then takes up this rejection as associated with the feminine in her chapter, 'The Pageant of Her Bleeding Twi-hard Heart: *Twilight*, Female Sexuality and Consumption'. Expanding upon arguments raised in our foreword, and Natalie Wilson's *Seduced by* Twilight: *The Allure and Contradictory Messages*,[3] Harman argues that 'the Saga's unofficial merchandising – ranging from cardboard cut-outs of Edward Cullen that "watch you while you sleep" to sparkling freezable dildos that promise "this vamp won't be the only thing coming for you in the night" – offers a rampant consumerism that also screams of a morbid eroticism.' This is located within the modern history of female fandom and consumption. These chapters directly approach the wide-ranging receptions of the series, confronting the love/hate dynamic engendered by *The Twilight Saga*.

From here, we move to further examinations of genre, through analyses of the mythical tradition as well as the creation of generic supernatural space in the section 'Werewolves, Lions and Lambs: Creating and Subverting the Generic Myth'. This begins with a chapter by Judith Kohlenberger entitled

'Why *Twilight* Sucks and Edward Doesn't: Contemporary Vampires and the Sentimental Tradition', in which she argues that *Twilight* bears less resemblance to the horror genre than to the romantic tradition. 'The (re-)romanticisation of the vampire, culminating in its refusal to suck human blood,' she explains, 'has come to serve as a central argument for why Edward and his siblings suck big time.' This notion is explored through an analysis of romantic genre tropes, drawing comparisons to other texts from the tradition. Caroline Ruddell follows this exploration of *Twilight*'s genre traditions in her chapter 'The Lore of the Wild'. By discussing the adaptation of *The Company of Wolves* (1984, dir. Neil Jordan), we start to get not only a sense of *Twilight*'s roots in folklore and mythology, and how the films both adhere to and subvert these traditions, but also an understanding of the symbiotic relationship between film, television, literature and folk stories. Coming full circle, perhaps, Wickham Clayton then attempts to relocate *The Twilight Saga: New Moon* (2009, dir. Chris Weitz) contrary to the previously discussed genre debates, to actually have one foot – or perhaps fang – within the horror genre through the absence and reappearance of the horrific supernatural in ' "Where Have All the Monsters Gone? Long Time Passing": The Aesthetics of Absence and Generic Subversion in *New Moon*'. He argues that, of the whole franchise, this second instalment undergoes an important aesthetic shift to foreground the absence of the supernatural within the narrative. By framing *The Twilight Saga* and its individual films within the context of generic expectation and established storytelling forms, we see how they can appeal individually to different segments of its audience, and simultaneously frustrate spectators by undermining what they anticipate in a viewing experience.

We then move away from genre to return to gender, this time textually in 'Romancing the Tomb: Sexual Dysfunction and Sexuality', opened by Ruth O'Donnell's 'My Distaste for Forks: *Twilight*, Oral Gratification and Self Denial'. Through an analysis of the implications of the films' 'vegetarian' vampires, O'Donnell uses psychoanalytic theories of oral fixation to explore the sexual dynamic of Edward and Bella's relationship, as well as their individual characters. The following chapter, 'Of Masochistic Lions and Stupid Lambs: The Ambiguous Nature of Sexuality and Sexual Awakening in *Twilight*', by Marion Rana, explores the saga's unique approach to the coming-of-age story and argues that the narrative creation of sexual awakening is not as clear as it would seem superficially. Rather than sexless 'abstinence porn', 'Bella and Edward's relationship finds its culmination in the biting scene near the end of *Twilight* ... [which] could hardly be more sexual', she states. 'Edward's obvious arousal, Bella's panting, his inability to stop, her obvious enjoyment, even the roaring fire in the background all illustrate that what we are perceiving is a substitute for sexual action from which both partners draw masochistic delight.' The issues of sex, sexuality and masochism versus sexual violence and their implications are then further explored by Mark Adams' 'Venus in Fangs: Negotiating Masochism in *Twilight*'. Here, the notion of both Edward and Bella as masochistic is explored to show in fact that they both inhabit alternating submissive/dominant roles. Through an examination of Victor Smirnoff's masochistic contract, Adams undercuts what he perceives to be the myth of Bella as a weak female, being dominated by a controlling male. Adams convincingly argues that the power dynamic effectively shifts between the two characters regardless of gender, resulting in a form of chaste masochism. Taking O'Donnell's, Rana's and Adams' chapters together then, we are asked to rethink the oft-raised criticism of *Twilight* – Edward's controlling of Bella, where her role cannot be understood as anything other than his passive victim. The reality, it would seem, is much closer to the Lions and Lambs analogy, but for sexualised reasons not overtly intended by the films, nor indeed Meyer. These explorations stab at the heart of cultural response: by utilising psychoanalytic traditions, we can observe what is both appealing and disruptive on a core psychological and sexual level, helping to explain viewer response, and ultimately representing a necessary approach to understanding the phenomenon.

From gender and sexuality, focus then turns to other dominant ideologies of identity, in the section 'The Politics of Pallor: Post-colonialism and Racial Whiteness, Queered?' Post-colonialism is the focus of Simon Bacon's chapter, 'The Cullens: Family, Mimicry and the Post-colonial Vampire'. Through a comparison to *The Lost Boys* (1987, dir. Joel Schumacher) amongst other politically comparative recent vampire films, Bacon analyses the representation of the Cullen 'family' as not inherently post-colonial, but a group of non-humans mimicking what appears to be dominant human post-colonial ideologies. This in turns reveals and subverts the innately problematic nature of post-colonialism. In the following chapter, 'Racial Whiteness and *Twilight*', Ewan Kirkland examines the films in their relation to the history of race and the vampire film, in conjunction with ideas of whiteness, moreover, stating that 'Castle Cullen [and its inhabitants]...evoke the fairy tale [of] whiteness...[and] the kinds of cultural capital which constitute the invisible and weightless knapsack of white privilege'. Kirkland thus exposes *Twilight*'s hidden yet always visible dominant ideology of cultural privilege as the preferred social position, particularly when considering voluntary familial attachment. This section closes with R. Justin Hunt's 'Scent, Siblings and the Filial: Queering *Twilight*'. Here, he argues that the Cullens, through their knowingly queer performance of the hetero-normative family, mirror and indeed perhaps exploit queer community structures. He explains that the films in *The Twilight Saga* 'queer for us notions of normative boundaries' precisely because it blurs clear relationship parameters and incorporates the troubling element of olfactory attraction and identification. What is clear from these three chapters is that the Cullens' queer family unit fails to convince with its performance of normality and fails to disguise its white privilege – forcing us to consider, perhaps, our own. Framing *The Twilight Saga* through a lens of politics, society and identity, an urgent element of the saga's cultural impact emerges: within our dominant structures and ideologies, how do the characters' identities in the *Twilight* films differ from the way we see ourselves and, more importantly, how are we similar?

Finally, we return to a consideration of the saga's fans and their own relationship to narrative, genre, identity, gender and sexuality through their creation of fan fiction in 'Slash and Burn: Deviating Fandom and Rewriting the Text'. Brigid Cherry's 'Defanging the Vampire: Projected Interactivity and All Human *Twilight* Fanfic', examines how the *Twilight* franchise is altered through 'all human' fan fiction, which removes the supernatural to explore what would happen if Forks' residents were indeed all human. She concludes with the words of 'LG412':

> I adore seeing these characters reinvented, and making them all human opens up such an array of possibilities for reimagining them. I think die-hard fans turn to fan-fic for MORE. More of their favorite characters, favorite relationships, etc. AH fic allows so many different ways to explore those characters and relationships, while also giving writers and readers a way to find pieces of their own lives in the stories.

We end this collection with 'Normal Female Interest in Vampires and Werewolves Bonking: Slash and the Reconstruction of Meaning' by Bethan Jones, who continues the examination of fan fiction through the sub-genre of slash – which 'posits a homoerotic relationship between two characters ... most commonly written about male pairings, although slash written about female/female pairings ('femslash') also exists' – examined here through Bella/Alice and Jacob/Edward ('Jakeward') pairings. These slash communities are observed and interviewed by Jones in order to demonstrate how sexual pairings unavailable in the original texts have been, and continue to be, reappropriated to create wholly different messages and meanings. Examining how *The Twilight Saga* functions within recognised fan practices, this section shows us how they can be identified as fan texts, as well as the potential narrative desires the films elicit in their fans. By addressing how fans address these desires, and what prompts them to do so, we ultimately observe a valuable insight into how these texts affect those who consume them – truly taking such a cultural phenomenon to its logical conclusion. With the relatively recent release – and indeed rerelease – of E. L. James' best-selling novel *Fifty Shades of Grey*,[4] itself having originated from a BDSM themed 'het'[erosexual] fanfic, we can begin to see not only an expansion of the 'canon' to include these differing texts, but also perhaps their entering into the legitimising mainstream. It is worth pondering, however, how far from the tree this particular heterosexual BDSM-themed apple has fallen, in contrast to those discussed herein by Cherry and Jones.

We hope that the chapters contained here will not only be of interest to academics, fans and 'acafans'[5] alike, but will also raise questions and discussions in you, the readers – not only regarding *Twilight*, but also for the consideration of future mainstream blockbuster franchises. If compiling this collection has taught us one thing, it is that, in the case of these texts, their cultural import can't be clearly distilled into whether the films are 'good' or 'bad'. Instead, a multitude of cultural, social and artistic framings are necessary to begin to understand why *The Twilight Saga* has permeated discourse in many arenas and critical platforms.

Notes

1. Based on figures from IMDb.com: http://www.imdb.com/title/tt1392170/business?ref_=tt_dt_bus (accessed 3 February 2013).
2. *The Twilight Saga: Breaking Dawn – Part 2* (2012, dir. Bill Condon) earned $141.1 million in its domestic opening weekend, according to IMDb.com: http://www.imdb.com/title/tt1673434/business?ref_=tt_dt_bus (accessed 3 February 2013).
3. Natalie Wilson, *Seduced by* Twilight: *The Allure and Contradictory Messages of the Popular Saga* (Jefferson, NC: McFarland, 2011).
4. E. L. James, *Fifty Shades of Grey* (Texas: The Writers' Virtual Coffee Shop 2011, and London: Arrow Books, 2012).
5. Matt Hills, *Fan Cultures* (London: Routledge, 2002).

PART 1

MUTE MONSTERS AND VOCAL [FAN/] CRITICS: GENRE AND RECEPTION

1

GUILTY PLEASURES: *TWILIGHT,* SNARK AND CRITICAL FANDOM

Francesca Haig

In July 2010 a colleague and I arranged to see the newly released film *The Twilight Saga: Eclipse* (2010, dir. David Slade). We referred to this as 'the excursion of shame', swearing to make no mention of it in the academic department where we work. We'd shared long conversations about the many things that appalled us about both Stephenie Meyer's books and the films themselves, but sheepish and critical as we were, there was no denying that we had some kind of affection for both the books and films and that our enthusiastic engagement with these texts was a source of pleasure. There was a similar combination of fervour and furtiveness in a series of exchanges I had with a PhD student: we had several passionate conversations about the manifold failings of the books and first two films, but these discussions culminated in her begging me to lend her *Breaking Dawn* (2008), the final book in Meyer's series (but to leave it in her pigeonhole in a brown paper bag). As I struggled to reconcile my own criticisms of the texts with my eager engagement with them, I began to see a similar form of critical *Twilight* fandom proliferating, from video parodies on YouTube to LiveJournal exchanges gone viral. At a 2011 academic conference on 'Modern Vampire Romance', many of the papers and much of the discussion centred on trenchant criticism of the *Twilight* books and films, from academics who had, none the less, evidently consumed the books and films with some pleasure.[1]

Since the start of the *Twilight* phenomenon, press attention has focused on the 'sincere' fans ('Twi-hards', the '*Twilight* Moms', etc.). However, *Twilight* seems also to have provoked an ironic, critical fandom in which readers and viewers bemoan the flaws of the books and films, while enjoying and keenly devouring (if sometimes furtively) the texts. Such engagement is sometimes described as 'snark' ('snark' is defined by the Urban Dictionary as a combination of 'snide' and 'remark'); while this term evokes the humorous and critical aspects of such fandom, it doesn't quite do justice to affectionate, immersive engagement with the texts. What does this conflicted form of fandom reveal about the *Twilight* phenomenon and the nature of the pleasures it provides? Is this critical, subversive fandom simply an attempt to justify the pleasure taken from *The Twilight Saga*, or does the criticism itself constitute a new kind of fan pleasure?

While this critical *Twilight* fandom is distinctive, theorists and fans have increasingly been aware that fandom often incorporates elements of criticism. Despite the popular perception of fandom as uncritical adoration, the definition of 'fandom' does nothing to exclude critical engagement with texts; Cornell Sandvoss defines fandom as 'the regular, emotionally involved consumption of a given popular narrative or text'.[2] The critical fandom generated by *Twilight* fits this definition in both its regularity and its emotional involvement: critical fans both devour each new book and film, and engage in sustained, passionate debates about the series and its flaws. However, the particular form of critical response generated by *Twilight* may help to clarify or expand existing theorisations of fandom.

In providing examples of this ironic fandom, it is perhaps simplest first to clarify what it does not include. Uncritical fandom, including much of the adoring, imitative *Twilight* fan fiction that floods sites such as fanfiction.net, often fits neatly into existing fandom stereotypes, and bears almost no relation to the kind of *Twilight* snark this chapter examines. While it is difficult to generalise about such fan fiction, due to both its volume (more than 185,000 *Twilight* stories on fanfiction.net, for example) and its range, the majority display an earnest mimicry of the characters, tone and tropes of the source texts, even while envisioning new events. The same is true of sites devoted entirely to *Twilight* criticism, or '*Twilight* Haters' sites (relatively few in comparison to 'fan' sites, it must be said). These include the GoodReads 'you know you hate twilight if...' site. This forum contains many relevant criticisms (commenter 'Gemma' writes: 'I sorta wanted to gouge my eyes out with dull toothpicks everytime [sic] stephanie [sic] meyer used the word "velvety"'[3]) but it lacks the affection that characterises the more complex engagements with the texts. Equally I would exclude the film *Vampires Suck* (2010, dirs Jason Friedberg and Aaron Seltzer), whose affection for the texts exists only on a mercenary level, and which lacks the wit and the intellectual acuity of much of the more sophisticated *Twilight* snark. As film critic Mark Kermode recently noted, such films have 'no parody in them'.[4]

Instead of those responses that simply adore or critique the series, the form of *Twilight* fandom that interests me is demonstrated on the 'Twatlight' website, a LiveJournal community specifically set up for *Twilight* snark. The site is for fans of the series, but with an explicitly critical bent; as they state: 'We're not anti-*Twilight*, but we're not a serious *Twilight* community. If you can't handle humourous [sic] discussion of the books, don't join'. In a similar vein are two of the most popular exemplars of *Twilight* snark: 'Growing up Cullen' and 'Twilight in Fifteen Minutes'. The former is a long exchange between two LiveJournal users ('oxymoronassoc' and 'welurklate'), in which they riff on possibilities offered by the text, with a focus on the hero's century of abstinence in a house filled with passionately bonking vampire couples. Parodying the prudish, controlling and emotional aspects of Edward's character, this text builds into a delicious series of imagined dialogues in which Edward channels his sexual frustration into an increasingly tenuous series of hobbies, while being mocked by his family, particularly Emmet. Constantly justifying his actions (including his stalking of Bella) to his family, Edward exclaims: 'Yes, I am doing that "Emo bullshit", I can feel if I want to.' A representative excerpt (in which both 'oxymoronassoc' and 'welurklate' are voicing Edward) shows Edward's response to a porn film that he has caught Emmet watching online:

Oxymoronassoc: Who has been looking at this vile filth on the computer? Who?

Oxymoronassoc: I am suspicious of their alleged love ... it is unpure ...

Welurklate: This film has failed to make me believe their relationship at all

Oxymoronassoc: Emmett you can see the boom mic

Oxymoronassoc: The production value is shoddy at best

Oxymoronassoc: Could they not afford more fabric for the costumes? ... I do not believe a lady cop would dress in such a manner ... it is terribly unprofessional

Welurklate: She has worked hard to be respected in a male dominated field ... she would not throw it away by sleeping with five members of the force at once

Oxymoronassoc: Why must we subjugate her in this manner?

Welurklate: they are NEVER going to catch the killer this way!

'Twilight in Fifteen Minutes' is another example of *Twilight* snark that has reached viral status. Based on Cleolinda Jones' LiveJournal site (titled 'Occupation: Girl'), it is the first in what became a series of sharp, parodic synopses of the *Twilight* novels and films, playing up the manifold absurdities of both the plot and style. Here follows an excerpt from Jones' recap of the first *Twilight* film (2008, dir. Catherine Hardwicke):

Bella: Wait, what's going on at the police station?

Edward: Wait, why is my not-dad there?

Carlisle: Bella, I'm so sorry... your father's weird friend was killed by a feral plot point.

Bella: I didn't even know we had those in this movie!

Carlisle [*significant look*]: I know. They're very rare in Forks.

Edward [*mind-reading*]: D:<

As a result of the popularity of 'Twilight in Fifteen Minutes' (and her other *Twilight* recaps) Jones has become something of a *Twilight* authority, quoted in publications such as *New York Magazine* and *Salon*.[5]

It is worth considering whether these texts would in fact count as a form of fan fiction. This practice, like most types of active media fandom, is commonly seen as shameful in non-fandom circles, an attitude encapsulated by the reference in the Jezebel blog to 'medieval-themed *Twilight* fan fic... from under the internet's mattress'.[6] I suspect that the authors might resist the fan fiction label, loaded as it is with connotations both of poor quality and of uncritical, obsessive fandom.[7] None the less, both of these memes, particularly 'Growing up Cullen', perfectly fit the definition: they are imaginative texts that play with and extend an existing canon, and which demonstrate an extensive knowledge of, and pleasure in, that canon.

As well as 'Twilight in Fifteen Minutes' and the related recaps, Jones' LiveJournal page also offers a considered analysis of the popularity of the *Twilight* series; called 'My thoughts on Twilight: Let me show you them'. The essay approaches the canon in a subversive and parodic manner. For example, she writes: 'it's totes okay for a guy to stalk you and watch you while you sleep so long as he's hot.' Commenters on this post join in, with criticisms in a similar vein; 'viorica8957' writes: 'it's totes okay for your boyfriend to break your car to keep you from going to see someone he doesn't like.' In a telling metaphor, Jones' article likens *Twilight* to 'Twinkies':

> If you want gourmet pastry, or even a homemade cake, you know where to get that. If you're eating a Twinkie, you clearly know what you want and why you're eating it, and you know that it's not good to eat very many of them, but ... you know ... sometimes you just want one.[8]

This idea that the series represents a mindless, sugary indulgence, which fans know is rubbish but enjoy none the less, is clearly one that resonates; fans commenting on Jones' article echo it again and again, referring to 'junk food', 'brain candy', 'candyfloss in paper form'. The same sentiment appears elsewhere: an anonymous commenter on a *Bitch* magazine article about the *Twilight* series argues:[9]

> The books are badly written, yes. It's pure escapism and fantasy and is aimed at people who want to escape from the real word [sic] for a while too. Yell about that, if you want, but don't make these books a 'social issue' when they're too fluffy and silly to even register on that scale.

It is clear that in both popular perception and self-justification, fandom is seen as uncritical, a switching off of critical faculties for trashy pleasure.

Jones evidently takes real pleasure from the *Twilight* books and films; of the first novel (which she read online) she states: 'If I had a hard copy, I would snuggle it.' There is, however, a disclaimer: she goes on to give other examples of her 'bad taste' in films and literature, noting 'my loving something is not the most ringing endorsement in the world'.[10] In fact Jones is oversimplifying her relationship to the series and not doing credit to her own critical analysis, which is often both witty and astute. This is the crucial flaw in the 'junk food' justification seized upon by her and so many others. When one enjoys junk food, one doesn't engage in a critical analysis of it. You know it's bad for you and take pleasure in it, but engaging in a detailed analysis of its dietary shortcomings isn't part of the pleasure. This is what seems to me to be distinctive about *Twilight* snark: the criticisms aren't incidental to the pleasure taken in the texts; they appear, in large part, to constitute that pleasure. This form of critical fandom does not simply recognise *Twilight* as rubbish and enjoy it *in spite of* that recognition; the recognition *itself* and the analysis, discussion and parody that it permits, provide much of the fans' pleasure. To dismiss this form of *Twilight* fandom as simply a 'guilty pleasure,' a knowing embrace of poor-quality pap, is something of an oversimplification. The comment by 'aome', agreeing fervently with Jones' article and describing the series as 'fluffy and sugary and totally brainless' doesn't accurately sum up the critical approach that Jones exemplifies; while the *Twilight* books and films themselves may indeed be 'totally brainless', in their critical grapplings with the texts, the brains of these critical fans are emphatically still engaged.

These critical forms of engagement with the texts are at odds with traditional perceptions of fandom as synonymous with unthinking passion for the canon. As Matt Hills notes: ' "love" and "affect" have been used to characterise fans' attachments to their texts', and the stereotypical fandom has been defined by its ' "irrationality" or "arationality" ',[11] a role filled to perfection by the 'Twihards' and '*Twilight* Moms' whose public squealing has been extensively covered by the media. Taking the stereotype even further, the press has gleefully reported the various incidents of physical violence, in which fans have attacked rivals, or those who dare to criticise the *Twilight* series (Gawker website published an article summarising some of these, entitled 'When Twihards Attack'[12]). Similarly uncritical adoration of the text was seen (and widely reported) in the case of a *Twilight* fan who accused the producers of Joe Johnston's 2010 *Wolfman* film of stealing the concept of werewolves from Stephenie Meyer.[13]

Despite the popular (mis)perceptions of fandom as uncritical, it has always contained critical aspects. Even in fan fiction, generally derided by non-fans as the ultimate indulgence of the acritical obsessive fan, there are elements of criticism or subversion of the canon. For example, in much of the *Harry Potter* slash fan fiction pairing Harry with Draco Malfoy there is an implicit critique of the heteronormativity of the canon. Similarly, the interactivity and reinvention offered by fan communities, particularly online, always permit an envisioning of textual alternatives: canonical character deaths are reversed, alternative endings explored, fan trailers produced to rival or counteract official trailers. In her book on fan fiction, Sheenagh Pugh distinguishes between two main fan motivations: fans wanting 'more of' their chosen text; and those who want 'more from' the text. As she notes: 'there is canon material which, though it draws its readers or viewers in, strikes them as being far from perfect or fully realised; they see possibilities in it which were never explored as they might have been.'[14] Even 'traditional' fandom, then, has always engaged with criticism.

However, because irrational passion has continued to dominate the popular understanding of fandom, academia has been relatively slow to engage with fandom, let alone to endorse it. Even a theorist such as Matt Hills, who coined the term 'scholar-fan' in acknowledgement that academia and fandom are not necessarily mutually exclusive, observes that 'where academics do take on fan identities, they often do so with a high degree of anxiety';[15] the furtiveness of my own 'excursion of shame' outing is far from unique. However, in contrast to the perceived opposition between 'rabid fandom' and critical analysis, there have increasingly been attempts to theorise the ways in which criticism and fandom overlap. In these formulations it is possible to recognise some aspects of the critical fandom demonstrated by many *Twilight* fans; however, there are also many points of difference that suggest that this mode of critical fandom still requires further exploration.

Almost all theoretical models of fandom have been influenced by Stuart Hall's identification of three modes of reading: oppositional, dominant or negotiated,[16] of which the critical fandom encouraged by *Twilight* is closest to the oppositional mode. While Hall's emphasis on the viewer's active construction of meaning is useful, his model imperfectly describes the interplay of pleasure and criticism that characterises much *Twilight* fandom. More recently, Jonathan Gray has recognised that media studies' focus on 'positive' fandom has been at the expense of the variety of possible forms of engagement with texts, which have been 'under theorized'.[17] Importantly, Gray has drawn overdue attention to what he calls the 'anti-fan', which he defines as 'he or she who actively and vocally hates or dislikes a given text, personality or genre'.[18] When conducting interviews about *The Simpsons*, Gray was struck by 'how many of the anti-fans and non-fans could provide a lengthy and impressive in-depth analysis' of the show,[19] and similarly I have found that it is the critical fans of *Twilight* who provide some of the most insightful critiques of the series.

Gray's theory of the 'antifan' is particularly useful in drawing attention to the affective power of dislike and criticism; the passionate response of critical fans to *The Twilight Saga* is reflected in Gray's statement that 'many of us care as deeply (if not more so) about those texts that we dislike as we do about those that we like.'[20] However, critical *Twilight* fans are recognisable in some aspects of Gray's 'antifandom', but not in others. He describes antifans as those 'who refuse to let their family watch a show, who campaign against the text, or who spend considerable time discussing why a given text makes them angry to the core';[21] critical *Twilight* fans certainly fit the last of these criteria, but fail absolutely to fit the first two.

An even more significant difference lies in Gray's view that antifans have a more distant relationship from the text than 'actual' fans. While 'antifans must find cause for their dislike in something', according to Gray this engagement with the text is unlikely to be sustained or close; it may not necessarily even involve viewing the primary text, but might be based on paratexts, such as previews, advertisements or reviews.[22] This 'lack of familiarity' with the text that

Gray ascribes to the antifan[23] is far removed from the avid yet critical engagement with *Twilight* texts that I have both witnessed and shared.[24]

Gray conceives of the antifan as differentiating between the multiple dimensions of a text ('moral, rational-realist, and aesthetic dimensions'); his or her disapproval of one dimension results in them being 'unwilling or unable to interact with all three levels'.[25] Gray's archetypal antifan is somebody whose disapproval of a text's moral dimensions means that they will not engage with the text on an aesthetic level. However, this view suggests an artificial distinction between dimensions of a text and fails to acknowledge that a reader may engage with different textual dimensions in different ways. Critical fans of *Twilight*, for example, may vocally disapprove of the series' moral dimensions (its pathologically self-sacrificing heroine, for example) or its 'rational-realist' dimensions (the term 'sparklevamp' has become an internet meme, summarising the popular criticism of Meyer's sparkling rendition of vampires). However, it is reductive to assume that disapproval of these aspects therefore precludes such fans from simultaneously engaging with, and taking pleasure from, the texts' aesthetic dimensions. As commenter 'My Way' notes on the Television Without Pity (TWOP) *Twilight* forum, 'I think Edward acted like a stalker and his behavior would never be acceptable in real life, yet I enjoyed the books.' A fan of the films may be acutely aware of the controlling characteristics of Robert Pattinson's Edward, but that would not preclude such a viewer from finding him good looking, or the action scenes engaging. Furthermore, Gray's model doesn't allow room for dissonance *within* any one of his posited dimensions: a critical fan of *Twilight* may enjoy certain aspects of the 'aesthetic dimension' of the series: they may take pleasure in Meyer's use of Gothic elements and idealised romance, while simultaneously objecting to her repetitive, hyperbolic prose. As commenter 'KisstheCook' notes on the TWOP *Twilight* forum: 'I liked the series very much, but I don't think they were especially well written.'

When academics have attempted to account for criticism within fandom, they have tended to focus on a particular mode of criticism, one largely driven by nostalgia for an earlier, 'purer' version of the text. Henry Jenkins has been influential in recognising that fandom contains elements that overlap with the critical analysis of academia; he goes so far as to claim that 'organized fandom is, perhaps first and foremost, an institution of theory and criticism'.[26] However, as an exemplar of this critical fandom Jenkins quotes a published letter by Joan Marie Verba, a self-identified *Star Trek* fan, who writes: 'To criticise *Star Trek* ... means that we enjoy *Star Trek* enough to want it to be the best it can be, and we wish to point out flaws in the hope of improvement ... If we didn't *care*, we wouldn't criticize.'[27] Once again, critical *Twilight* fans will spot important similarities and differences between their practice and this formulation. Such fans would (albeit sheepishly) acknowledge that they care about the texts: the time commitment of reading the four substantial books, watching the films and engaging in discussions about the texts is testament to this. However, Verba's justification of her criticism as an attempt to improve the text is unlikely to resonate with critical fans of *Twilight*. I would have been horrified if the later *Twilight* books, or the film versions, had been a dramatic improvement on the earlier ones; rather than affirming my fandom, it would have undermined its main pleasure. Before the release of Slade's *Eclipse* film, 'furrylump' wrote on the TWOP *Twilight* forum: 'I want *Eclipse* to be hilariously terrible.' Similarly, when a fellow poster suggested some sensible ways in which the writers of the screenplay for the *Breaking Dawn* movies might tone down some of the novel's more outlandish plot issues, 'Scarynikki12' responded: 'I want to see BD in it's [sic] completely effed up glory!' While Jenkins does recognise that fandom 'typically involves not simply fascination or adoration but also frustration and antagonism', his view of fan criticism as a way by which the fan can 'try to find ways to salvage them [the texts] for their interests'[28] does not seem to reflect the gleeful, critical pleasure involved in much *Twilight* fandom, in which criticism constitutes a principal interest.

Johnson addresses a similarly nostalgic mode of fan criticism when he gives the example of fans of Joss Whedon's *Buffy the Vampire Slayer* (1997–2003), many of whom took to internet forums to express dissatisfaction with the show's sixth season. Considering whether these might fall under Gray's classification of 'anti-fans', Johnson is keen to recuperate them for 'mainstream' fandom:

> the militancy of these *Buffy* viewers remained symptomatic of fandom, not of anti-fandom in its own right... [A]nti-fans who hate a program (without necessarily viewing it) must be differentiated from disgruntled fan factions who hate episodes, eras, or producers because they perceive a violation of the larger text they still love.[29]

The critical fandom provoked by *Twilight* seems to fit neither of these definitions. In Johnson's insistence on differentiating between fans' criticism of the present state of the text and their 'pleasurable engagement with the diegetic past'[30] he fails to recognise that, for many fans, criticism itself can be a form of 'pleasurable engagement'. Theorisations of critical fandom have failed to acknowledge that, for some fans, criticism is not a mode of reclaiming a once-loved text, but rather a pleasurable form of engagement with the text.

The nostalgic mode of criticism is particularly ill suited to the critical fandom of so many *Twilight* readers and viewers. It is true that the books have arguably become increasingly absurd; the plot of Meyer's *Breaking Dawn* defies both parody and synopsis, including as it does an accelerated pregnancy with a monster foetus, caesarean delivery by vampire teeth and a werewolf falling irrevocably in love with a baby. However, far from complaining of a decline in quality over the course of the series, the absurdities of the final book have been greeted with glee by its critical fans. While disappointed 'sincere' fans complained about *Breaking Dawn*, even launching a campaign to return the book to stores,[31] critical fans have embraced the novel; Jones, in her LiveJournal summary of the final section of *Breaking Dawn*, describes it as 'possibly the most awesome crackfic of any of the series so far'.

The false dichotomy between fandom and criticism derives in part from the perceived opposition between the irrational, affective nature of fandom and the analytical nature of criticism. Grossberg reflects the popular view of fandom when he notes that 'the fan's relation to cultural texts operates in the domain of affect or mood'.[32] However, a distinction between the affective and critical response is tenuous; to assume that an affective response cannot be critical is reductive. When I respond with eye-rolling at yet another act of self-sacrifice on the part of Bella, I do not first step outside of my affective engagement with the text in order to don my 'academic, feminist' hat; my response is as visceral and instinctive as my response to the swelling use of Muse's 'Supermassive Black Hole' in Hardwicke's *Twilight* film. My revulsion at Edward's controlling behaviour in all of the films is as instinctive and compelling as my response to Pattinson's good looks. My affective responses are ideologically and socially conditioned; indeed, to see some responses as 'innate', 'natural' or 'affective', while dismissing others as subsequent rationalisations, exposes a deep-seated essentialism (my ideological positioning as a feminist is no more constructed than my social position as a heterosexual or as a woman). While in subsequent *Twilight* discussions with friends we move beyond a purely affective response, as we construct and probe rational arguments about the text, the driving force of these critical discussions remains an affective response to the text's limitations and absurdities.

Fandom itself has begun to articulate this engaged, critical drive, often more convincingly than academia. The 'Fanlore' wiki site offers the term 'ironic distance', defining it as 'the simultaneous impulses to mock and to squee'.[33] An even more detailed definition appears in a glossary of *Twilight*-related terms coined by Jones: 'Lolfan: ... the kind of people (i.e., me) who read these books for the sole purpose of snarking on them. Levels of affection for the subject matter may vary ... .'

While I hope that this chapter will broaden definitions of fandom to include persistently critical engagements with texts, I do not seek to subsume this critical fandom into a monolithic or homogeneous notion of fandom. Fandom has always been subject to factions, or 'fan-tagonism', a term coined by Johnson.[34] Indeed, the critical fans described in this article seem keen to make a distinction between themselves and 'sincere' fans. On the TWOP *Twilight* forum, poster 'tip and fall' comments on a fellow poster's suggestion for a (mocking) costume to wear to the opening of Hardwicke's film, writing: 'Ah, I would *so* steal that, except I don't [sic] to be mistaken for a completely-in-earnest fan. I have my pride.' The fact that a person sufficiently engaged with the texts to read the novels, post on a *Twilight* forum, and to attend the opening of the first film (possibly in costume) is none the less anxious to maintain the distinction between his/her critical engagement and that of a 'completely-in-earnest fan', aptly demonstrates the persistence of reductive and tenuous (mis)conceptions of fandom.

The question of what it is about the *Twilight* films and books that has produced such a cluster of ironic fandom is perhaps beyond the scope of this chapter. However, as the vast majority of the detailed criticism of the series seems focused on its gender politics (particularly the controlling nature of Edward and the passivity of Bella), it seems clear that the series' self-evidently objectionable gender politics is encouraging, if not demanding, critical engagement. At the same time, most of this critical engagement seems to come from the female audience at which the series is so obviously pitched. In aiming so squarely at a female audience, and yet employing such conspicuously problematic gender politics, it is arguable that *Twilight* has created the perfect storm of conflicted, critical fandom. Even within the groups that one might assume would be uncritically in favour of the texts, the fandom is more complex than the media coverage has suggested. In a recent article, Anna Silver has observed criticism of the series' gender dynamics taking place even 'from inside the sometimes rabid fan community',[35] in such sites as the Feminist Mormon Housewives blog or the '*Twilight* Moms' Facebook group. Chelsea, writing on Feminist Mormon Housewives, posts, 'I find the message to young girls disturbing. That love is an irresistible force that precludes making any rational decisions. That it's OK (even noble) to sacrifice your personal safety if you "really" love someone.'[36]

This type of criticism proliferates in *Twilight* forums. For example, the 'Fanpop' website hosts a forum titled 'critical analysis of twilight'; and a post from 'persephone 713' is representative of the criticism taking place:

> I am not a feminist by any means – Hell I collect Disney Princesses. But if all girls/women were like Bella Swan the world would be even more pathetic. And for creating the notion that its 'Romantic' for your so called lover to stalk you, leave you – then come back, watch you etc. NOT COOL.

When Mormon housewives and collectors of Disney princesses drawn to the 'Fanpop' website are critiquing the series' gender politics, it is evident that *Twilight* is a breeding ground for critical fandom.

The fact that the most popular *Twilight* memes seem to be on LiveJournal also provides food for thought – the explicitly interactive nature of this forum (far more so than an ordinary blog, and yet more public than the restricted networks of Facebook) lends itself perfectly to the kind of critical interaction encouraged by *Twilight*. Academia, traditionally dismissive of both fandom and collaboration, remains relatively ill equipped to deal with co-authored, conflicted fan fiction such as 'Growing Up Cullen'.

If we can get beyond the false dichotomy between fandom and critical analysis, it is possible to argue that *Twilight* encapsulates an exciting new development in fandom, in which we see people loving this series not *in spite* of the criticisms which we can level at it, but *because* of these criticisms, and the analytical, interactive and parodic opportunities that it presents. One of the main *Twilight* fan websites, '*Twilight* Moms', neatly demonstrates the reductive popular view of fandom; the rules of their forum specifically state: 'No character bashing. This is a site for FANS of Stephenie Meyer, her stories and creations.' As long as fandom is seen to exclude criticism, the full extent and complexity of the *Twilight* fan experience will go unrecognised.

A reductive view of what fandom is, and a refusal to acknowledge the critical elements that can, and have, constituted an important part of fandom, will keep critical fandom of *Twilight* (and of other popular texts) in the closet, and will limit serious critical consideration of such texts. As long as enthusiastic engagement with a popular text is seen as inimical to criticism, such criticism will be stifled, and dimensions of both texts and fandom will be left unexplored. However, a recognition of the critical potential of fandom, and of the fact that this criticism might not be incidental, but central, to the pleasures provided by texts such as *Twilight*, allows us a new lens through which to understand the *Twilight* phenomenon.

Notes

1. 'Vegetarians, VILFs and Fang-Bangers: Modern Vampire Romance in Print and on Screen', a one-day conference at De Montfort University, Leicester, Wednesday 24 November 2010. This chapter represents a development of ideas presented in my paper at this conference.

2. Cornell Sandvoss, *Fans: the Mirror of Consumption* (Malden, MA: Polity, 2005), p. 8.

3. For ethical reasons, I have only quoted from open forums, where posters use pseudonyms. As Gray notes, in such forums 'posters are fully aware of the public, open nature of the forum' (Jonathan Gray, 'Antifandom and the Moral Text: Television Without Pity and Textual Dislike', *The American Behavioral Scientist* 48/7 (2005), pp. 840–58, p. 847).

4. Mark Kermode and Simon Mayo, 'Kermode and Mayo's Film Review', BBC Radio 5 Live radio broadcast, 15 November 2010.

5. *New York Magazine*, 'Did *Breaking Dawn* ruin the *Twilight* series?', 5 May 2008, http://www.vulture.com/2008/08/did_breaking_dawn_ruin_the_twi.html (accessed 5 May 2012); Sarah Hepola, '"Twilight" of our youth', *Salon*, 17 November 2009, http://www.salon.com/2009/11/17/twilight_of_our_youth/ (accessed 5 May 2012).

6. Margaret Hartmann, 'Michael Sheen Does A Dramatic Reading Of Twilight Fan Fiction', Jezebel blog, 27 May 2011, http://jezebel.com/5806180/michael-sheen-does-a-dramatic-reading-of-twilight-fan-fiction (accessed 5 May 2012).

7. While fan fiction encompasses a range of practices, it is increasingly recognised that such fiction does not always deserve the mockery levelled at it. Sheenagh Pugh's *The Democratic Genre: Fan Fiction in a Literary Context* (Bridgend: Seren, 2005) is an excellent exploration of the complexities and potential of fan fiction.

8. Cleolinda Jones, 'Occupation: Girl' (LiveJournal page) (2011), http://cleolinda.livejournal.com (accessed 5 May 2012).

9. Christine Seifert, 'Bite Me! (Or Don't)', *Bitch: Feminist Response to Pop Culture* 42 (2008), pp. 23–5, http://bitchmagazine.org/article/bite-me-or-dont (accessed 5 May 2012).

10. Jones, 'Occupation: Girl'.

11. Matt Hills, *Fan Cultures* (London: Routledge, 2002), p. 22. This derogatory characterisation of fandom has, of course, been gendered: as Gray observes, 'behaviour perceived as fundamentally irrational, excessively emotional, foolish and passive has made the fan decisively feminine' (Jonathan Gray, 'New Audiences, New Textualities: Anti-Fans and Non-Fans', *International Journal of Cultural Studies* 6 (2003), pp. 64–81, p. 67). Given that the *Twilight* novels and films are solidly pitched at a young, female audience, and famously embraced by other female groups such as the '*Twilight* Moms', it seems clear that the media focus on 'hysterical' *Twilight* fan behaviour has been inflected by persistent assumptions about gender.

12. One of the attacks, in which a young woman reported being bitten by a stranger as she left a screening of *New Moon*, was subsequently revealed by police to be fabricated by the ostensible victim (Heather Lynn Peters, 'Police: Teen exaggerated story about being bitten in movie theater; alleged "biter" no longer sought', *The Muskegon Chronicle*, 25 November 2009, http://www.mlive.com/news/muskegon/index.ssf/2009/11/

police_teen_exaggerated_story.html (accessed 5 May 2012)). This fabrication itself, however, remains a dramatic example of extreme *Twilight* fandom (just as the widespread, credulous reporting of her initial story may indicate the media's eagerness to embrace examples of extreme *Twilight* fandom).

13. George Roush, 'Taylor Lautner Fan Letter to Universal: Your Wolfman Ripped Off *Twilight*', *Latino Review*, 18 February 2010, http://www.latinoreview.com/news/taylor-lautner-fan-letter-to-universal-your-wolfman-ripped-off-twilight-9247 accessed 27 June 2011 (link no longer working).

14. Sheenagh Pugh, *The Democratic Genre: Fan Fiction in a Literary Context* (Bridgend: Seren, 2005), p. 43.

15. Hills, *Fan Cultures*, p. 12.

16. Stuart Hall, 'Encoding, Decoding', in Stuart Hall, Dorothy Hobson, Andrew Lowe and Paul Willis (eds), *Culture, Media, Language: Working Papers in Cultural Studies, 1972–1979* (London: Unwin Hyman, 1980), pp. 128–38.

17. Gray, 'New Audiences, New Textualities', p. 75.

18. Gray, 'Antifandom and the Moral Text', p. 840.

19. Gray, 'New Audiences, New Textualities', p. 65.

20. Ibid., p. 73.

21. Gray, 'Antifandom and the Moral Text', p. 840.

22. Gray, 'New Audiences, New Textualities', p. 71.

23. Ibid., p. 74.

24. While Gray mainly sees antifandom as involving 'audiencehood from afar', he does acknowledge that sometimes antifandom can involve a close engagement with the text, though he still specifies that such an engagement must necessarily be 'devoid of the interpretive and diegetic pleasures that are usually assumed to be a staple of almost all media consumption' (Gray, 'Antifandom and the Moral Text', p. 843). However, he does provide one example that comes close to the sort of critical fandom examined in this article, when he observes that some viewers who are highly critical of the show *The O'Reilly Factor* none the less remain avid viewers: 'many keep going back for more. ... Some viewers ... appear to engage actively in their antifandom, watching O'Reilly precisely to raise their blood pressure or, as the predominantly intellectual-rational tone of their posts suggests, as somewhat of an intellectual-rational challenge' (Ibid., p. 854).

25. Ibid., p. 844.

26. Henry Jenkins, *Textual Poachers: Television Fans and Participatory Culture* (New York and London: Routledge, 2009), p. 86.

27. Ibid., p. 86.

28. Ibid., p. 23.

29. Derek Johnson, 'Fan-tagonism: Factions, Institutions, and Constitutive Hegemonies of Fandom', in Jonathan Gray, Cornell Sandvoss and C. Lee Harrington (eds), *Fandom: Identities and Communities in a Mediated World* (New York and London: New York University Press, 2007), pp. 285–300, p. 293. Jenkins gives a similar example of nostalgia-driven criticism, citing *Star Wars* fans who are critical of later manifestations

of the text but remain fans because of their love for earlier episodes/films (Jenkins, *Textual Poachers*, pp. 97–8).

30. Johnson, 'Fan-tagonism', p. 294.

31. 'Did *Breaking Dawn* ruin the *Twilight* series?', *New York Magazine*, 5 May 2008, http:// www.vulture.com/2008/08/did_breaking_dawn_ruin_the_twi.html (accessed 5 May 2012).

32. Lawrence Grossberg, 'Is there a Fan in the House? The Affective Sensibility of Fandom', in Lisa Lewis (ed.), *Adoring Audience: Fan Culture and Popular Media* (London: Routledge, 1992), pp. 50–65, p. 56.

33. The term 'squee' is increasingly popular on the internet as an expression of an enthusiastic response. It is worth noting that definitions usually link it to fandom; the Urban Dictionary, for example, defines 'squee' as '[a] noise primarily made by an over-excited fangirl'.

34. Johnson, 'Fan-tagonism', p. 287.

35. Anna Silver, '*Twilight* is not Good for Maidens: Gender, Sexuality, and the Family in Stephenie Meyer's *Twilight* Series', *Studies in the Novel* 42/1 and 2 (2010), pp. 121–381, p. 22.

36. Ibid., p. 122.

2

'CUE THE SHRIEKING VIRGINS'?: THE CRITICAL RECEPTION OF *THE TWILIGHT SAGA*

Mark Jancovich

As Anne Billson has noted, one of the most striking things about *The Twilight Saga* has been the response to it by critics. More than simply 'gleeful in their derision', many critics have attacked the saga with an animosity that is rare and considerably more extreme than is usually directed against 'any other non-sense aimed at the young male demographic'.[1] Their outrage is not simply an expression of critical impotence, but is also bound up with their conception of the audience's gender. As we will see, despite a rhetoric of feminist politics that castigates the films as politically conservative, most reviews display a sense of revulsion at the presumed audience for these films, an audience that is presented as unruly, irrational and dehumanised. Many of these critics are proudly liberal and tolerant, and would rarely present other social groups in this way. The fact that they feel comfortable characterising young girls (or as we will see femininity more generally) in this way is deeply troubling, but can be understood in relation to Joanne Hollows' discussion of the ways in which the opposition between feminism and femininity, an opposition that frequently presents femininity as the other of feminism, as that which feminism exists to challenge and correct.[2] However, while this often creates a problematic opposition in some feminist work between the figures of the feminist and the ordinary woman, in the case of *The Twilight Saga*, this opposition is used to legitimate a situation in which predominantly (although not exclusively) male critics adopt the mantle of feminism to condemn women.

Furthermore, these women are not only figured as living in false consciousness, but are often presented as lacking consciousness altogether. For example, the saga's 'core target demographic' is described as 'hormonally unbalanced teenage girls'[3] or even as 'zombies' – dead, brainless bodies without minds, that will form the 'slack-jawed legions who will stagger into theatres this weekend' to see the latest offering.[4]

Other reviewers predict that fans will be 'entranced' by the films[5] but not in the positive sense of being enthralled by their magic. Instead it is suggested that the audience is dominated by the films and kept in a hypnotic state where they are unable to tell fantasy from reality or indeed able to make any sort of distinction. For example, Corliss describes the audience as one distracted by trivia and prone to 'emit an awestruck sigh, as if they'd seen Zac Efron in the flesh or a puppy on YouTube'.[6]

If the tastes of this audience inspire pure horror in many critics, their behaviour is imagined as a virtual nightmare of mindless bodies out of control that unthinkingly react to external stimuli: 'Cue the shrieking virgins.'[7] One reviewer describes the audience as 'a cinema full of young girls who, when they weren't texting friends and guzzling soft drinks, giggled, sighed and exhaled with a passion',[8] while Ebert describes something that he sees as even more terrifying: 'The last time I saw a movie in the same theatre, the audience welcomed it as an opportunity to catch up on gossip, texting and laughing at private jokes. This time the audience was rapt with attention.'[9] If critics repeatedly condemn contemporary audiences for not treating films with due seriousness and concentration, for having the temerity to view cinemagoing as a social activity in which they can interact with others, these same critics are all the more outraged when audiences treat the wrong sort of film with seriousness and concentration.

None the less, despite their differences, both these audiences are depicted as having one thing in common: an indulgence in sensation. Rather than engaging in cerebral forms of aesthetic appreciation, they are depicted as consuming wantonly; chattering with friends (whether verbally or electronically) in ways that are presumed to be meaningless and trivial; or in greedily consuming the images on screen, not as an intellectual act but as a bland and mindless pleasuring of themselves. It is therefore common for critics to suggest that the films are little more than female pornography: 'I felt like I was attending a Barely Legal Chippendales show.'[10] However, no one explains why this is bad, or why it is any worse than the materials directed at male teenagers.

This disgust at the saga's audiences and their bodily enjoyment reaches its zenith in one critic's claim that, in *The Twilight Saga: Breaking Dawn – Part 1* (dir. Bill Condon, 2011) the depiction of Bella and Edward's wedding night leaves 'the bed in tatters, and the audience, presumably, in a puddle of ecstasy'.[11] The criticisms of the saga are therefore part of a larger history of associating the dangers of mass culture with femininity and vice versa,[12] dangers that are often conveyed through metaphors of fluidity, such as when mass culture is described as a morass, or ooze, that spreads, absorbs and engulfs everything.[13]

No attempt is therefore made to make sense of the pleasures that audiences might actually derive from watching these films. Instead, the audience is seen as a homogeneous one, the experiences of which are completely other and irrelevant to those of the critic or other rational viewers. If 'all 13-year old female' viewers should run 'to the nearest multiplex', the rest of us 'needn't run. Or walk.'[14] These films, it is posited, have nothing to offer anyone outside the target audience other than boredom or incomprehension.

If this Othering of the audience were not worrying enough, there is also an insidious creep in the categorisations. Although some reviewers suggest that the audience is teenage girls, it soon becomes clear that it is not simply *some* teenagers but 'seemingly every teenage girl on the planet [who is] lapping it up',[15] a category that starts to spread still further. For some critics, the audience is '13-year-old' girls';[16] for others, it is the '14-year-old girl';[17] and for yet more others it is '16-year-old girls and their grandmothers'.[18] For the *Mail*, it is 'aimed at girls between 13 and 15. That's IQ, by the way, not age',[19] and while this might sound like a narrowing of the category, other critics start filling in the remaining female demographics. For *Christianity Today*, the audience is a pre-teen or 'tween' one[20] and, for another critic, men 'get dragged to cinemas to see it by their wives and girlfriends'.[21] Very soon, it seems, no distinction between women needs to be made and the fantasy of the mindless teenage girl is applicable to all women everywhere.

Ironically, this attack is often done under the guise of feminism. Of course, if this kind of hypocrisy weren't so prevalent elsewhere, it might be amusing to find publications such as *SFX* denouncing *The Twilight Saga: New Moon* (2009, dir. Chris Weitz) as 'a century of feminism down the drain'[22] or *Film Threat* attacking the film for its 'anti-feminist ideology' and for having 'reversed everything that Joss Whedon did for female empowerment'.[23] Neither publication takes the same stance against the anti-feminist politics of more male-centred films and it is strange to find Joss Whedon as not only the key figure to advance 'female empowerment' but also posed against Stephenie Meyer. Certainly, women are not automatically feminist any more than men are automatically anti-feminist, but it does seem odd that a man is the only figure who can be found to authorise feminism, and that a woman represents the problematic gender politics of contemporary media.

Indeed, the attack on the saga often works to legitimate the gender politics of contemporary media. It condemns these films through their supposed association with the far right in a manner that suggests that most media products are somehow unproblematic. For example, the saga's central relationship between a female human and a male vampire is claimed to be complicit in the New Right's campaigns against sexual liberalism and particularly 'the burgeoning pro-abstinence ideology of Christian organisations such as True Love Waits' that promote celibacy among the young.[24] *The New York Times*, for example, claimed that the first film was a 'romance for the hot-not-to-trot abstinency set',[25] while *Time Out London* claimed that 'it's hard not to read this as some slightly sinister metaphor for the perils of fornication and the wonders of abstinence'.[26] The main evidence for such a reductive reading is highly circumstantial. The *Guardian* describes Meyer as 'a Mormon mother of three from Arizona',[27] as though this explains everything, while *Christianity Today* claimed that 'Meyer, a Mormon, interjected her book with moral themes with which Christians resonate',[28] despite its own reservations about the film. For example, its review of *New Moon* dismissed the film as 'essentially uncritical celebrations of that overwrought, obsessive passion that is the hallmark of immaturity'.[29] It did not sympathise with the film's supposed Christian morality but rather condemned its 'immaturity' and its refusal to offer any suggestion of 'what "losing one's soul" or being "damned" means'.

The problems here are numerous. Mormons, whatever their politics, are not simply synonymous with the evangelical Christian Right, and these two religious groupings have quite major differences. In other words, even extreme Christians are not all the same, nor are all Mormons. Furthermore, little evidence (never mind detail) is given about Meyer's actual Mormon morality and, even if it were, this does not mean that the books, and much less the films, could be contained by these politics. It has long been standard that critics see literary and film texts as complex systems that cannot be simply reduced to their authors' intentions and may in many ways exceed and even contradict those intentions.

Other evidence is also mobilised such as an implied association between the films and 'OJD (Obsessive Jonas Brothers Disorder)'.[30] This suggests that the audience for the films is basically the same as that for the publicly celibate boy band, although no evidence is actually provided to substantiate this link. Similarly, there are a series of rather smug associations implied with the

conservative philosophy that wives are happier if they 'surrender' to their hus-
bands' authority. For example, Ebert claims of the audience that 'Edward seems
to stir their surrender instincts'.[31] The film is therefore damned not through
explicit or developed critique but through rumour and innuendo that associates
it with the Right and with censorship.

Furthermore, these reviews are often contradictory and reveal some of the
problems with the readings that they offer. For example, the *Daily Mail* expresses
some sense of confusion at criticisms of the film. At a point when many sections
of the press and even certain feminists are attacking the supposed sexualisation of young girls,[32] the *Daily Mail* claims to be bemused that the film is
condemned 'in the *Guardian* for ... encouraging teenagers to embrace celibacy.
This is, apparently, a bad thing.'[33] The point here is not to endorse the *Daily
Mail*'s own extremely contradictory and hypocritical stance on the sexualisation
of young girls (it also condescendingly attacks the film as 'High School Musical
without the Sex'). Instead, this example simply demonstrates the contradictions
inherent in these discourses. Indeed, the *Guardian* review did not conform to
the *Mail*'s description but offered a more sophisticated analysis of the film's
politics: the film 'also in a strange, unexpected way, responds to the Just Say
Yes movement. When anything and everything is sexualised in the media,
when women and women's bodies are obsessively presented in sexual terms,
then what happens when you don't fit in?'[34] In other words, debates over young
people's sexual activity are far more complex than many reviews acknowledge,
and an encouragement for young people to practise sexual restraint is not simply equivalent to the New Right's position on abstinence.

Descriptions of the film also seem to undermine the film's supposed abstinence agenda or at least to significantly complicate it. As most reviewers
acknowledge, it is not Bella who won't but Edward who won't let her: 'However
much [Edward] wants to give in to his feelings for Bella in the bedroom department – and however much *she might want him to* – he cannot.'[35] Here Bella is not
a chaste young virgin but an actively desiring one, something that is strongly
conveyed by references to her 'increasingly feverish pleading'.[36]

Indeed, the barrier to the sexual consummation of Bella and Edward's
romance is a quite familiar dynamic of romantic fictions in which romance is
intensified through its frustration, a technique that long predates abstinence
debates. Many reviewers even acknowledge as much, so that *The New York
Times* claims: 'Like all vampire stories, "Twilight" is about repressed desire and
untamed hunger.'[37] Such a statement does not conform to the association with
the politics of abstinence, but undermines it. It demonstrates that the concern
with repressed desire is a feature of vampire narratives that long predates the

politics of abstinence; and that it is not simply about female sexuality but sexuality more generally. It is not just young girls who find sex both attractive and frightening; and it is precisely this ambivalence that is often associated with male-oriented horror by its critics.

Indeed, romantic frustration is clearly linked by critics to long-established generic features beyond horror. Most critics note that *New Moon* actively associates Bella and Edward with Romeo and Juliet, lovers whose desires are frustrated by their familial backgrounds. In other words, romances frequently create tensions through the class or ethnic backgrounds of their lovers. As Corliss notes, 'Bella could be any Hollywood heroine in love with a good boy whom society callously misunderstands.'[38]

Furthermore, the vampire's kiss is often claimed to be associated not only with sex but with perverse sexualities, a claim that could suggest that the saga's sexual politics are far more complex than the version of straight sex that most reviewers imply is the normal and healthy option that the films deny, i.e. the saga and its fans might be much more interesting than the critics who attack them.

These difficulties become particularly apparent when critics try to tackle the main characters, and while some see Bella as a figure of passivity and conformity, others read her very differently. *Film Threat*, for example, describes her as a 'typical teenager' and as 'useless', a position that implies absolute dependence and a lack of agency.[39] *Christianity Today* similarly presents her as 'not the brightest crayon in the box'.[40] For others, her passivity is seen as so extreme that it is positively perverse. Ebert describes her as a 'thantophile', a figure so passive that she is in love with death and embodies 'the sentiment, "I'd die for you"'.[41] Alternatively, *Time Out London* claims that her 'insistence that she doesn't mind the bruises [after her first night of sex with Edward] is downright masochistic',[42] while *Variety* claims that 'the spirit of masochistic self sacrifice ... has defined the series'.[43] Nowhere is there an acknowledgement that, again, such romances with death and masochistic desires are common to a range of more legitimate and even canonical works; and that masochistic desires may not be as simple as they seem.[44]

It is hardly surprising, then, that some critics have seen Bella as far less conventional, even though this acknowledgement often contradicts their more general claims. Most notably, the *Guardian* makes special mention of a scene in the film in which 'we see her looking poignantly from a window of a speeding car at these very same nice, normal people emerging from a diner, a veritable tableau of the nice, safe normality that could have been hers'.[45] This scene presents Bella as anything but the average teenager. On the contrary, it is suggested

that she is someone whose desires define her as abnormal and perverse, someone with a profound sense of alienation from normality. For other critics, she is
'articulate, quite attractive, intelligent';[46] seen as having a 'tremulous intensity
and a slight snarl'[47] and described as a 'spiky, populist heroine'.[48] Furthermore,
her sexuality is not seen as normal or safe but indeed quite the reverse. The
Telegraph notes that 'boy, does she have terrible taste when it comes to the opposite sex', so much so that it asks: 'How disappointed would you be if you raised
a child who, confronted with a chap announcing "I'm designed to kill you",
replied: "I don't care"?'[49] Her desires, it is claimed, are perverse and should be
a worry to parents.

This dichotomy is also seen in discussions of Kristen Stewart, who plays Bella,
and while some complain of the 'lead actors' lack of emotional range',[50] others identify her performance as 'strong' and 'consistently excellent'.[51] Moreover,
those who are most positive also seem most aware of her previous roles, and
vice versa – those who are least positive seem least aware. For example, *The
Telegraph* unwittingly disparages the films' fans with the claim that they 'think
of [Stewart] as some kind of Jodie Foster in waiting'.[52] The irony here is that
the critics who praise Stewart draw attention to her earlier performances in
Into the Wild (2007, dir. Sean Penn) and *Panic Room* (2002, dir. David Fincher),
the latter of which featured Stewart as Jodie Foster's 'androgynous offspring'.[53]
With Foster as her mother, a star who had long attracted a lesbian following
due to public speculation about the star's own sexuality,[54] and given Stewart's
'androgynous' styling in the film, the young actress brought unconventional
star image to her role as Bella.

If critics seemed divided on whether Bella represented a conventional figure of femininity, or quite the opposite, there was general agreement that the
objects of her desire were not simply dangerous and inappropriate men (neither
of them are seen as safe figures of asexuality) but not even really masculine.
Instead, reviewers often displayed a sense of deep-seated homosexual panic, as if
the virulence of the attacks on the films was due to a desperate need to disavow
any pleasure in the images on screen. Edward is not only described as 'a bore'[55]
but as too feminine, 'looking at Bella intensely, up through his eyelashes, as if
in homage to Princess Diana'.[56] Similarly, he is supposed to have the 'peevish-
ness of a guy who just lost a Greta Garbo lookalike contest'.[57] Alternatively, the
Daily Mail predictably refuses such subtlety:

> Unlike real heterosexual boys, he is ready at all times to talk about feel-
> ings ... For much of the time he instructs her as though he's a middle-aged
> agony aunt ('Take Control! You're a strong, independent woman!') He

even has an eating disorder which practically makes him an honorary girl.[58]

Even Jacob (a werewolf who also woos Bella) is seen as 'gay', largely because he is clearly not the real subject of desire but its object. Critics repeatedly complain that he seems to 'never wear shirts'[59] or jokingly suggest that 'his torso remains so central a character it should be given its own credit line'.[60] As *Empire* puts it so honestly: 'The plethora of shirtless men (sometimes shot in – God help us – slow-motion) and general fetishisation of Bella's love interests may raise a giggle or an eyebrow in audiences more accustomed to seeing women in their scanties.'[61] There are even sniggery references to *Brokeback Mountain* (2005, dir. Ang Lee) with Ebert commenting on the 'Brokeback spirit' of *The Twilight Saga: Eclipse* (2010 dir. David Slade),[62] while others observe: 'Suddenly, it's eyelash-fluttering *Brokeback Eclipse*, and quite hilarious.'[63]

Not only are the male characters seen as too feminine but there are continual claims about the saga's reputed lack of violence. For *Time Out London*, the need for a 'tween-acceptable rating' meant that 'blood-drenched carnage isn't an option',[64] and this failure is seen as emblematic of the saga's failings, which is supposed to have 'drained the blood from the vampire genre and replaced it with sugared water; no wonder teenage girls flock around like humming birds'.[65] Edward is therefore supposed to 'sully the entire vampire tradition', due to his 'fears [of] sullying Bella's pure soul; what kind of vampire worth the title frets about that sort of thing?'[66]

This complaint becomes a recurring theme among critics, for whom it also affords an opportunity for fun. Rather than take the saga seriously, critics demonstrate their disdain not simply through what is said but through the flippant way in which they say it. *The New York Times* therefore punningly suggests that the lack of violence and gore makes *New Moon* 'juiceless' and 'near bloodless',[67] while others shift the terms of the pun, to claim that the films are 'not so much undead as entirely devoid of life'[68] or 'missing any animating pulse'.[69]

For all these critics, however, the problem is the same: the saga's monsters are simply not violent enough. The *Guardian* even published an article that claimed that *The Twilight Saga* strategy for success was one in which

the lead vampire in *New Moon* isn't a Romanian with slicked back hair who shouts 'I vant to suck your blood!' and then turns into a bat – he's a sallow-looking chap who talks about his feelings and sparkles like a *fairy* whenever the sun gets too bright. And, unless I am mistaken, the werewolf appears to be Mr September model from the Moody Topless hunks calendar.[70]

It is then suggested how other monsters 'can successfully reinvent themselves as sappy romantic leads in their own teenage dramas'.[71] The irony is, of course, that many of the monsters that they discuss (the Creature from the Black Lagoon and Hannibal Lector) explicitly engaged in dark romances with their leading ladies – Clarice and Lector even became an odd couple by the end of Harris' *Hannibal*.

The lack of violence is not simply supposed to demonstrate the saga's lack of quality but even to disqualify it from the category of horror altogether. As *Empire* puts it, 'Despite the presence of vampires, *Twilight* is romance, not horror, and anyone hoping to sink their teeth into a juicy gore-fest will be disappointed.'[72] Despite the long and well-established association between romance and horror, the two are presented as distinct categories and the saga is therefore seen as a kind of category violation.

As if to emphasise the point, critics repeatedly contrast the saga with *Buffy the Vampire Slayer*, the latter being seen as both 'real horror' and 'real feminism'. Even Billson asserts 'God knows I'm Team Buffy not Team Bella, and I prefer my vampires evil',[73] a position that uncharacteristically forgets one of Whedon's key characters: Angel, the vampire with a soul, who was Buffy's love interest for three seasons until he left to become the subject of his own spin-off series. Furthermore, *Buffy* was hardly original here and erotic tensions between vampires and humans could even be said to be a central, or at least predominant, feature of the vampire tale throughout its history, even in nineteenth-century literary versions such as Bram Stoker's *Dracula* (1897).

Denied the category of horror, the saga is associated with a series of derided genres. The films are therefore ridiculed through their association with the less legitimate end of teen TV and it is claimed that ' "Twilight" isn't quite "Transylvania 90210", but ... close'.[74] However, the most common generic association is with the 'daytime soap-opera'[75], and even then it is seen as a poor example of the type: 'a formless, gormless soap opera'.[76] Similarly *New Moon* was described as 'feeling like *The Da Vinci Code* mashed up with a feminine-hygiene commercial'.[77]

In this context, it should be noted that the most critically lauded instalment in the saga was the third, *Eclipse*, precisely due to its violence and action. As the most 'guy friendly film of the series',[78] it attracted a series of positive reviews that also demonstrated quite how despised the saga was as a whole, even as they praised this latest addition. *SFX* started its review with a strange sentence phrased as an announcement but followed by a question mark, as if it could not quite believe its own statement: '*Twilight* film in "not gut-wrenchingly awful" shocker?'[79] In addition, *Village Voice* referred to the film as 'the least laughable instalment yet in the series',[80] while *The Wall Street Journal* claimed: 'for the first time in the series I felt I'd seen a real movie.'[81] In other words, if some condemned the saga by excluding it from the category of horror, others even went so far as to claim that they were not just bad films but did not even properly qualify as 'real' films or even as cinema. For *Variety*, then, *Eclipse* differed from earlier instalments, being 'the most cinematic of the series so far',[82] and the justification for all of these comments was the film's choice of director, David Slade, who had made his name with gory and violent horror films, *Hard Candy* (2005) and *30 Days of Night* (2007). For *Hollywood Reporter*, the saga '*finally* nails the right tone' with 'action' that is 'nifty enough that young men may get into the series too'[83] – Slade is thus given 'much of the credit for the success'. *SFX* also claims that 'the right director can make all the difference' and praises Slade's 'visceral set pieces' and 'pacier structure',[84] while the *Sun* also praises Slade for the film's 'action' and for 'a brilliantly executed fight' near its close.[85]

However, despite all the praise for Slade's action and violence, there is virtually no interest in judging the saga as romance, other than to complain that it privileges romance over sex. In other words, we return to a quite reductive suggestion that romance is only ever a repression of sexuality and that it is used to oppress women.[86] Only *Christianity Today* makes the distinction between sex and intimacy and claims of *Twilight* that 'tender loving moments' are 'what the film does best: quiet moments of intimacy – not sex, but more innocent intimacy like when the infatuated Bella and Edward lie in the grass with their hands barely touching, or when they first kiss'.[87] This point is not a return to the issue of abstinence but may, on the contrary, clarify what the claims about abstinence obscure.

To come at the issue from another direction, *Time* was one of the few publications to discuss the film in the context of the complaints levelled at contemporary Hollywood by older viewers (or more accurately, alienated non-viewers) who see the obsession with sex as having displaced the romance of classical Hollywood cinema. Consequently, while *Time* seems to accept the association of the film with the abstinence campaigns, it also acknowledges that this association may have had unintended consequences. If the film 'is faithful to the book's chaste eroticism ... waiting has its own delicious tension',[88] and the film's success was the way in which it rekindled 'the warmth of great Hollywood romances, where foreplay was the climax and a kiss was never just a kiss'.[89]

Indeed, as much of the contemporary scholarship on film censorship has pointed out, censorship can be extremely productive in a way that explicitness is not.[90] For example, in a discussion of the ironies of the Hollywood Production Code Administration, Henry Jenkins demonstrates the ways in which the prohibition against the depictions of the vampire's kiss often resulted in an absence or gap – the vampire moves in to his victim's throat, the screen goes black and a scream is heard. But such techniques did not simply deny the audience an image of the vampire's kiss. It activated their imaginations, encouraged audiences to read for connotations and, in the process, enabled them to fill in such ellipses in multiple different ways. In other words, the attempt to prohibit can give licence to the imagination and to the imagining of perversities that cannot be named, perversities that may even gain their very power from not being named.[91]

Notes

1. Anne Billson, 'I Know *Twilight* is Awful, but ... ', *Guardian Film Blog*, 24 November 2011.
2. Joanne Hollows, *Feminism, Femininity and Popular Culture* (Manchester: Manchester University Press, 2000).
3. Dominic Power, 'Film Review: The Twilight Saga – New Moon', *SFX*, 24 November 2009.
4. Michael O'Sullivan, 'A Modern "Romeo" With a Bite', *The Washington Post*, 20 November 2009.
5. Mark Adams, 'Teen Flick is Bloody Romantic', *Mirror*, 19 December 2008.
6. Richard Corliss, '*Twilight* Review: Swooningly True to the Book', *Time*, 20 November 2008.
7. Manohla Dargis, 'The Love that Dare Not Bare its Fangs', *The New York Times*, 20 November 2008.
8. Sakhdev Sandhu, '*Twilight* – Review: First Love and Fresh Blood', *The Telegraph*, 19 December 2008.
9. Roger Ebert, 'Don't Say You'll Die for Me Unless You Really Mean it', *Chicago Sun Times*, 19 November 2008.
10. Jessica Baxter, 'Review of *The Twilight Saga: New Moon*', *Film Threat*, 19 November 2009.
11. Justin Chang, 'Review of *The Twilight Saga: Breaking Dawn – Part 1*', *Variety*, 11 November 2011.
12. Andreas Huyssen, 'Mass Culture as Woman: Modernism's Other', in Tania Modleski (ed.), *Studies in Entertainment* (Bloomington: Indiana University Press, 1986), pp. 188–207.
13. Mark Jancovich, 'A Real Shocker: Authenticity, Genre and the Struggle for Cultural Distinctions', *Continuum: Journal of Media and Cultural Studies* 14/1 (2000) pp. 22–35;

see also Janice Radway, 'On the Gender of the Middlebrow Consumer and the Threat of the Culturally Fraudulent Female', *South Atlantic Quarterly* 93/4 (Fall 1994), pp. 871–93.

14. Joe Morgenstern, '"Twilight" Barely Sips at Juicy Vampire Genre', *Wall Street Journal*, 21 November 2008.
15. Power, 'Film Review: The Twilight Saga – New Moon'.
16. Morgenstern, '"Twilight" Barely Sips at Juicy Vampire Genre'.
17. Adams, 'Teen Flick is Bloody Romantic'.
18. Ebert, 'Don't Say You'll Die for Me'.
19. Chris Tookey, '*Twilight*: A Teen Flick You Can Sink Your Teeth into', *Daily Mail*, 19 December 2008.
20. Todd Hertz, 'Review', *Christianity Today*, 21 November 2008.
21. Anon., 'New Moon for Monsters: Which Movie Beasts Need a Makeover', *Guardian*, 25 November 2009.
22. Power, 'Film Review: *The Twilight Saga – New Moon*'.
23. Baxter, 'Review of *The Twilight Saga: New Moon*'.
24. Sandhu, '*Twilight* – Review: First Love and Fresh Blood'.
25. Dargis, 'The Love that Dare Not Bare its Fangs'.
26. Trevor Johnston, 'Review', *Time Out London*, 18–31 December 2008.
27. Helen Pidd, 'Stephenie Meyer Turns Rainy Little Forks – and the World – into a Twilight Zone', *Guardian*, 13 November 2009.
28. Hertz, 'Review'.
29. Steven D. Greydanus, 'Review of *The Twilight Saga: New Moon*', *Christianity Today*, 19 November 2009.
30. Dargis, 'The Love that Dare Not Bare its Fangs'.
31. Ebert, 'Don't Say You'll Die for Me'.
32. See Linda Papadopoulos, *Sexualisation of Young People Review*, Home Office (2010), http://webarchive.nationalarchives.gov.uk/+/http:/www.homeoffice.gov.uk/documents/Sexualisation-of-young-people2835.pdf? date last accessed view=Binary; Angela McRobbie, *The Aftermath of Feminism: Gender, Culture and Social Change* (London: Sage, 2009); and for a critique of this kind of work see Linda Duits and Liesbet van Zoonen, 'Coming to Terms with Sexualization', *European Journal of Cultural Studies* 14/5 (2011), pp. 491–506; and Clarissa Smith and Feona Attwood, 'Lamenting Sexualization: Research, Rhetoric and the Story of Young People's "Sexualization" in the UK Home Office Review', *Sex Education: Sexuality, Society and Learning* 11/3 (2011), pp. 327–37.
33. Tookey, '*Twilight*'.
34. Peter Bradshaw, 'Girl Meets Vampire. Girl Loves Vampire. Girl and Vampire Go to the Prom ... Peter Bradshaw Enjoys this Unorthodox but Sweet and Satirical Take on the Teen Vampire Movie', *Guardian*, 19 December 2008.
35. Bradshaw, 'Girl Meets Vampire'.
36. Manohla Dargis, 'Abstinence Makes the Heart ... Oh, You Know', *The New York Times*, 19 November 2009.
37. Dargis, 'The Love that Dare Not Bare its Fangs'.
38. Corliss, '*Twilight* Review: Swooningly True to the Book'.

39. Baxter, 'Review of *The Twilight Saga: New Moon*'.
40. Greydanus, 'Review of *The Twilight Saga*'.
41. Roger Ebert, 'Worse than Being a Vampire is Being a Vampire's Lover', *Chicago Sun Times*, 18 November 2009.
42. Anna Smith, 'Review of *The Twilight Saga: Breaking Dawn Part One*', *Time Out London*, 17–23 November 2011.
43. Chang, 'Review of *The Twilight Saga: Breaking Dawn – Part 1*'.
44. For work on the complexities of sexuality, see Carole S. Vance (ed.), *Pleasure and Danger: Exploring Female Sexuality* (London: Routledge, 1984). See also Adams and Rana in this collection.
45. Bradshaw, 'Girl Meets Vampire'.
46. Sandhu, '*Twilight* – Review: First Love and Fresh Blood'.
47. Dargis, 'The Love that Dare Not Bare its Fangs'.
48. Dan Kois, 'Blood is Thicker than Blood', *Village Voice*, 16 November 2011.
49. Sandhu, '*Twilight* – Review: First Love and Fresh Blood'.
50. Claudia Puig, '*Twilight* Barely Gets the Blood Flowing', *USA Today*, 19 November 2008.
51. Will Lawrence, 'Review of *Twilight*', *Empire* (November, 2008).
52. Sakhdev Sandhu, '*Twilight: Eclipse* – Review', *Telegraph*, 8 July 2010.
53. J. Hoberman, 'Prisoners' Songs', *Village Voice*, 26 March 2002.
54. Clare Whatlin, *Screen Dreams: Fantasising Lesbians in Film* (Manchester: Manchester University Press, 1997).
55. Bradshaw, 'Girl Meets Vampire'.
56. Ibid.
57. A. O. Scott, 'Global Warming Among the Undead', *The New York Times*, 29 June 2010.
58. Tookey, '*Twilight*'. In fact, this dialogue is from Bella, not Edward, and therefore illustrates the cavalier ways in which many critics discuss the saga. This lack of attention to detail not only undermines the reliability of claims about the saga's sexual politics but also the sincerity of these discussions of sexual politics. Once again, sexual politics seems to be largely mobilised as a stick to beat the saga, not as a topic about which critics demonstrate much commitment more generally.
59. Roger Ebert, 'Bella & Edward, Bella & Jacob, Edward & Jacob', *Chicago Sun Times*, 28 July 2010.
60. Nancy Gibbs, '*New Moon* Review: Team Jacob Ascending', *Time*, 19 November 2009.
61. Helen O'Hara, 'Review of *Twilight: New Moon*', *Empire* (n.d., 2009).
62. Ebert, 'Bella & Edward'.
63. Peter Travers, '*Twilight Saga, Eclipse*', *Rolling Stone*, 29 June 2010.
64. Johnston, 'Review'.
65. Philip French, 'Review: *The Twilight Saga: New Moon*', *Observer*, 22 November 2009; See also Edwards-Behi's article in this collection for a discussion of these issues.
66. Joy Tipping, 'Review of *The Twilight Saga: New Moon*', *Dallas Morning News*, 23 November 2009.
67. Dargis, 'Abstinence Makes the Heart…Oh, You Know'.

68. Chris Tookey, '*Twilight New Moon*: First Review of Long Awaited Sequel', *Daily Mail*, 25 November 2009.

69. Tim Robey, '*The Twilight Saga: New Moon*, First Review', *The Telegraph*, 16 November 2009.

70. Anon., 'New Moon for Monsters: Which Movie Beasts Need a Makeover' (my emphasis).

71. Ibid.

72. Will Lawrence, 'Review of *The Twilight Saga: Eclipse*', *Empire* (July 2010); again for further discussion see Edwards-Behi.

73. Billson, 'I Know Twilight is Awful, but ...'

74. Anon., 'Love Sucks (Blood)', *The Washington Times*, 21 November 2008.

75. Peter Debruge, 'Review of *The Twilight Saga: Eclipse*', *Variety*, 27 July 2010.

76. Robbie Collin, '*Twilight Saga: Breaking Dawn, Part One*, Review', *The Telegraph*, 16 November 2011.

77. Ann Hornaday, '*The Twilight Saga: Eclipse*', *The Washington Post*, 29 June 2010.

78. Anon., 'Have Men Got the Guts to Enter the Twilight Zone?', *Guardian*, 24 June 2010.

79. Jordan Farely, 'Review of *The Twilight Saga: Eclipse*', *SFX*, 5 July 2010.

80. Dan Kois, *The Twilight Saga: Eclipse* Serves Fans and Brand', *Village Voice*, 29 July 2010.

81. Joe Morgenstern, ' "Eclipse" Makes "Twilight" a Bit Brighter', *The Wall Street Journal*, 9 July 2010.

82. Debruge, 'Review of *The Twilight Saga: Eclipse*'.

83. Kirk Honeycutt, '*The Twilight Saga: Eclipse* – Film Review', *Hollywood Reporter*, 14 October 2010.

84. Farely, 'Review of *The Twilight Saga: Eclipse*'.

85. Anon., 'Bright Stars at Twilight', *Sun*, 9 July 2010.

86. For a longer discussion of these issues, see Hollows, *Feminism, Femininity and Popular Culture.*

87. Hertz, 'Review'.

88. Corliss, '*Twilight* Review: Swooningly True to the Book'.

89. Ibid.

90. See, for instance, Matthew Bernstein, *Controlling Hollywood: Censorship and Regulation in the Studio Era* (London: Athlone, 2000).

91. Henry Jenkins, 'Reception Theory and Audience Research: The Mystery of the Vampire's Kiss', in Christine Gledhill and Linda Williams (eds), *Reinventing Film Studies* (London: Arnold, 2000), pp. 165–82.

3

'FLICKS FOR CHICKS (AND CHICKS WITH DICKS) WHO CAN'T TAKE SERIOUS HORROR': THE GENERIC MISRECOGNITION OF *THE TWILIGHT SAGA*

Nia Edwards-Behi

To be a *Twilight* fan and to be a horror fan are, if some online critics are to be believed, two incompatible positions. An examination of the online horror community's reception of *The Twilight Saga*, via the attitudes found in popular horror websites and blogs, reveals an apparent misinterpretation of *The Twilight Saga* as a straightforward horror franchise. The three sorts of materials under consideration – user comments written by visitors to a website, news items, and reviews, which are written by the website's regular contributors – will mostly be taken from the self-proclaimed 'number one source for horror'.

BloodyDisgusting.com is widely considered to be one of the most frequently visited horror news and review websites and, as such, it provides a useful primary focus point for such an investigation.[1] Although such websites are only a specific representation of part of the online horror fandom, they do shed light on the sorts of attitudes and opinions expressed by invested followers of a particular genre within this locale. Most coverage given to *The Twilight Saga* on BloodyDisgusting.com conforms to Lisa Bode's findings that of all sorts of critical spaces, specialist blogs tend to provide 'the most highly negative reviews' and write 'most condescendingly of the teen girl audience'.[2] This provides the two primary criticisms upon which reviews and comments on BloodyDisgusting. com focus: negative accounts of the film itself, and the hyperbolic criticism of its target teen girl audience.[3]

While 'anti fandom' and *The Twilight Saga* has been discussed elsewhere[4] the specific examination of the horror community's apparent rejection of the saga is more in line with what Matt Hills describes as 'a kind of fan protectionism, and boundary maintenance, that can be analysed as inter-fandom'.[5] As Hills argues, this is an important line of investigation, and taking one particular arena of inter-fandom under consideration allows for a greater specificity in the results.

Criticising the Films

Tellingly, a news posting announces the first official image from *The Twilight Saga: Eclipse* (2010, dir. Slade) as 'super-duper lame', and asks the question '[W]hy can't they ever release something cool?'[6] A similar promotional news item by MrDisgusting brands a ten-second teaser trailer 'super annoying'.[7] In the latter, MrDisgusting addresses the apparent concerns of users at the posting of *The Twilight Saga* news on the website by stating such news items will be kept to a minimum, and that 'we listen to your feedback!' A similar article announcing a 14-second teaser released to promote *The Twilight Saga: New Moon* (2009, dir. Weitz) proclaims him to be 'insanely sick of reporting on these movies' and he complains that 'the rest of you can just skip over this crap, meanwhile I *have to* read everything'.[8] Perhaps conversely, he defends the coverage of *The Twilight Saga* on the website in response to an irate user, through the fact that 'more people read this article in 5 minutes than the *All About Evil* poster we've had up for a few hours'.[9] This highlights two questions that *Twilight* raises for such a website (and for generic debate moreover): how should 'horror' be defined, and why should attention be given to films that do not meet this definition?

Scholarly conceptions of the horror genre[10] are partially reflected in typical fan/user comments which articulate specific complaints about the films themselves. Comments from users include 'Could someone please enlighten me as to why this not-horror news is featured on a horror site? Anyone?'[11] and 'This has pretty much nothing to do with horror, why is this even being covered here? It gets plenty of coverage on other sites, this is for the horror community!'[12] Some users argue that *The Twilight Saga* falls into the category of 'sci-fi and fantasy type' films[13] which are indeed also given some coverage on BloodyDisgusting. com, while others argue that the film 'still has horror elements' and that

'therefore it belongs on this website'.[14] As the saga progresses, more comments
appear in defence of the coverage, both from fans – 'I've seen all the *Twilight*
movies ... and you know what else, I like them!'[15] – and those who are happy to
ignore it – 'BD has covered this pablum since it started ... so everyone get over
it and don't click.'[16] Yet these voices tend to appear in minority to the more
overwhelmingly common response: 'Fuck those Twilight movies in the ear! I
hate that garbage, stop posting news about them!!!!!!!!!!'[17]

While these user comments express confusion and dismay as to the saga's
continued horror website coverage, some also present a plausible, alternative
explanation. Comments such as 'how much do they pay you to promote this
shit?' and 'can I have the money you make from covering this on a horror site?'[18]
accuse BloodyDisgusting.com of providing coverage of *The Twilight Saga* purely
for financial reasons, which is in opposition to the website's relatively independent nature. To a degree, this also conforms to the predominant conceptions of
fans of 'marginal' texts – such as horror films – as masculine and resistant to
the mainstream,[19] and in this particular instance financial gain is positioned as
the mainstreaming of an independent horror website.[20]

Furthermore, these criticisms levelled towards the films appear to position
them as failed horror products, implying (and assuming) that *The Twilight Saga*
was intentionally made to be 'horror' and thus should be assessed accordingly,
and not in terms of other generic concerns. Indeed, criticisms tend to focus on the
lack of balance between action and dialogue – 'minimal action, minimal plot,
and people talking to each other about the same things over and over again'.[21]
This generic distinction, as identified by Bode,[22] clearly sees critics and fans
define horror or vampire cinema in a particular way. Bode attributes this distinction to the critics' 'patrolling of male-coded horror and action genre boundaries'
against contamination by aspects deemed 'feminine'.[23] What these responses
demonstrate is the increasingly slippery nature of defining the horror genre,
whereby fans of more traditional conceptions of it respond in increasingly defensive ways to a greater sense of fluidity as to what constitutes a 'horror film'.

Criticising the Fans

Criticising *The Twilight Saga* against generic expectations also encompasses and
facilitates the criticism of the saga's fans.[24] Fans are more often than not assumed
to be teenage girls who take the franchise very seriously, or indeed perhaps 'too'
seriously, an assumption I examine below. There is certainly no consideration
that those who enjoy the films may do so through an appreciation of the saga
as 'bad'[25] – and certainly never as 'paracinema'.[26] There are three primary ways

the fans of *The Twilight Saga* are criticised in such articles: through their intelligence, their appearance, and their taste. The first and the third are somewhat intertwined, with the fans – 'the girls' – in question not expected to know any better due to their age and their gender, attesting to their lack of cultural capital. Offering an alternative form of criticism to the majority of online horror articles, one review bemoans the fact that fans of the books have probably never heard of Judy Blume, and pinpoints the futility in advising 'young fans' to steer clear of the film *New Moon*, the implication being that they'll see it regardless of negative reviews.[27] This stance assumes a more paternal but none the less patronising role, in which the reviewer is positioned above the fan through their superior knowledge, taste, and thus cultural capital.

These more engaged criticisms of the assumed fan's literary scope are, however, often coupled with an attack on the fans' physical appearance. The aforementioned review of *New Moon* describes a typical book fan as 'some pimply, braces-wearing seventh grade girl'.[28] Further user comments are particularly explicit in their rejection of the films as feminine, seeking to reinforce an 'authentic' horror canon: 'it's a romantic horror flick for chicks who can't take serious horror grow the fuck up and watch some real horror you bitchs [sic]'[29] Notably, a parodic review of *New Moon* from genre website LatinoReview sees its reviewer describe Robert Pattinson as 'the stuff fat 14 year old girls dream of'.[30] Although the review is a parody, its vernacular is not, and as such it appears to astutely explicate many of the attitudes underlying more straight-faced reviews of the films. A large number of user comments employ homosexuality as a means to deride *The Twilight Saga*, often in as simple a manner as the word 'gay' being left as a comment,[31] or with slight elaboration, 'BD getting all gay up in here!'[32] 'Ugh, gay!!!!!! Death to *Twilight*!!'[33] It is impossible to gauge to what degree this might demonstrate an inherent homophobia, or to what degree the term 'gay' is being bandied around as a more generic insult. However, an apparent alignment of female, teen taste with homosexual taste as indiscriminating is apparent. The dismissive attitude is evident in a reviewer writing 'sorry girls (and gays),' before criticising Taylor Lautner as a weak link in the film. Although difficult to determine how consciously these alignments are made, the trend nevertheless seems to seek to reject *The Twilight Saga* as a feminised product[34] and ratify the space as hyper-masculinised and heteronormative.

The distinction between 'proper', male-coded horror and the feminine 'mainstream' has been noted by several scholars in the response to the 2009 San Diego Comic Con *New Moon* panel. The response to the inevitable *Twilight* fan presence at the convention is that they supposedly 'ruined' the event.[35] This rejection of *The Twilight Saga* presence at such a convention is once again a gendered disavowal, since 'franchises and fan activities', it is understood, 'are for boys and men'.[36] George 'El Guapo' Roush of LatinoReview authored another bitingly parodic blog post in advance of a *The Twilight Saga: Breaking Dawn – Part 1* (2011, dir. Condon) panel session at the more recent 2011 San Diego Comic Con, in which he offered a list on how to cope at a Comic Con when *Twilight* fans are present. The piece demonstrates many of the familiar criticisms expected of similarly dismissive articles, from the derisive description of the fans as 'rabid ... 12-year-old girls' to the undermining of female fan production, through his assertion that the fans contribute little 'besides making shitty YouTube compilation videos'.[37] Further, Roush recommends that the serious (and thus male) Comic Con attendees who dislike the saga 'fight back ... in the most violent ways possible'.[38] He then contentiously suggests 'or do what this guy did last year and just stab a bitch,' referring to an actual incident which saw a male Comic Con attendee attack another man with a pen.[39] Perhaps best demonstrative of the gendered divide is the number one piece of advice on the list: 'bring a rape prevention kit'. Roush outlines that only 'little girls and their single moms' would attend a *Twilight* panel, and that because the saga is aimed at women, 'there is a 99.9% chance' that any man who attends 'is a rapist'.[40] This demonstrates an assertion of appropriate masculine behaviour in addition to the derisive accounts of femininity. Thus, once more, fans are positioned as incomprehensible and worthy of derision, and are blamed – rather than the filmmakers – for enabling what could be termed a 'pseudo-horror' franchise to become so commercially dominant.

Problematising Genre

If horror is still often popularly thought of as a 'masculine' genre and a franchise such as *Twilight* is seen as 'feminine', then the rejection of one by the other can be argued as the demonstration and posturing of gendered attitudes. This is in line with the dismissal of melodrama, 'women's pictures' and soap operas precisely for their apparent nature as gendered feminine.[41] However, it is problematic to reduce such a clash of taste to issues of gender, insofar that such a claim only reduces the argument to conceptions associated with traditional gender roles. There are arguably as many female voices of dissent against *The Twilight Saga* as there are male, but their complaints are often made in much the same capacity and through the same terms, that the films are failed horror and that the fans are foolish for enjoying the saga. As such this could be read as what Hollows has termed playing at being 'one of the boys'.[42] For example, Brittney-Jade Colangelo's prominent Day of the Woman horror blog features around 40 *Twilight*-bashing posts, which she derogatorily refers to as 'twatlight'.[43] She complains that 'it's next to impossible to rock a fanged t-shirt without being bombarded by teenage girls asking where we got it'.[44] Although her blog is dedicated to 'the feminine side of fear', the criticisms of the saga found in her blog might be seen as conforming to assertions of women behaving as 'one of the boys'. Although gendered distinctions between critics pose an interesting avenue of further investigation, I would argue that, regardless of a critic's gender, foremost to the, at times, hyperbolic nature of online criticism is the issue of genre. Through online critics and user comments, *The Twilight Saga* is assessed in relation to specific conceptions of the horror genre, and as such rejected. This occurs in spite of the saga's lack of clear textual markers that position it as intentionally 'horror', and as such the apparent reasoning behind the vitriolic attacks on the films, the fans, and consumers of the franchise are ultimately erroneous and flawed.

The horror genre is an important intertext for *The Twilight Saga*, and by extension the genre's community of fans and enthusiasts are an important location of inter-fandom for the saga. Thus, further investigation into the horror community's reception of *The Twilight Saga* (particularly in relation to individuals or groups who may enjoy *both* horror and *The Twilight Saga*) will no doubt expand this complex picture. Further still, such an investigation should be revealing of what degree issues of genre and genre hybridity play into a film's reception, particularly when said film or film series is marketed in a particular way. *The Twilight Saga* thus offers a rich case study for further investigation into convergent issues of marketing, reception and inter-fandom.

Notes

1. Marc Graser, 'Collective Nabs Bloody-Disgusting', *Variety*, 12 September 2007, http://www.variety.com/article/VR1117971910?refCatId=1238 (accessed 5 May 2012).
2. Lisa Bode, 'Tastes: Teen Girls and Genre in the Critical Reception of *Twilight*', *Continuum* 24/5 (2010), pp. 707–19.
3. I would argue that the online horror community's criticism of the saga as an intended horror product is a misrecognition of the intended generic concerns of the saga. Although the saga features the semantic elements of a horror film, arguably the saga is a melodrama of the sentimental tradition. Marketing of *The Twilight Saga* employs non-horror generic conventions in order to sell the film, by offering a generic appeal – to melodrama – that the producers assume the audience wants to see (Lisa Kernan, 'Trailer Rhetoric', in *Coming Attractions: Reading American Movie Trailers* (Austin: University of Texas Press, 2004), pp. 36–77, pp. 44–5). With this in mind, it seems that to criticise *The Twilight Saga* for being too melodramatic seems to be as redundant as criticising horror films for being too scary, given its generic concern.

4. See Jessica Sheffield and Elyse Merlo, 'Biting Back: *Twilight* Anti-Fandom and the Rhetoric of Superiority', in Melissa Click, Jennifer Stevens Aubrey and Lissa Behm-Morawitz (eds), *Bitten By Twilight: Youth Culture, Media and the Vampire Franchise* (New York: Peter Lang, 2010), pp. 207–22; Jacqueline M. Pinkowicz, '"The Rabid Fans that Take [*Twilight*] much too Seriously": The Construction and Rejection of Excess in *Twilight* Antifandom', *Transformative Works and Cultures* 7 (2011), http://journal.trans-formativeworks.org/index.php/twc/issue/view/8. (accessed 5 May 2012).

5. Matt Hills, '"Twilight" Fans Represented in Commercial Paratexts and Inter-Fandoms: Resisting and Repurposing Negative Fan Stereotypes', in Anne Morey (ed.), *Genre, Reception and Adaptation in the "Twilight" Series* (Farnham: Ashgate, 2012), pp. 113–30, p. 115.

6. MrDisgusting, 'A Super-Lame Romantic Look at "The Twilight Saga: Eclipse"', 22 December 2009, *Bloody Disgusting*, http://www.bloody-disgusting.com/news/18481 (accessed 5 May 2012).

7. MrDisgusting, '"The Twilight Saga: Eclipse" Trailer Debut March 11, 10 Second Teaser NOW', 10 March 2010, *Bloody Disgusting*, loody-disgusting.com/news/19410/the-twilight-saga-eclipse-trailer-debut-march-11–10-second-teaser-now/ (accessed 5 May 2012).

8. MrDisgusting, 'Watch 14 Seconds of the Trailer for "New Moon"', 29 May 2009, *Bloody Disgusting*, http://www.bloody-disgusting.com/news/16343 (accessed 5 May 2012).

9. MrDisgusting, 'Full Trailer for "The Twilight Saga: Eclipse"', 11 March 2010, *Bloody Disgusting*, http://www.bloody-disgusting.com/news/19429 (accessed 5 May 2012).

10. For example see Robin Wood, 'The American Nightmare: Horror in the 70s', in *Hollywood from Vietnam to Reagan* (New York: Columbia University Press, 1986), pp. 70–94; Andrew Tudor, *Monsters and Mad Scientists: A Cultural History of the Horror Movie* (Oxford: Basil Blackwell, 1989); Peter Hutchings, *The Horror Film* (Harlow: Pearson-Longman, 2004).

11. 'Gunmetal' in MrDisgusting, 'No Teases This Time – It's the Full "Breaking Dawn" Trailer'.

12. 'SentinelPrimeX', Ibid.

13. 'evilfairydust', Ibid.

14. 'drmb1990', Ibid.

15. 'niuq' in MrDisgusting, 'First "Breaking Dawn" Image – A Whole Lotta Humpin' Going On!', 7 January 2011, *Bloody Disgusting*, http://www.bloody-disgusting.com/news/23061 (accessed 5 May 2012).

16. 'Nothing333' in MrDisgusting, 'No Teases This Time – It's the Full "Breaking Dawn" Trailer'.

17. 'EvilDeadFridaythe13thfan' in MrDisgusting, 'Hi-Res Image Gallery for "The Twilight Saga: Breaking Dawn Part 1', 2 February 2011b, *Bloody Disgusting*, http://www.bloody-disgusting.com/news/24371 (accessed 5 May 2012).

18. Both from user 'ThunderDragoon', in MrDisgusting, 'Hi-Res Image Gallery for "The Twilight Saga"' and MrDisgusting, 'No Teases This Time – It's the Full "Breaking Dawn" Trailer'.

19. Melissa A. Click, Jennifer Stevens Aubrey and Elizabeth Behm-Morawitz (eds), *Bitten By* Twilight: *Youth Culture, Media and the Vampire Franchise* (New York: Peter Lang, 2010), p. 7; see also Brigid Cherry, 'Refusing to Refuse the Look: Female Viewers of the Horror Film', in Mark Jancovich (ed.), *Horror, The Film Reader* (London: Routledge, 2001), pp. 169–78; Joanne Hollows, 'The Masculinity of Cult', in Mark Jancovich (ed.), *Defining Cult Movies: The Cultural Politics of Oppositional Taste* (Manchester: Manchester University Press, 2003), pp. 35–53; Jacinda Read, 'The Cult of Masculinity: From Fan-boys to Academic Bad-boys' in Mark Jancovich, *Defining Cult Movies: The Cultural Politics of Oppositional Taste* (Manchester: Manchester University Press, 2003), pp. 54–70.

20. BloodyDisgusting.com was bought in 2007 by management company The Collective; however, its content remains independently under the control of the original site founders (see Graser, 'Collective Nabs Bloody-Disgusting').

21. David Harley, 'BD Review: "The Twilight Saga: Eclipse" Doesn't (Quite) Bite', 29 June 2010, *Bloody Disgusting*, http://www.bloody-disgusting.com/news/20750 (accessed 5 May 2012) and 'Blu-Ray Review: "The Twilight Saga: Eclipse"', *Bloody Disgusting*, 30 November 2010, http://www.bloody-disgusting.com/news/22558 (accessed 5 May 2012).

22. Bode, 'Tastes', p. 710.

23. Ibid., p. 711.

24. See Jancovich, this collection, for a broader consideration of how critics have viewed the films' audience.

25. See Haig, this collection.

26. Jeffrey Sconce, '"Trashing" the Academy: Taste, Excess, and an Emerging Politics of Cinematic Style', in Ernest Mathijs and Xavier Mendik (eds), *The Cult Film Reader* (Milton Keynes: Open University Press, 2003 [1995]), p. 101.

27. Chris Eggertsen, 'Review: The Twilight Saga: New Moon' *Bloody Disgusting*, 19 November 2009, http://bloody-disgusting.com/film/111742/twilight-saga-new-moon/?tab=bd-review (accessed 5 May 2012).

28. Ibid.

29. 'flesheater123' in MrDisgusting, 'Hi-Res Image Gallery for "The Twilight Saga"'.

30. George Roush, 'Fans, It's the Review You Deserve! El Guapo Gives New Moon an A+!', *Latino Review* (2009), http://www.latinoreview.com/news/fans-it-s-the-review-you-deserve-el-guapo-gives-new-moon-an-a-8587 (accessed 8 February 2012) (link no longer working).

31. 'ollie23', in MrDisgusting, 'Full Trailer for "The Twilight Saga: Eclipse"'.

32. 'Jcrimes' in MrDisgusting, 'No Teases This Time – It's the Full "Breaking Dawn" Trailer'.

33. 'Dutchess' in MrDisgusting, 'A Super-Lame Romantic Look'.

34. See Harman in this volume.

35. Click et al., *Bitten By Twilight*, p. 6; Natalie Wilson, *Seduced by* Twilight: *The Allure and Contradictory Messages of the Popular Saga* (Jefferson, NC: McFarland & Co., 2011), p. 201.

36. Click et al., *Bitten By* Twilight, p. 6.

37. George Roush, '5 Ways to "Twilight" Prepare Yourself for This Year's Comic-Con', *El Guapo TV* (2011), http://elguapotv.blogspot.com/2011/06/el-guapo-presents-5-ways-to-twilight.html (accessed 5 May 2012) (link no longer working).

38. Ibid.

39. Lewis Wallace, 'Comic-Con Eye-Stabbing Leaves 1 Injured, 1 Jailed', *Wired.com*, 25 July 2010, http://www.wired.com/underwire/2010/07/comic-con-stabbing/ (accessed 5 May 2012).

40. Roush, '5 Ways to "Twilight" Prepare Yourself'.

41. See Barbara Klinger, 'Tastemaking: Reviews, Popular Canons, and Soap Operas', in *Melodrama and Meaning: History, Culture and the Films of Douglas Sirk* (Indianapolis: Indiana University Press, 1994), pp. 69–96.

42. Hollows, 'The Masculinity of Cult', p. 39.

43. The significance of her use of the word 'twat' as derogatory, given its feminine connotations, perhaps suggests another avenue of potential investigation, yet is beyond the scope of this specific chapter.

44. Brittney-Jade Colangelo, 'How to Fix Twilight', *Day of the Woman: A Blog for the Feminine Side of Fear* (2010), http://dayofwoman.blogspot.com/2010/06/how-to-fix-twilight-yes-its-possible.html (accessed 5 May 2012) (link no longer working).

4

THE PAGEANT OF HER BLEEDING TWI-HARD HEART: *TWILIGHT,* FEMININITY, SEXUALITY AND FEMALE CONSUMPTION

Sarah Harman

The Twilight Saga is continually maligned and problematised through its association with the feminine. Take for instance Stuart Heritage's recent anti-*Twilight* 'humorous' rant in the *Guardian*:

> It's become passé to blame *Twilight* for everything, but that doesn't mean that *Twilight* isn't actually to blame for everything. Most bad things, if you work hard enough, can be traced back to *Twilight* ... But *Twilight's* biggest crime – bigger than getting away with having a soggily submissive female as its lead character, bigger even than making grown women refer to themselves as 'Team Jacob' without any trace of shame or irony – is what it's done to the undead ... [N]ow vampires are little more than sensitive glittery emo types who enjoy poetry and actually *like* people. It's a disgrace ... Now the supernatural is just about as mainstream as it gets ... This leaves us with two choices: we either ignore or embrace the madness. One choice involves wilfully missing out on a vast slice of popular culture. The other involves dressing cats up as butlers and kissing posters of Robert Pattinson before you go to bed. I think I'll take my chances with the former.[1]

Undoubtedly this reinforces Edwards-Behi's assertion in the previous chapter that this masculine horror traditionalist position rejects the saga through 'an apparent alignment of female, teen taste with homosexual taste as indiscriminating ... [wherein fans are] not expected to know any better due to their age and their gender, attesting to their lack of cultural capital'.[2] But how might these gendered assumptions figure into a legacy of femininity and consumption in the meta-world outside of these debates? What might this say about contemporary feminine (and indeed feminist) identity? This chapter thus seeks to unpack just what is at 'stake' behind the figures of the 'Twi-hard' and '*Twilight* Mom'[3] kissing their posters of Robert Pattinson before they go to bed' and thus their role within capitalist consumption and consumerism.

Consuming consumption

In her 1996 book *The Sex of Things: Gender and Consumption in Historical Perspective*, Victoria de Grazia explains through rhetoric the indivisible nature of femininity and consumption within capitalism:

> What more precisely is the identification of femininity, of the female sex, of womankind generally with sumptuary laws, shopping sprees, and domestic display, not to mention the mundane chores of purchase and provisioning with which women are so familiarly associated? Is this only a time-worn trope of patriarchal culture? Or does it bare deeper social processes?[4]

Similarly, the problematic of the feminine in capitalist patriarchy presents as a recurring trope in the theorisation of postmodern feminism. Echoing the sentiments of de Grazia within a somewhat more polemical context, Nina Power has stated in the preface to her feminist monograph, '[i]f the contemporary portrayal of womankind is to be believed, contemporary female achievement would culminate in the ownership of expensive handbags, a vibrator, a job, a flat and a man – probably in that order.'[5] Certainly, as these two statements observe, within popular culture women are viewed as consumers, and since the economic boom of the 1950s and subsequent increase in multimedia marketing and advertisements, female identity has become [m]aligned with consumption. While Marxist-feminists have problematically sought to 'liberate women from the oppression of capitalism', 'post-feminists' now seek to reframe or perhaps *repackage for sale* this 'oppression' as 'liberation and power' in economic terms.

The situation that the contemporary feminist woman finds herself in is a quandary that Power satirises:

> Feminism offers you the latest deals in lifestyle improvement, from the bedroom to the boardroom, from guilt-free fucking to the innocent hop-skip all the way to the shopping mall – I don't diet so it's ok! *I'm* not deluded! I can buy what I like! Feminism™ is the perfect accompaniment to femme-capital™: politics, such as it is, belongs to the well-balanced individual (the happy shopper), sassiness is like, *so* where it's at (customer confidence) and, most of all, one must never, ever admit to cracks in the facade (ideology). This foundation is flawless! And it lasts all night! Not like men, titter, titter, etc. etc.[6]

Thus the very act of consumption itself is gendered and in the power economics of post-modernism and post-feminism, the exploration of femininity and consumption becomes increasingly crucial, yet increasingly rejected through this gendered rubric. Thus it is imperative to unpack how such a feminised popular culture phenomenon as *The Twilight Saga*, being as it is aligned with notions of rabid consumption and consumerism, functions in this socio-political and economic context.

Herstories of hysterical consumption

The popularity of *The Twilight Saga* and its consistent gendering as feminine can of course be attributed to the high visibility of its female fans and the level of merchandising which leads critics to state, '*Twilight* fans will buy anything.' The consumption of this – by no means atypical – branding of *Twilight* can undoubtedly be seen to link into a projection of identity formation and belonging, as well as a desire of proximity to the text. Yet the characterisation of this hysterical,[7] indiscriminately consuming fan is of course by no means a recent phenomenon. As Barbara Ehrenreich et al. discussed in their 1992 paper 'Beatlemania: Girls Just Want to Have Fun,'

> hysteria was crucial to the marketing of The Beatles. First there were reports of near riots in England. Then came a calculated publicity tease that made Colonel Parker's manipulations look oafish by contrast: five million posters and stickers announcing 'The Beatles Are Coming' were distributed nationwide ... By the time The Beatles materialised, on *The Ed Sullivan Show* in February 1964, the anticipation was unbearable ... By the time The Beatles hit America, teens and pre-teens had already learned

to look to their unique consumer subculture for meaning and validation ... For girls, fandom offered a way not only to sublimate romantic and
sexual yearnings but to carve out subversive versions of heterosexuality.[8]

The complexity of this fandom is thus made clear. It seemingly offers the
means by which to evade the pre-conceived life of the 'nice girl' and is framed
as potentially rebellious against gendered behaviour expectations. Yet it is
entirely rooted in heteronormative consumerism.

In *Twilight* specifically, we see this in the figure of the '*Twilight* Mom' as well
as the younger 'Twi-hard'. Media coverage, it would seem, not only propels
these stereotypes, but leads the hysteria and hype:

> 'I was so excited,' Sarah O'Regan from London tells us. 'I won tickets on
> In4merz, which is the *Twilight* street team where I had to blog about *New
> Moon* and *Robsessed* for a week solid to win. I got to the *Robsessed* premiere
> and it was rammed with fans, I wasn't even late, but I didn't find out
> about the free Robsessed posters till they were all gone. Then I spotted
> one on the table at the same time as another girl and we both ran for it. I
> grabbed it first but then she snatched it off me! ... I was totally Robsessed
> and I had fire in my heart! It all happened so quickly. I ended up on the
> floor and my arm and cheek were in terrible pain, so my friend had to
> take me to hospital.' Sarah's Robsessed poster was torn in the scuffle, but
> she's glad she kept 'the better half' showing Rob's face.[9]

This media-created notion of *Twilight* fandom thus remains heternormative,
patriarchal and capitalist, as Natalie Wilson indeed notes: 'By buying into
Twilight, so to speak, fans buy into the ... message that wealth is desirable (and
attainable), that someday their prince will come – and he will be a rich vampire
able to rescue them from their woes, economic and otherwise.'[10] Further, she
notes, *Twilight* fans 'quite literally, become consumed by the franchise [and] just
as the *Twilight* texts frame women in such a way ... so does the *Twilight* franchise
court, construct, and perpetuate the notion of woman as consumer.'[11] Yet this
reaches beyond Summit and Meyer's realm, for the saga's unofficial merchandising – ranging from cardboard cut-outs of Edward Cullen that 'watch you while
you sleep' to sparkling freezable dildos that promise 'this vamp won't be the only
thing coming for you in the night' – offers a rampant consumerism that also
screams of a morbid eroticism. This seems very much at odds with the dominant
masculine horror fan complaints and criticisms of the films, which is indeed to
put it lightly.[12] Yet the popular and perhaps not unfounded characterisation

of this femininity as morbidly erotic, indiscriminately consuming and naive teenage hysteria overlooks the very reasons *Twilight* appeals to the feminine.

[Re]sexualised vampire pathos for sale?

Milly Williamson has stated that the pathos-ridden Byronic vampire pre-dates the horror communities' definitive vampire, Dracula, and has strong roots within the largely feminine Gothic melodrama genre. In her 2005 monograph she states: '... there has long been a devalued association of femininity with the Gothic Vampire and this is linked to the feminisation of "popular" or "mass" culture more generally which can be found in critical and even fannish discourses.'[13] Additionally she explains,

> the vampire's rebel-status comes to belong to the arena of the self, or rather, of making a spectacle of oneself – of making the 'self' a spectacle of the unconventional and the rebellious.[14]

So what might this feminine 'self' in *The Twilight Saga* convey? As discussed elsewhere[15] the films continue the romantic tradition of the gothic melodrama through multiple positions of both the 'Outsider' and the cruciality of family.[16] Further, in both Bella and Edward we observe the feminine self in a variety of covert and overt permutations, most crucially within the romance of a teenage girl with a sexless, yet sexualised twenty-first-century Vampire-with-a-Soul, embodying the battleground of female sexual-identity formation. Bella, as an 'unremarkable looking' teenager, a clumsy awkward outsider who finds love and an increasing awareness of her own sexual desire, is clearly a central identification point for the 'average' teenage female reader/viewer. In addition, through her relationship with Edward, abstinence becomes across the saga analogous with developing female sexuality, imbued with danger and the fear of male sexuality.

In the first instalment specifically, Edward describes himself to Bella thus: 'I'm the world's most dangerous predator, Bella. Everything about me invites you in. My voice, my face, even my smell. As if I would need any of that ... as if you could out-run me ... as if you could fight me off. I'm designed to kill' (*Twilight*, 2008, dir. Catherine Hardwicke). *Twilight* is thus a somewhat troublesome romance for most – being a romance of obsession – reflecting the relentless nature of teenage 'first love' and desire, but further the gravitation towards another which tends to displace the formation of self, projected onto the idea of 'completion', or perhaps, *adulteration* with an Other. Furthermore, this love is contradictory, at once both danger and safety; Edward: 'Bella, your number was up the day I met you'[17] and yet, 'I feel very ... protective of you.'[18] Yet although this may at first present as a fear of Edward's primal quintessentially masculine sexuality which threatens to devour Bella – and thus a fear here performed by an abject-yet-sexualised Other – it is in fact a story of the conflict of desire and resistance towards her own female sexuality and becoming a woman. However, this desire is a danger in itself and can and does bring about changes to render Bella, and indeed the feminine, irreparably transmogrified.

This is achieved via a number of processes or events: the loss of the family of her youth – the breaking away from her childhood; the loss of her innocence and purity as encompassed in her vampiric turning and the loss of her 'soul'; her vampiric transformation into a beautiful graceful 'woman', comfortable in her own skin and no longer an Outsider, of sorts; as well as the literal loss of her virginity, her pregnancy and eventual motherhood. Thus certainly in *The Twilight Saga* sexual change and the fear thereof is a conflict of desire and fear of the sexualised feminine self and its seemingly inevitable, irreparable ramifications. Clearly this is a key universal theme for female teens struggling to come to terms with the change of their own identity and movement away from the family into independence and sexuality – a transformation which is both desired and feared. In addition it is also a way for those older female fans to come to terms with their own changed identity, and to romanticise this 'turning'.

Concluding the saga of *Twilight*

Thus for the female within postmodern post-feminist patriarchy the struggle of heteronormative concurrent societal demands is both concerned with the formation of an adult sexual feminine identity, as well as being disavowed. For fans of *The Twilight Saga* this is manifest in the rejection, and manufacturing, of this hysterical sexual identity and its crucial role in the formation of a feminine 'self'. Yet the transgressive nature of this rebellious teenage desire is never really resolved or sated, but suspended, as the older female fans of *Twilight* demonstrate. This performative and ultimately conformative femininity is never truly resolved, as it exists as a mirror to masculinity. Yet with each new generation it re-emerges, recultivated, occupying this somewhat contradictory position of both conforming and transgressing. *The Twilight Saga*, then, is simply yet another example of how, disavowed by the patriarchal family whilst conversely eroticised, female hysterical desire is ultimately cultivated by patriarchy and propelled by consumerism.

Notes

1. Stuart Heritage, 'Being Human, I'd say True Blood is in its Twilight years', *Guardian*, 4 February 2012, http://www.guardian.co.uk/film/2012/feb/04/being-human-true-blood-twilight (accessed 28 April 2012).

2. Cf. Camille Bacon-Smith, *Enterprising Women: Television Fandom and the Creation of Popular Myth* (Philadelphia: University of Pennsylvania Press, 1992); Brigid Cherry, *Screaming for Release: Femininity and Horror Fandom in Britain*, in Julian Petley and Steve Chibnall (eds), *British Horror Cinema* (London: Routledge, 2002); Joanne Hollows, 'The Masculinity of Cult', in Mark Jancovich, Antonio Lazaro Reboll, Julian Stringer and Andrew Willis (eds), *Defining Cult Movies: The Cultural Politics of Oppositional Taste* (Manchester: Manchester University Press, 2003); Jacinda Read, 'The Cult of Masculinity: From Bad Boys to Academic Bad-Boys' in Mark Jancovich et al. (eds), *Defining Cult Movies*; and Sarah Thornton, *Club Cultures: Music, Media and Subcultural Capital* (Cambridge: Polity Press, 1995).

3. Which of course, while forming the most immediately visible and identifiable mode of *Twilight* fandom, is indeed not representative of all fans – see Haig, Cherry and Jones in this collection for two more pieces of this jigsaw of fanship.

4. Victoria de Grazia, *The Sex of Things* (Berkeley: University of California Press, 1996), p. 3.

5. Nina Power, *One Dimensional Woman* (Winchester: Zero Books, 2010), p. 1.

6. Ibid., p. 29.

7. See further Melissa A. Click (2009), '"Rabid", "Obsessed", and "Frenzied": Understanding Twilight Fangirls and The Gendered Politics of Fandom', FlowTV, Department of Radio, Television, and Film at the University of Texas at Austin, http://flowtv.org/2009/12/rabid-obsessed-and-frenzied-understanding-twilight-fangirls-and-the-gendered-politics-of-fandom-melissa-click-university-of-missouri/comment-page-1/ (accessed 28 January 2013).

8. Barbara Ehrenreich, Elizabeth Hess and Gloria Jacobs, 'Beatlemania: Girls Just Want to Have Fun', in Lisa A. Lewis (ed.), *The Adoring Audience: Fan Culture and Popular Media* (London: Routledge, 1992), pp. 99–100.

9. *Heatworld*, 'Meet the Robert Pattinson fan who ended up in hospital', 20 November 2009, http://www.heatworld.com/Celeb-News/2009/11/Meet-the-Robert-Pattinson-fan-who-ended-up-in-hospital/ (accessed 4 April 2012) (link no longer working).

10. Natalie Wilson, *Seduced by* Twilight: *The Allure and Contradictory Messages of the Popular Saga* (Jefferson, NC: McFarland & Co., 2011), p. 185.

11. Ibid., pp. 186–7.

12. Again, see Edwards-Behi's chapter.

13. Milly Williamson, *The Lure of the Vampire* (London: Wallflower, 2005), p. 56.

14. Ibid., pp. 37–8.

15. See Kohlenberger and Rana in this collection.

16. See Bacon and Hunt in this collection.

17. Williamson, *The Lure of the Vampire*, p. 56.

18. Ibid. In addition this is replicated in Edward's thoughts in Meyer's unfinished, leaked *Midnight Sun,* 'How ironic that I'd wanted to protect this human girl ... She would never need protection from anything more than she needed it from me' (Stephenie Meyer, *Midnight Sun,* 2008, www.stepheniemeyer.com/midnightsun.html (accessed 5 May 2012), p. 17 (link no longer working). Whether this additional narrative will enter the cinematic canon has yet to be seen.

PART 2

WEREWOLVES, LIONS AND LAMBS: CREATING AND SUBVERTING THE GENERIC MYTH

5

WHY *TWILIGHT* SUCKS AND EDWARD DOESN'T: CONTEMPORARY VAMPIRES AND THE SENTIMENTAL TRADITION

Judith Kohlenberger

Is it high art? No. But it's not trying to be.[1]

Archetypal character constellations, prescribed plot structures and conventional denouements suggest that *The Twilight Saga* and its screen adaptations owe less to the classic Gothic tale and the horror film genre but, rather, perpetuate sentimental traditions. Indeed, the screen representations of *Twilight*'s vampires mirror many of the concerns and dynamics of sentimental literature, the dominant literary genre in Europe and the USA between 1820 and 1870. Since the early twentieth century, critics have characterised these novels as devoid of literary value, damaging to women through the propagation of gender stereotypes, and stylistically flawed. This parallels popular responses to the *Twilight* films, whose (re-)romanticisation of the vampire, culminating in its refusal to suck human blood, has come to serve as a central argument for why Edward and his siblings suck big time.

In accordance with Jane Tompkins'[2] proposed reconsideration of the sentimental mode as a sense-making scheme in literature and film, *Twilight* ought to be taken seriously for the cultural work it performs, which is tightly linked to the vampire's metaphorical potential. In doing so, we are confronted with potentially far-reaching consequences for the figure of the vampire: what happens to the formerly malevolent fanged fiend when expelled from his natural habitat and unwontedly transferred to the sentimental mode for an almost exclusively female spectatorship? Or is this transference unwonted and even indeed unprecedented?

Tracing blood: the vampire and romantic tradition(s)

Early cinematic renderings of the vampire – such as F. W. Murnau's *Nosferatu* (1922) and Bela Lugosi's performance as Universal's *Count Dracula* (1931, dir. Browning) – tend to represent the figure as a veritable creature of the night and foreground his monstrous rather than human nature.[3] Many visualisations focus on his pale appearance, topped off with frizzy black hair and prominent fangs, his status as an eternally damned and undead being and his insatiable appetite for human blood, preferably from a young virgin. This common cultural image of the demon was predominately shaped by Bram Stoker's *Dracula* (1897)[4] and later cultivated by Hollywood's horror flicks. While the humane, soulful and compassionate bloodsucker may seem a recent phenomenon which has only lately found its culmination in *The Twilight Saga*, there are both fictional and cinematic instances of sympathetic vampires long before Anne Rice's influential *Vampire Chronicles*.[5] Although the supposed domestication of the vampire has been the subject of several extensive studies,[6] contemporary tame versions of the once wicked creature have a long history, as Nina Auerbach argues: 'Until the coming of the impersonal, imperial Dracula in 1897, [the] friend-seeking vampire dominated the nineteenth-century.'[7] In fact, the figure of the vampire emerged conspicuously in the Romantic era and thus allows for the detection of several deeply Romantic traits. Interestingly, even Stephenie Meyer, having majored in English literature, acknowledges the Romantic roots of her characters: 'You just need to go back to Byron and it's all there.'[8]

Not merely the modern-day Cullens, but the figure of the vampire as a literary character originates in the Romantic era, as Milly Williamson has pointed out, '[F]rom its entry into the novel, the popularised image of the vampire in Europe and the Anglo-American world had become fused to Byronic images of glamorous outsiderdom, morose fatalism, sexual deviancy and social and artistic rebellion.'[9] According to popular belief, Byron composed the Gothic horror tale *The Vampyre* (1819) during the same legendary ghost-story competition at Villa Diodati in Switzerland which gave birth to Mary Shelley's *Frankenstein* (1818).[10] While the story was in actual fact contrived by Byron's contemporary John Polidori,[11] it was the confusion with the much more popular persona of Byron which promoted the vampire's appeal.[12] In the twentieth century, Mario Praz's notorious *Romantic Agony* (1933) further emphasised the conflation of Byron and the vampire: 'For, once fashion is launched, the majority imitate its external aspects without understanding the spirit which originated it. The same can be said of Vampirism, and for this fashion also Byron was largely responsible.'[13] Far from being a soulless, bloodthirsty monster, the early vampire is above all conceived of as a Byronic hero, a proud, moody and contemplative character, who is 'fated to live ... outside the society of companionable men, ostracised and isolated'.[14]

In spite of his augmented narcissism and hedonistic lifestyle, the Byronic figure proves to be a deeply moral character, acting on his own rules of conduct, which is perfectly illustrated by the following lines from Byron's poetic closet drama *Manfred* (1817):

My joys, my griefs, my passions, and my powers,

Made me a stranger; though I wore the form,

I had no sympathy with breathing flesh.[15]

It hence appears to be sensible to suggest that the vampire, from its earliest conceptualisations, retains an unmistakably Byronic air and thereby poses as a quintessentially Romantic character. This is also noted by Praz when he argues that via Byron's fictionalisations 'the vampire ... took on a Byronic colour'[16] and, conversely, reveals 'the vampire loves of the Byronic Fatal Man'.[17] Hence, it is not only time-wise that Elke Bartel, with reference to Margaret L. Carter's eminent critical bibliography *The Vampire in Literature* (1988),[18] claims that 'the vampire is very much a product of the Romantic movement',[19] whereas Candace Benefiel marks the vampire's 'great debt to the brooding Byronic heroes of British Romanticism'.[20]

While 'the association between rebellion and a doomed but glamorous outsiderdom which marked the Romantic idea of vampirism'[21] has receded in the aforementioned vampire horror films, the portrayals found in *Twilight*'s screen versions highlight the vampire's Romantic roots as a tortured soul. Edward can be classified as a prototypical Byronic character who appears to be in a constant state of agony and internalised guilt. His cynical, detached air is soon exposed as an elaborate mask, revealing deep emotions and a high sensitivity underneath. Like Byron's brooding yet compassionate heroes, Edward is depicted as 'capable of deep and strong affection'.[22] This is well reflected in the dream-like sequence of the first movie: seated at an impressive black piano Edward plays a lullaby, thus wooing his lover next to him. The scene, filmed with slow camera movement encircling the piano as the centre of focus, emphasises Edward's melancholy and contemplative nature, as does his love of literature, classical music and the uncountable diaries he has been keeping since his conversion.[23] Edward's Romantic air as revealed in this sequence is well grounded in the long-standing tradition of sympathetic vampires, which, as has been established, even surpasses the genealogy of the villainous Dracula. Contrary to the Ricean and similarly introspective, soulful vampires, however, the tame creatures of the *Twilight* universe have provoked dismay among audience and critics alike. The saga's reputation as a particularly fallacious specimen of pulp cinema thus hardly concurs with the literary legacy of Byron's lofty and critically acclaimed poetry, but rather mirrors the reactions faced by sentimental writers.

Generations of trash: from scribbling women to Team Edward

'What is the mystery of these innumerable editions of *The Lamplighter*, and other books neither better nor worse?', Nathaniel Hawthorne irritably wondered when facing the rocketing sales figures of Maria Cummins' eponymous romance and the equally successful works of her colleagues.[24] While books like *The Lamplighter* (Maria Susanna Cummins, 1854),[25] *The Wide Wide World* (Susan Warner, 1850)[26] or *Linda* (Caroline Lee Hentz, 1850)[27] were major best-sellers in their time, Hawthorne's *The Scarlet Letter* (1850)[28] only sold 10,000 copies in his lifetime and was thereby easily surpassed by his female rivals.[29] Eventually, however, 'Hawthorne has had his revenge': it is *The Scarlet Letter* rather than Cummins' tearful story of a poor orphan girl that is nowadays considered part of the American literary syllabus.[30] Browsing any online forum devoted to cinema and fandom, one will inevitably stumble upon myriad charges: users despairing over the sheer popularity of this 'piece of trash' or, in view of *Twilight*'s unparalleled box office revenues, bewilderedly asking, 'Has the world gone absolutely insane?' resurrect Hawthorne's rage in the twenty-first century.[31] Websites dedicated to the logical and stylistic flaws in Meyer's oeuvre or the inaccurate representation of vampires who, by their very nature, do not sparkle, provide ample material to fuel their indignation.[32] Apart from these rather humorous approaches, recurrent accusations against *Twilight* concern its conservative morality; the stereotypical, one-dimensional portrayal of its characters; its formulaic plot and conventional denouement; and its immense popularity. The exact same notions served as supposedly informed arguments against the canonisation of most sentimental fictions.

The term sentimental fiction, also referred to as domestic or women's fiction, denotes the dominant literary genre in Europe and the USA in the middle of the nineteenth century. Broadly speaking, sentimental fiction can be classified as novels by, for and about women, which witnessed their height between 1820 and 1870.[33] The plot, promoting compassion, moral rectitude and self-denial, characteristically evolves around an adolescent girl, who has to pass through a series of trials until she finally finds her place in the world. Similar to the discussion surrounding vampire romances today, sentimental fiction provoked both scholarly and public debate. The authors' (predominantly male) contemporaries bemoaned the lack of moral and stylistic accuracy and condemned their creators as a 'damned mob of scribbling women' who occupied 'the public taste … with their trash'.[34] Nina Baym's seminal *Woman's Fiction* (1978) unearths the underlying motivations that fuelled these and similar accusations:

> [M]any clerical opponents of the novel thought that women were trying to take over their functions and hence attacked them all the more fiercely. Similarly, male authors felt threatened by the apparently sudden emergence of great numbers of women writers. Their distress showed itself in expressions of manly contempt for the genre, its authors, and its readers.[35]

Retrospective canonisations of the twentieth century, such as the infamous study *American Renaissance* (1941) by literary scholar F. O. Matthiessen, equally marginalised or entirely ignored the contributions of female authors. According to Matthiessen, the literary scene in nineteenth-century America consisted of only five male writers, namely Emerson, Thoreau, Hawthorne, Melville and Whitman. No other literary production could possibly 'equal [their oeuvre] in imaginative vitality'.[36] While Matthiessen and similar accounts, dating from the beginning of the last century, have by now been subjected to thorough and wholesale critique,[37] sentimental fiction continues to occupy a controversial position in literary scholarship. Recently, Ann Douglas issued a devastating critique of sentimental novels and their – in her opinion – non-existent literary value. Douglas' comprehensive study *The Feminization of American Culture* (1977) maintains that sentimental novels require no thinking, reproduce and construct stereotypes and prove to be damaging to women through the perpetuation of clichéd representations, and are written in a horrible, unimaginative style. They exemplify the beginnings of a degenerated mass culture that swallowed up more valuable literature and thought.[38]

It is in response to the underlying gender dynamics of these retrospective assessments that Jane Tompkins suggested a reconsideration of sentimental fiction. Tompkins' often quoted analysis, which can be and was read as a sharp repartee to Douglas' off-putting verdict,[39] persuasively demonstrates how the specific concerns and structural properties of sentimental novels perform vital cultural work. The sentimental mode is understood as a sense-making scheme, offering women a rare chance of reading about their own experience. Interestingly, the terms Tompkins chooses to dissect prevailing criticism and reveal its phallocentric underpinnings sound uncannily familiar:

> [T]wentieth-century critics have taught generations of students to equate popularity with debasement, emotionality with ineffectiveness, religiosity with fakery, domesticity with triviality, and all of these, implicitly, with womanly inferiority. In this view, sentimental novels written by women in the nineteenth century were responsible for a series of cultural evils whose effects still plague us ... the rationalization of an unjust economic order, the propagation of the debased images of modern mass culture, and the encouragement of self-indulgence and narcissism in literature's most avid readers – women ... In contrast to male authors like Thoreau, Whitman, and Melville, who are celebrated as models of intellectual daring and honesty, these women are generally thought to have traded in false stereotypes, dishing out weak-minded pap to nourish the prejudices of an ill-educated and underemployed female readership.[40]

Substitute the nineteenth century with the twenty-first, and we are confronted with an adjustable template for much current discourse on vampire fiction. Paralleling recurrent responses to sentimental novels, *Twilight*'s major appeal to a typically young and female audience is equally interpreted as 'evidence of the deplorable feminine taste in literature'.[41] Baym's and Tompkins' pointed analyses thus reveal the highly misogynist undercurrents informing the majority of criticism on sentimental storylines, be it directed towards nineteenth-century domestic novels or *Twilight*'s screen adaptations. Whereas the educational value of vampire films situated in the male-connoted horror and splatter genres might just be as questionable, these productions never provoked a public outcry as tremendous as the one inspired by the (equally fictional) feminine sentimental world of *Twilight*.

Sentimental schemes and subversive tendencies in *Twilight*

In addition to these similarities in their reception, nineteenth-century sentimental novels and the modern *Twilight* saga reveal a number of other parallels. In both cases, criticism is directed towards several specific structural, formal and contents-related features, which characterise the sentimental mode both then and now. In this respect, the *Twilight* films can be regarded as a continuation of many of the concerns, ideological perspectives and societal functions of sentimental literature.

Characteristics shared between the two are principally found at the structural level and involve archetypal character constellations, a prescribed and thus highly predictable plot structure and a conventional denouement. It is Bella, the human, female protagonist of the narrative, who determines the perspective of the story and serves as a point of identification. Just like sentimental novels, the *Twilight* saga thus employs a first-person narration and internal focalisation via the diary form, which enhances identification with the protagonist. The cinematic adaptations preserve this property by capitalising on figural shots from Bella's perspective: the world of the movie is explored, represented and made sense of through the heroine's eyes, which largely corresponds with the structure of sentimental fiction. The story's solid centre remains the adolescent female protagonist, who has to pass through a series of emotional and physical trials until she eventually 'awakens ... to her inner possibilities',[42] as Baym argues with regard to sentimental literature. Bella is indeed cast in the tradition of the typical sentimental heroine, whose mediocre looks and physical abilities are repeatedly stressed in order to arouse the reader's sympathy and allow for unproblematic, rapid identification. Meyer's novels contain uncountable instances of Bella's clumsiness and her limited self-esteem. This is aptly realised in the cinematic adaptations, where the (critically disparaged) expressionless, introverted acting of Kristen Stewart as a passive receptacle can well be understood as further enhancing identification by the viewers. Rather unusually for a film pentalogy directed towards an adolescent and thus fashion-conscious audience, Bella is regularly clad in simple, mud-and-cream-coloured-outfits, such as jeans and bulky sweaters. In contrast to the stylish (upper-class) vampires, her look remains unobtrusive and modest. None the less, both her clothes[43] and, even more importantly, her personality undergo development in the course of the narrative, as Bella has to learn how to exert self-mastery and control over her emotions. Conquering her regular outbursts of passion constitutes a fundamental goal for the nineteenth-century heroine.[44] By the end of the story, she will have substantially matured, 'so much that what was formerly denied her now comes unsought'.[45]

In addition to the rather stereotypical characterisation of its heroine, *Twilight*'s storyline works in a similarly formulaic manner. The films appear to follow a prescribed master plot, which ends in a highly predictable denouement. Sentimental novels consistently conclude with marriage as the only conceivable happy ending, and this fate is eventually also met by the protagonists

of *Twilight*. In that respect, the figure of the literally toothless and thus mar-
riageable vampire appears to facilitate, if not generate several vital characteristics of the sentimental mode. The domesticated, figuratively impotent and thus
neutered vampire serves the conservative viewpoint of the saga and continues to
elicit heavy criticism. Equally, the cluttered and highly emotionalised style in
which the novels are composed had to endure the critics' derision. Whereas sentimental fiction is characterised by a 'language of tears',[46] involving excessive
weeping and characters bursting into tears at any occasion, *Twilight* is dominated by a rather cluttered, overflowing dictum, which involves a high density
of symbols and metaphors.[47] Tompkins herself called attention to the writer's
'intellectual complexity, ambition, and resourcefulness',[48] and yet her main
target in reassessing sentimental fiction was anything but its literary value.
Accordingly, scholars tend to refrain from claiming stylistic brilliance for any of
the scrutinised works.[49] The cultural work performed by sentimental fictions,
however, remains indisputable, which appears to be even enhanced by the symbolically charged figure of the *Twilight* vampire.

The vampire's feasibility as an adaptive metaphor for sexual relations, mat-
ing and blood-transmitted diseases has been the subject of countless studies.[50]
The act of feeding and the potential conversion via sucking blood from the
victim's neck does not only figure, however, as a thinly disguised analogy for
physical intimacy, but also presents a subversion of the reproductive act. When
performed by a vampire, sucking does not signify intercourse without reproduction, but reproduction without intercourse. Additionally, 'the parent of the vampire is the vampire who made it':[51] its ability to create new vampires establishes
it as an essentially maternal figure. This dimension is exploited to its fullest by
the Cullen family in *Twilight*. Indeed, the alternative non-consanguine vampire
family figures as a central motif in the saga and appears to serve as a corrective
to the more troublesome human families: Bella's divorced parents appear to be
neither capable of nor particularly interested in taking care of their child's needs.
Following O'Donnell's psychoanalytical paper in this collection, Bella is hence
constructed as the symbolic neglected child and consequently projects her oral,
rather than genital desires on Edward. *Twilight* thereby advances a specific version of the happy vampire family motif, which Hunt's insightful contribution
in this anthology also investigates with regard to queer community structures.
Accordingly, the films might be understood as elaborating a paradigm which
already emerged conspicuously in Neil Jordan's *Interview With The Vampire*
(1994), based on Anne Rice's eponymous novel. Here, Louis and Lestat convert
the little Claudia and thus form an alternative, yet well-functioning family
unit. Paralleling the adoption system of the Cullens, this odd little ménage 'is

so close to the norm as to constitute a parody'.[52] Joel Schumacher's *The Lost Boys* (1987) explores similar concerns, yet ultimately provides a much more disturbing vision of a potential vampire family. Even *Dracula* (1931) shares his castle with three brides who, due to their common origin, could equally be read as his daughters. Francis Ford Coppola's *Dracula* (1992) seemingly elaborates on this possibility by drawing attention to the extreme age differences between the parental Dracula and his offspring, eventually also including Jonathan after his erotic assimilation into the family.

In no previous narrative, however, does the vampire family seem to be attributed a role as pivotal as that in *Twilight*. Not surprisingly, this aspect again aligns the saga with sentimental fiction as its ideational predecessor. The revision of traditional kinship structures and the critical scrutiny of the nuclear family constitute central concerns in sentimental fiction. Contrary to popular presuppositions, the conventional family model of blood-related mother, father and children is surprisingly rare in these novels. In its most frequent version, the heroine begins as an orphan or 'has by necessity been separated from her parents for an indefinite time'.[53] While she thereby has to suffer under the hands of her only remaining relatives, she will have found a non-consanguine mother and/or father surrogate by the end of the narrative. According to Cindy Weinstein, this ineffectiveness and symbolic destruction of the biological family was utilised to define kinship in terms of love rather than blood: '[T]he cultural work of sentimental fictions is nothing less than an interrogation and reconfiguration of what constitutes a family ... [C]onsanguinity becomes one more choice to be made.'[54] This vision of a family is also represented by the Cullen family, which is formed by mutual conversion and adoption and united by a common ideal, i.e. their ethically motivated 'vegetarian' lifestyle. What connects the different generations of vampires are literally subverted, rather than traditional, blood bonds. Like the classic sentimental heroine, the divorce child Bella, who experiences her new home Forks as an exile, eventually finds the Cullens as a new, surrogate family she fits into perfectly. The viability of these appropriated kinship structures is well reflected by the great popularity with which the Cullens have been met by their teenaged audience.

Far from constituting yet another instance of *Twilight*'s reassuring moral standpoint, the pronounced emphasis on a distorted vampire, rather than a nuclear human family, complicates both blood and love relationships and eventually undermines the conservative bias. Hence, the elder vampire acts as both lover and parent of the newly converted creature, which results in a 'relationship [that] is oddly incestuous'.[55] This constellation adds a subversive dimension to most pairings in *Twilight*, similar to the way the extraordinary kinship structures in sentimental fiction served as a counter narrative to the hegemonic nineteenth-century discourse of the bourgeois family. Beyond the picket fence surface, the little family of Bella and Edward indeed reveals a peculiar set-up. Not only should their love relationship and eventual marriage in *Breaking Dawn – Part I* (2011, dir. Bill Condon) be understood as an interspecies union, it ultimately leads to Bella's conversion, making Edward both her husband and her vampire parent. Similarly to several preceding vampire films, *Twilight's* creation of a new vampire is paradoxically projected as an act of simultaneous birth, death and lovemaking. This is already prefigured in the first screen instalment of the saga. When James, leader of the villainous vampire gang, traps Bella and initiates the conversion by injecting venom into her body, she suffers from violent convulsions while she moans and cries in apparent agony. Tellingly, her moaning is difficult to categorise: the film implies that Bella, despite the pain she is enduring in this scene, is well aware that this could make her one of Edward's kind. Hence, the scene portrays an odd intermingling of pleasure and pain, which leads to an utter loss of both physical and mental control. In that sense, it potentially offers further fuel for criticism as alleged evidence for Bella's and Edward's violent relationship, whose underlying dynamics are skilfully dissected in Adams' article within this book on masochism in *Twilight*. In this particular scene, however, Bella's positioning – she is lying on her back, with trembling extremities and accompanied by deep moans – makes the aforementioned comparison of the conversion to a sexual act even more conceivable. Not only has she been bitten by a male, highly sexualised vampire,[56] who intends to revenge himself on his rival, but the scene is also preceded by the flight from her father's house and a staged break-up with Edward. This makes her figuratively free for a new partner. The analogy of Bella's almost-conversion with an orgasmic experience is enhanced by the tools that necessarily accompany any vampiric act: on the one hand the penetrating fangs and on the other hand the oral cavity, the mouth, which receives the blood. Additionally, the liminal state which the victim thereby undergoes involves both a destruction, the symbolic death of the human being, and a creation, the birth of the new vampire.

These symbolic implications suggest that even a text as supposedly formulaic and reassuring as *Twilight* is corrupted by the presence of the vampire and its metaphorical force. Similar to a variety of vampire movies, both *Twilight's* camera work and its conventional plotline are latently destabilised, 'as if the bodies of the films themselves were progressively contaminated with the presence of radical Otherness',[57] a trope which both Bacon and Kirkland adeptly explore in their respective contributions within this edition. The alternative kinship relations necessarily provoked by the figure of the vampire complicate and ultimately undermine the conservative angle of the story. The wish for a nuclear, intact family, which majorly informs the plot and has served as a central point of criticism, is thereby exposed as a condoned desire for a distorted kinship model based on incestuous relationships, noticeably opposed to conventional, human families. Accordingly, the seemingly natural prohibition against pre-marital sex, coded as literally unsafe due to Edward's ultimately uncontrollable thirst for blood, is perceptibly reversed: in this reading, Bella's wish of joining the Cullens, which functions as a fundamental motif in advancing the saga's plot, is decoded as a craving for deviance, which is acted upon in repeatedly bizarre ways. Consequently, *Twilight* could be understood as yet another example of how the figure of the vampire metaphorically infuses its venom into the conservative surface and derives a vampiric, oppositional subtext from it. Destroying the original fabric to create a new, physically improved, immortal being, the vampire reveals various degrees of inconsistency, and thereby aids to uncover the deviant, non-conformist tendencies dormant in *Twilight*'s subtext.

The legacy of sentimentality

Weinstein's argument demonstrates how sentimental fictions could provide a powerful, if latent, discourse of reconfiguring conventional notions of love, family and sexuality, whose active revision also emerges in *Twilight*. Correspondingly, the tame and toothless vampire might prove to be a more suitable metaphor than Dracula, whose appearances in earlier master narratives of the genre are thus contested in the best postmodern manner. Indeed, the figure of the vampire can well be regarded as eliciting the cultural concerns and structural qualities which Meyer's saga shares with sentimental fiction. Regardless of questions of taste and literary quality dominating the majority of public discussions, *Twilight* has to be treated as a cultural artefact which reflects and constructs, yet also challenges present discourses. *Twilight* thus exemplifies how sentimental narratives, be it literary or cinematic productions, must be appreciated, yet also comprehensively scrutinised for their 'monumental effort to reorganize culture'[58] via diverse approaches. Dismissing the sentimental mode in form and content as trash, an unqualified verdict in which scholarly critique more often than not effortlessly matches the general public tenor, equals foregoing a potentially precious opportunity to gain insights into both hegemonic and residual societal discourses. As prior studies of sentimental narratives have amply demonstrated, dissecting the highly ambiguous tendencies latent in sentimental fictions' superficially reassuring texts can yield remarkable and otherwise inaccessible analyses. In the case of *The Twilight Saga*'s cinematic renderings, it is primarily the symbolically charged figure of the vampire which allows for alternative readings of its understructure that surprisingly do not suck at all.

Notes

1. Melissa Rosenberg, screenwriter of *The Twilight Saga* (qtd in Marshall Heyman, 'From Dawn to 'Twilight'', in the *The Wall Street Journal Online* (2010), http://online.wsj.com/article/SB10001424052748704895204575321012753160750.html?mod=rss_Lifestyle (accessed 7 June 2012).

2. Jane Tompkins, *Sensational Designs: The Cultural Work of American Fiction 1790–1860* (Oxford: Oxford University Press, 1985).

3. For a detailed historical overview of the cinematic depiction of vampires, see Alain Silver and James Ursini, *The Vampire Film: From* Nosferatu *to Bram Stoker's* Dracula (New York: Limelight, 1993).

4. Bram Stoker, *Dracula* (Westminster: Constable & Co., 1897).

5. Cf. for instance Erle C. Kenton's *House of Dracula* (1945), in which the vampire yearns to overcome his monstrous existence. Le Fanu's *Carmilla* (1872) is an often-cited example of a friend-seeking vampire in literature (Nina Auerbach, 'My Vampire, My Friend: The Intimacy Dracula Destroyed', in Joan Gordon and Veronica Hollinger (eds), *Blood Read: The Vampire as Metaphor in Contemporary Culture* (Philadelphia: University of Pennsylvania Press, 1997), pp. 11–16).

6. See for instance Atara Stein, 'Immortals and Vampires and Ghosts, Oh My! : Byronic Heroes in Popular Culture', in Laura Mandell and Michael Eberle-Sinatra (eds), *Romanticism and Contemporary Culture*, Romantic Circles Praxis Series (2002), http://www.rc.umd.edu/praxis/contemporary/stein/stein.html (accessed 3 May 2011).

7. Auerbach, 'My Vampire, My Friend', p. 11.

8. 'Extras', *Twilight*, DVD, directed by Catherine Hardwicke, Concorde Home Entertainment, 2008.

9. Milly Williamson, 'Spike, Sex and Subtext: Intertextual Portrayals of the Sympathetic Vampire on Cult Television', *European Journal of Cultural Studies* 8/3 (2005), pp. 289–311, p. 294.

10. For a more detailed account of the famous ghost-story contest see, for instance, Siv Jansson's introduction to Mary Shelley's *Frankenstein; Or, the Modern Prometheus* (London: Wordsworth Classics, 1999), pp. vii–xxv.

11. John Polidori, *The Vampyre; a Tale* (London: Sherwood, Neely and Jones, 1819).

12. Frances Wilson (*Byromania: Portraits of the Artist in Nineteenth- and Twentieth-Century Culture* (London: Macmillan, 1999) offers an insightful and entertaining account of the cult surrounding Byron's persona.

13. Mario Praz, *The Romantic Agony*, trans. Angus Davidson (1933; London: Collins, 1960), p. 95. Apart from emphasising the Byronic and thereby essentially Romantic traits of the archetypical vampire, Praz also fuelled the myth of Byron as the creator of the modern vampire legend by claiming that he 'composed part of a "tale of terror", so that 'Dr Polidori [merely, one might say] elaborated the sketch' (ibid.).

14. Peter L. Thorslev, *The Byronic Hero: Types and Prototypes* (Minnesota: University of Minnesota Press, 1962), p. 104. These and similar Byronic traits have evidently been influenced by Byron's scandalous life, featuring, among other scenarios, an alleged incest with his half-sister, dozens of hetero- as well as homosexual affairs, illegitimate children, voluntary participation in Greek and Italian wars of independence, several years in self-chosen exile and great financial debt. See Jerome J. McGann's concise and readable introduction to Byron's *oeuvre* (in Jerome J. McGann (ed.), *Lord Byron: The Major Works* (Oxford: Oxford University Press, 1986), pp. xi–xxiii) and Gross (Jonathan David Gross, *Byron: The Erotic Liberal* (New York: Rowman and Littlefield, 2001)) for a detailed account of the poet's sexual and political liberalism.

15. George Gordon Byron, *Manfred* [1817], in McGann, *Lord Byron*, pp. 274–314, pp. 2.2.50–7.

16. Praz, *The Romantic Agony*, p. 97.

17. Ibid., p. 99.

18. Margaret L. Carter, *The Vampire in Literature: A Critical Bibliography* (Ann Arbor: Umi Research Press, 1989).

19. Elke Bartel, 'From Archfiend to *Angel*: Dracula's Political Dimension', *Studies in Popular Culture* 27/3 (2005), pp. 15–25, esp. p. 22.

20. Candace R. Benefiel, 'Blood Relations: The Gothic Perversion of the Nuclear Family in Anne Rice's *Interview with the Vampire*', *The Journal of Popular Culture* 38/2 (2004), pp. 261–73, p. 262.

21. Williamson, 'Spike, Sex and Subtext', p. 293.

22. Macaulay, quoted in Lamont, Claire, 'The Romantic Period', in Pat Rogers (ed.), *The Oxford Illustrated History of English Literature* (Oxford: Oxford University Press, 2001), pp. 274–325, esp. p. 297.

23. Apart from this individual scene, *Twilight*'s *mise-en-scène* is generally dominated by gloomy colours. Long shots of the regularly dark, overcast sky, impressive mountain ranges, thunderstorms and lightning establish a prototypical Romantic scenery.

24. Nathaniel Hawthorne in a letter to his publisher William D. Ticknor in 1855 (Nathaniel Hawthorne, *The Letters, 1853–1856*, ed. Thomas Woodson, L. Neal Smith and Norman Holmes Pearson (Columbus: Ohio State University Press, 1987), p. 304).

25. Maria S. Cummins, *The Lamplighter* (Boston: John P. Jewett & Co, 1854).

26. Susan Warner, *The Wide, Wide World* (1850; New York: Cosimo, Inc., 2005).

27. Caroline Lee Hentz, *Linda; or, The young pilot of the Belle Creole* (Philadelphia: T.B. Peterson, 1850).

28. Hawthorne's *Scarlet Letter* (*The Scarlet Letter* (Boston: Ticknor, Reed, and Fields, 1850).

29. Hawthorne's 10,000 copies had to compete with 100,000 annually sold copies of *The Lamplighter* (Nina Baym, Introduction to Maria S. Cummins, *The Lamplighter* (New Brunswick: Rutgers University Press, 1995), pp. ix–xxxiv).

30. Ibid., p. ix.

31. 'Twilight = Trash', Searching for Liminality blog, http://ciaee.livejournal.com/4497. html (accessed 22 April 2011); and 'I want to beat Edward Cullen with a stick', Not

Overburdened With Subject blog, http://otahyoni.livejournal.com/130432.html (accessed 22 April 2011).

32. Cf. for instance 'Reasoning With Vampires', http://reasoningwithvampires.tumblr.com/ (accessed 22 April 2011).

33. While it partly derives from the eighteenth-century novel of sensibility, represented for instance by Henry Mackenzie's *The Man of Feeling* (London: T. Cadell, 1771) or Oliver Goldsmith's *The Vicar of Wakefield* (1766; Oxford: Oxford University Press, 2006), sentimental fiction constitutes an independent literary genre. See Donna M. Campbell, 'Domestic or Sentimental Fiction, 1820–1865', *Literary Movements*, Department of English, Washington State University, last modified 21 March 2010, http://www.wsu.edu/~campbelld/amlit/domestic.htm (accessed 2 December 2010) for a detailed overview of its scope and origins.

34. Hawthorne, *The Letters*, p. 304.

35. Nina Baym, *Woman's Fiction: A Guide to Novels by and about Women in America, 1820–1870* (Ithaca: Cornell University Press, 1978), pp. 22–3.

36. F. O. Matthiessen, *American Renaissance: Art and Expression in the Age of Emerson and Whitman* (Oxford: Oxford University Press, 1941), p. vii.

37. See for instance the edited collection by Walter Benn Michaels and Donald E. Pease (*American Renaissance Reconsidered* (Baltimore: Johns Hopkins University Press, 1989)), and especially Jonathan Arac's contribution on 'F. O. Matthiessen: Authorizing an American Renaissance', pp. 90–112.

38. Ann Douglas, *The Feminization of American Culture* (New York: Knopf, 1978), esp. pp. 253–6.

39. Laura Wexler, *Tender Violence: Domestic Visions in an Age of US Imperialism* (Chapel Hill: University of North Carolina Press, 2000), specifically refers to the Douglas–Tompkins debate and thereby marks the seminal impact of this progressing scholarly dispute.

40. Tompkins, *Sensational Designs*, pp. 123–4.

41. Baym, *Woman's Fiction*, p. 14.

42. Ibid., p. 19.

43. Bella's style adapts to the vampires' in the course of the narrative. She increasingly dons clothes in cold colours, such as grey, steel blue and white.

44. Baym, *Woman's Fiction*, p. 25; Tompkins, *Sensational Designs*, p. 176.

45. Baym, *Woman's Fiction*, p. 19.

46. Campbell, 'Domestic or Sentimental Fiction'.

47. Apparently, the movies attempt to remain faithful to Meyer's original writing and incorporate the symbols used in the novels. A case in point is the deep-red apple which adorns the cover of the first instalment and foreshadows its epigraph from the Book of Genesis. Meyer herself suggests that the apple as the biblical forbidden fruit stands for Edward, and that Bella has to decide between good and evil, i.e. between taking or leaving the apple ('Extras', *Twilight*, DVD, directed by Catherine Hardwicke, Concorde Home Entertainment, 2008). In the movie, Edward catches the apple at the school buffet and thereby demonstrates his superhuman skills.

48. Tompkins, *Sensational Designs*, p. 124.

49. See, for instance, June Howard, 'What Is Sentimentality?', *American Literary History* 11/1 (1999), pp. 63–81.

50. Cf. Terry L. Spaise, 'Necrophilia and SM: The Deviant Side of *Buffy the Vampire Slayer*', *The Journal of Popular Culture* 38/4 (2005), pp. 744–62 and Deborah Wilson Overstreet, *Not Your Mother's Vampires: Vampires in Young Adult Fiction* (Plymouth: Scarecrow, 2006).

51. Benefiel, 'Blood Relations', p. 262.

52. Ibid., p. 264.

53. Baym, *Woman's Fiction*, p. 35.

54. Cindy Weinstein, *Family, Kinship, and Sympathy in Nineteenth-Century American Literature* (Cambridge: Cambridge University Press, 2004), p. 9.

55. Benefiel, 'Blood Relations', p. 263.

56. Throughout the saga as well as in this particular scene, James is wearing tight jeans and an unbuttoned leather jacket, revealing his muscular chest. His status as a tracker, a vampire obsessed with the hunt for humans, might equally be read as expressive of his attitude towards women, his figurative prey.

57. Martine Beugnet, 'Figures of Vampirism: French Cinema in the Era of Global Transylvania', *Modern & Contemporary France* 15/1 (2007), pp. 77–88, p. 81.

58. Tompkins, *Sensational Designs*, p. 124.

6

THE LORE OF THE WILD

Caroline Ruddell

Myth and folklore (often the original source for literary fairytales) provide a backdrop to *The Twilight Saga*, and this is in part due to other contemporary popular tales of the supernatural owing a debt to such roots. Myth and folklore can largely be understood as 'oral prose narrative' and, like fairytale, such narratives morph and change in different historical and cultural contexts. Mikel Koven, on discussing another contemporary vampire series, *True Blood*, suggests that it functions broadly as fairytale in that it makes use of 'oral prose narrative' and is set in a fictional supernatural world.[1] In a very similar way *The Twilight Saga* can be considered as fairytale where a fantasy diegetic world allows supernatural figures to exist alongside their human associates, and it makes use of oral prose narrative, particularly in relation to the werewolf community's history and heritage. While much of the thematic content surrounding werewolf and vampire narratives has been driven by film and popular culture, it is important to acknowledge that the fairytale also provides impetus for understanding many of the themes and, importantly, the representation of gender and sexuality in these texts. While the films and books are a little 'bloodless',[2] in that they shy away from gore and sexual content, they do provide an intriguing representation of both the 'monster' and the heroine, which can be viewed as an example of fairytale reworked. This chapter will chart the representation of Bella in *The Twilight Saga* with a specific focus on the fairytale, where gendered relations are problematic, and the reworking of fairytale by authors such as Angela Carter can provide a framework for negotiating the moral implications that can be both explicit and implicit in the fairytale.

In *The Twilight Saga* fairytale, folklore and mythology, as strictly mediated through contemporary popular media, are central to the characterisation of and thematic content related to the werewolf, vampire and human characters. Common themes related to popular vampire narratives are evoked in the diegetic world of *Twilight*. For example, vampires are created once bitten by another vampire; they drink blood to survive; they often live in covens; and they are sexually attractive. In addition, the werewolf characters are mostly male, as is common in werewolf narratives in popular culture; they change during adolescence, again a common trope; and, particularly highlighted through Jacob's change, their shapeshifting is seen, at least initially in *The Twilight Saga*, as a curse. The books and films therefore make use of werewolf and vampire characterisations in contemporary popular culture to drive the narrative. Also noteworthy is that much of the werewolf mythology related to Jacob's pack is told around campfires as oral storytelling. Here, the ancestry of the Quileute Native Americans is interlinked with their history of members becoming werewolves during adolescence, although it should be noted that the representation of Quileute culture is by no means faithful in the texts.[3] Equally, the Cullens' vampirism is explained through various common vampire tropes such as difficulty in coping with immortality, and their potential for immorality. Rosalie typifies this theme through her struggle to come to terms with her vampiric existence and wishes for a human 'normality', that being marriage and children. Such issues draw on other contemporary vampire narratives such as Anne Rice's legacy, wherein Louis rages against his immortal existence, viewing himself as a monster.

The books and films therefore do not necessarily make use of traditional werewolf and vampire mythology, folktale and legend in light of folktale studies. Instead, they draw on and subvert tales of the werewolf and the vampire as they have been told in more contemporary popular film, television and fiction. For example, the vampires do not explode into ashes upon meeting the sun; rather, they glitter and shimmer in daylight, reworking the vampire trope.[4] While the vampires must still hide from the sun it is not for the usual reasons of avoiding death; instead it is a way of hiding their supernatural magnificence from the human population and demonstrates their ability to appear as if 'like angels'.[5] The Cullens are also 'vegetarian' in that they only drink animal blood; this softens the usual hankering after human blood that many vampire tales centre upon. The werewolf characters, once established in their new identity, revel in their metamorphosis from human to animal, whereas traditionally this incorporates a great deal of pain – as is the case in the famous transformation scene in *An American Werewolf in London* (1981, dir. John Landis). Tanya Krzywinska argues that 'when humans become beasts it is almost always figured as either a return of the repressed, the dominance of instinctual drives and throwing off the shackles of civilisation, or as an exaggerated literal demonstration of the material "otherness" of the body.'[6] Werewolves in popular culture therefore usually embody a lack of civilisation or 'culture', where nature or the instinctual dominates. However, the *Twilight* werewolves also 'imprint' on characters, which is an unusual subversion of the werewolf tale that true love can cure. In several tales of the werewolf, and in true fairytale fashion, one of the only ways to stop being a werewolf is to find true love. This is evident in films such as *Curse of the Werewolf* (1961, dir. Terence Fisher) for example. The books and films have therefore drawn on popular tales of the supernatural and reworked various elements presumably in order to appeal to (new) audiences; it is often the case that genre films somewhat subvert conventions in order to revitalise potentially predictable narratives. Marijane Osborn notes, 're-imagined vampires are not unique to Twilight, however, for within the last generation or so, thanks especially to the innovative efforts of Joss Whedon, vampire tradition has been rapidly changing.'[7] This chapter, whilst acknowledging that tropes within *The Twilight Saga* are subject to a continual reworking in line with shifts in genre and popular culture, argues that viewing the saga through the framework of the fairytale allows for interrogating the gendered power relations evident in the texts. The chapter will then chart the Gothic elements apparent in the films and suggest that the saga can be viewed as Gothic fairytale.

The Twilight Saga and fairytale

While the *Twilight* films are not marketed as fairytales, they fit into the current trend for films that draw upon fairytale; this is clearly demonstrated by Catherine Hardwicke, who moved on from directing *Twilight* (2008) to *Red Riding Hood* (2011). Further examples include *Ever After: A Cinderella Story* (dir. Andy Tennant, 1998) and the television series *Grimm* and *Once Upon a Time* (both 2012). In addition, the characters, narrative and themes of the film series (and books) also feature many elements in common with the fairytale in a broad sense. For example, storytelling and narrative are often told through the perspective of folklore and myth, such as Bella's research into both the vampire myth and the Quileute and, as noted, the oral storytelling of the Quileute.

Traditionally fairytale can be thought through as cautionary or warning tales for children, where events in the various narratives are designed to keep children on the 'straight and narrow', and within a patriarchal framework of the 'normative' such as traditional family values. As Bruno Bettelheim notes of Perrault's version of *Little Red Riding Hood*, where the wolf devours the child at the close, it is 'a cautionary story which deliberately threatens the child with its anxiety-producing ending ... It seems that many adults think it better to scare children into good behaviour than to relieve their anxieties as a true fairy tale does.'[8] What a 'true fairy tale' is might be open to debate, but he goes on to state, 'Perrault wanted not only to entertain his audience, but to teach a specific moral lesson with each of his tales.'[9] The moral lesson of Perrault's version of *Little Red Riding Hood* is that young girls should not 'stray from the path' and be swayed by unsavoury characters, such as the wolf, and should do what they are told. In many versions of the tale the little girl climbs into bed with the wolf, believing it to be her grandmother, and therefore the tale also has a distinctly sexual element. Fairytale is clearly open to subversion, reworking and reimagining, and Carter provides such examples of fairytale that are aimed more at an adult readership – this will be explored below.

In *The Twilight Saga*, various moral lessons are detectable. Readings of the books and films have often equated the moral compass of the texts with author Stephenie Meyer's Mormon faith. Film reviews have often noted her Mormon status,[10] while scholars have interrogated the relationship between sexual abstinence in the texts and religious faith; exploring the evidence of Mormonism in the series, Sarah Schwartzman writes:

> One message conveyed is that sexual relations before a sealed marriage can be both unnerving and dangerous ... There is no doubt that Meyer's active membership in the Mormon church has a significant influence on her writing. Her religion should be understood as informing her writing, laying the foundations for what it means to be an eternal couple, a vegetarian vampire, and an empowered mother.[11]

While the films make much of Bella's attraction to both Jacob the werewolf and Edward the vampire, for both narrative drive and spectacle, they are also distinctly conservative in their representation of gender dynamics and sexual politics. Abstinence is largely promoted; Bella and Edward do not have sex until married. Bella's psychological and sexual journey leads her into the clutches of the monster, and hints at a transgressive relationship between a supernatural being and a female human where the 'monster' desires her sexually and craves her blood. Yet the texts often do not deliver on these hints; the films are titillating in that they constantly focus on the intense desire between Bella and Edward, but the lovers refuse to consummate their relationship until after wedlock. The book even cuts from before the wedding night to the morning after so there is no depiction of the sexual act, an anticipated event that has underpinned much of the narrative drive up to that point. However, it should be noted that *Breaking Dawn – Part 1* (2011, dir. Bill Condon) does include slightly more sexual content than that which is apparent in the book. This is clearly a narrative device in this film as the plot revolves around Bella's unexpected pregnancy, and the conception of their child is an important part of the story. However, usually the moral lesson encoded in the films is that it is acceptable to flirt with both danger and sexual desire – apparent in Bella's relationship with both Edward and Jacob – but that good girls should ultimately position themselves within a normative patriarchal framework of marriage and children, and sex is a topic not to be discussed, or explicitly represented in these fictions.[12] While it is fruitful to investigate such issues in relation to Meyer's religious leanings, such moral coding in this series also lends itself well to the context of the fairytale, which has been much discussed in relation to conservatism and moral instruction.

For example, Jack Zipes writes that 'the literary fairy tale was designed both to divert as amusement and instruct ideologically as a means to mould the inner nature of young people'.[13] In line with this view, the *Twilight* texts are large-scale mainstream films that are produced with a high budget and have performed well at the box office, entertaining a large audience. The target audience is young teenagers and the films are designed to titillate such an audience, whilst being ideologically conservative in nature, carrying the message that sex before marriage is wrong. This is most clearly apparent in Bella's relationship with Edward. While Bella views pre-marital abstinence as outdated and unrealistic in contemporary times, Edward enforces this tradition in order to 'save her soul'. While rather melodramatic, the films, whilst acknowledging this outdated view, romanticise Edward's attitude to the end that Bella is seduced by it, ultimately agreeing to marriage despite this going against her instincts. The films also 'instruct ideologically' by placing Bella firmly within a patriarchal framework. This is not unusual to the Gothic tale or the fairytale,[14] and concomitantly there is a limit to the extent to which Bella can negotiate her independence within the social structure that she finds/places herself in. Thus she becomes trapped, albeit willingly, within a distinctly patriarchal system.

Moving from a life with her mother to the small community of Forks to live with her father, the Sheriff, Bella's mother fades significantly into the background; although depicted as loving and caring, she becomes largely absent in Bella's life, a point that is explored in more depth by O'Donnell in this collection. This latter theme is also common to the fairytale, in which good maternal figures are often absent.[15] Bella's life therefore becomes dominated by the men that surround her: not only her father, but also Edward and his family, where the doctor-cum-surrogate-father figure, Carlisle, is the head, and where the mother figure, Esme, has a very limited presence. Bella's friend Jacob gradually involves her in the werewolf pack (all male bar one) and the Quileute family, again distinctly lacking in female presence. Bella's school friends are a mixed group; the first film allows some room for female friendship with Jessica and Angela but these friendships are ultimately shown to be unfulfilling for Bella who much prefers the company of men (and the company of wolves). In addition, as Schwartzman argues, 'there is a paternalistic quality to nearly all of Bella's relationships with men'.[16] In this sense the film fits squarely into the view that mainstream cinema usually leaves female relationships and friendships unexplored, as Yvonne Tasker explains:

> Across the majority of its genres, the popular American cinema has marginalised representations of female friendship, more often favouring glamorous stars seen to exist in spectacular isolation, supportive figures who exist almost exclusively in relation to the hero, or women set in competition with each other.[17]

It should be acknowledged here that Bella is the protagonist and does not play a supportive role, nor is she glamorised to the degree that Tasker is discussing in relation to other examples of popular Hollywood cinema. However, she does exist largely in isolation from influential female figures and takes much more interest in her male friendships and relationships. This suggests a slight refraction from Tasker's argument but one that stands in that she does not have fulfilling female friendships, with the possible exception of that with Alice. The question arises here as to whether the films are simply 'instructing ideologically' or whether they are highlighting the difficulties of a particularly female experience, and the concomitant problems involved in moving from adolescence into adulthood.

When interrogating the representation of sexual and gender identity it is useful to consider Zipes' arguments concerning the ideological traditions and later reworkings of the fairytale. Zipes argues that tales such as those written by the Grimm brothers and their imitators have come to be regarded as conservative, 'indoctrinat[ing] children ... thus curtailing their free development'.[18] He instead argues that later writers from the 1960s onwards began reworking fairytales 'to write innovative, emancipatory tales, more critical of changing conditions in advanced technological societies based on capitalist production and social relations'.[19] While Zipes focuses largely on German writers it can be instructive to turn here to Angela Carter, who has interrogated the fairytale with reference to social and political concerns regarding the female role and experience. Such writings are in line with Zipes' argument that some reworkings take a critical stance towards the ideological implications of the traditional fairytale.

One of the most significant of Carter's reworking of fairytales is 'The Company of Wolves' (1979),[20] a version of *Little Red Riding Hood*. In her narrative, the central female protagonist actively seeks out the company of the wolves in her home in the forest. Cinematically adapted in 1986 (directed by Neil Jordan and co-written by Carter), the film extends the story into a dreamlike world in which the protagonist, Rosaleen, embraces the wolves to the extent that she becomes one herself. Carter's reworking of this familiar tale is interesting in that it allows the young female protagonist to embrace her own sexuality, and rather than the wolf devouring her at the close of the narrative, she becomes instead actively engaged in the course of her life. The film also has a clear sexual element in which the wolf is linked to both puberty and sexuality. Rosaleen's act of seeking out the wolf suggests a clear desire on her part to involve herself in the realm of the wolf, and this realm is made sexual by the many references to the wolves' voracious appetite and the attraction they hold.

The Twilight Saga as Gothic fairytale

Rather than being afraid, as in the traditional renditions of this tale, Rosaleen overcomes her fear and embraces the physicality of the male wolf. This is undoubtedly similar to the classic Gothic tale where the heroine is often driven by curiosity. In reading the *Twilight* films as negotiating a slippery line between 'ideological instruction' and a mediation of the female experience, it can also be useful to consider another important element of the texts: that of the Gothic. There is a complex relationship between cinema that draws on horror tropes and the Gothic tradition, as Peter Hutchings points out:

> Many critics have also seen gothic literature as providing another important source for the horror film. However, establishing the precise nature of the connection between gothic and horror is complicated by the fact that the term 'gothic' itself can be just as vague and imprecise as the term 'horror' ... The relationship between gothic and horror is not always clear. In some instances, the terms are used as if they are interchangeable,

while in other circumstances 'gothic horror film' denotes a type of horror cinema reliant on period settings (Hammer horror, for example). The more common approach is to see gothic literature as a precursor to and influence upon horror cinema.[21]

The series' relationship to the Gothic is ambiguous, as Lori Branch notes; on one hand the saga moves away from Gothic with its vegetarian vampires, and an emphasis on sunlight, and on the other hand 'more traditional Gothic spectacles' are apparent in, for example, the aristocratic vampire rulers, the Volturi.[22] The films can be viewed as Gothic tales in the sense that they feature the supernatural, a secretive past that inhibits the present (a feature of the vampire tale generally), recognisable monstrous figures and the Gothic heroine. In *The Twilight Saga*, the Gothic heroine, Bella, finds herself in dangerous territory amongst a number of potentially monstrous and supernatural characters; here the past continually unhinges the present as the supernatural characters usually have long histories and their memories and actions of times long past seep into the present. Further examples of the Gothic resonate in the series through its setting and landscape. In discussing traditional Gothic landscapes such as dark forests, mountainous terrain, moorlands and violent seas, Emma and James McElroy suggest of *Twilight* that, '[I]t is amidst such alluring topographies, whether wilderness or other, that the Gothic and like-minded fictions prepare their ecological narratives so that nature and culture, as suppositional binaries, can come into play.'[23] The interplay between nature and culture is perhaps best demonstrated through the Cullens' residence; a light, spacious and distinctly modern abode, populated with cultural products such as pianos, music and books, is set amidst the wild forests that circulate Forks. Here, the binaries of culture and nature exist alongside each other and demonstrate one of the Gothic elements of the series.[24] The series, it appears, negotiates the Gothic in a number of ways – both utilising Gothic tropes and reworking them for a (post)modern audience.

The Gothic tale can also be read as an adult fairytale where a number of themes, such as rites of passage, and 'a journey', carry over. One of the strongest elements in common between the Gothic and the fairytale is the oscillation between the supernatural and magic, and the real. The dialogue between these different realms allows for reading the fairytale and the Gothic both metaphorically and psychologically. As Marina Warner points out on fairytale, 'The double vision of the tales, on the one hand charting perennial drives and terrors, both conscious and unconscious, and on the other mapping actual, volatile experience, gives the genre its fascination and power to satisfy.'[25] Such an argument could certainly be related to the Gothic tale also. The layers of meaning that both the Gothic and the fairytale can provide, or different ways in which they might be read and interpreted, are another key crossover between these genres, or modes of storytelling. Further, both genres often feature a female protagonist who oscillates between being in and out of control of the circumstances she finds herself, or chooses to be, in.

At the close of the first film, and in order to save her mother, Bella chooses to go to the vampire villain James, who is intent on killing her; she actively goes to what she thinks will be her death. This is on the one hand an active choice that she makes independently, and on the other an act that involves her surrender to a more powerful (and male) being. Although there is a limit to how this narrative turn of events can be considered progressive, Bella's multi-faceted embrace of the monster can be considered similar to Carter's reframing of female experience, or more accurately, drawing attention to issues of female identity, and to a lesser extent, agency. Being active and curious are major components here in relation to the female protagonist as Gothic heroine, as Bella is shown to actively seek out Edward, despite his early attempts to avoid her, and her embrace of the Cullens' vampire world comes without hesitation. She does not usually show fear at the strength and power the vampire characters demonstrate (James being an exception), and in fact actively desires to become one herself. In effect, Bella rejects the human world and finds comfort in the more exciting world of the supernatural. This is clearly demonstrated by her conversation with Edward in *Eclipse* (2010, dir. David Slade) in which she finally agrees to marry him; she states explicitly that she feels more at home in the supernatural world. This is certainly not unlike Rosaleen's attitude in Carter's 'The Company of Wolves'.

What is apparent particularly in relation to the characterisation of Bella is that she is neither immersed in the world of the human nor fully engaged in the realm of the supernatural until she becomes a vampire, instead occupying a space somewhere in between. This is, to a point, symbolised through a split between her own family and her potential future family; Charlie represents a wholesome, loving although somewhat reserved father figure in a family context, while the Cullens provide Bella with wealth, endless love and attention, but also vampirism. The monstrosity of the Cullen family is veiled, and in this sense the films shy away from any potential horror and move towards a romance where luckily for our protagonist the in-laws are not really the monsters-in-law they have the potential to be. On the contrary, the series makes it explicit that Bella's lifestyle will be vastly improved by wealth and a loving and caring extended family, as well as immortality. Branch notes that the family in the *Twilight* texts plays a key role in relation to the Gothic, where she argues:

> it negotiates a particular set of concerns that hearken back to the Enlightenment origins of Gothic literature – guilt and forgiveness, desires and fears related to the family, and the tensions of belief and hope in an increasingly rationalized world – yet in a way peculiar to our own postmodern moment.[26]

Bella, for the majority of the series, ultimately becomes caught between two rather opposing family systems, which is epitomised by Charlie's suspicion of Edward and the Cullens, despite their appearing to be the most desirable of future in-laws for his daughter.

Bella's 'in-betweenness' is reflective of how unsure she is of her place in the world, and in particular as a female subject, which is a traditional Gothic representation of female identity. As Manley writes of Carter's protagonist in 'The Bloody Chamber' (1979)[27] (an adaptation of the Bluebeard tale), 'she is not always passive, however, but rather oscillates between being insecure and feeling sure of herself. She is a woman in process, someone who is exploring her subject position and beginning to tell her own story.'[28] In Carter's 'The Bloody Chamber' the female protagonist is married to a domineering and murderous man who has killed many of his former wives, and she becomes isolated in his castle. Although Bella is not in the same kind of danger from Edward, they are similar in that Bella is immersed completely into a very ordered and patriarchal system (albeit a liberal one), dominated by the law of the father. These two central characters differ from Rosaleen in 'The Company of Wolves', whose trip into the forest, to eventually be one with the wolves, is a much more archaic tale of physicality and desire. The wolves are not civilised and they reject the more ordered world of the human population, choosing to live in the wild forest; they are represented as animalistic and even id-driven in their pursuit of food and sex. Bella's embrace of the monster is a different beast entirely. The Cullens are the epitome of (white) civilisation,[29] signalled by the father figure as a doctor and well-respected pillar of the community.

In conclusion, on first reading, the *Twilight* films appear to offer a very conservative message in relation to the rites of passage in growing up. The texts suggest very strongly that abstinence is romantic and sexy; as is the case with certain fairytales, they are ideologically instructive in suggesting that sex should not precede marriage. Romanticising this view can be considered deeply conservative and at odds with the contemporary cultural moment. Yet I would also argue that the series leans towards (as well as leaning away from) the Gothic in that Gothic goes hand-in-hand with fairytale; they are titillating tales that function both to ignite curiosity in the 'other' whilst simultaneously warning us of the potential horrors of not conforming to the ordered social world. Therefore, it could be argued that by viewing the films through the lens of the Gothic and the fairytale, and by acknowledging the politics and potential of their reworkings, the films could be offering a representation of a young female experience as a continual negotiation within a world dominated by patriarchy. How Bella's journey is interpreted is a point of debate as discussed here, and there is room to map a reworking of Gothic fairytale on to the *Twilight* texts – both in the sense that the films conform to and subvert traditional supernatural tales, and in that Bella is active, curious and embraces the 'monster'. Yet, while Rosaleen's enjoyment of the company of wolves allows her sexual liberation and freedom from civilised society, Bella's embrace of the vampire enables her to become a very wealthy wife and mother – two very different fairytale endings.

Notes

1. Mikel Koven, ' "I'm a Fairy!? How Fucking Lame!": *True Blood* as Fairytale', in Brigid Cherry (ed.), *True Blood: Investigating Vampires and Southern Gothic* (London: I.B.Tauris, 2012), pp. 59–73.
2. Ben Walters, 'Review of *Twilight*', in *Sight and Sound*, February (London: BFI Publishing, 2009).
3. Kristian Jensen, 'Noble Werewolves or Native Shape-shifters', in Amy M. Clarke and Marijane Osborn (eds), *The* Twilight *Mystique: Critical Essays on the Novels and Films* (Jefferson: McFarland, 2010), pp. 92–106, p. 92.
4. See, for example, Osborn's discussion of the possible literary and folklore sources that relate to the Meyer vampires' glittering skin (Marijane Osborn, 'Luminous and Liminal: Why Edward Shines', in Clarke and Osborn, ibid., pp. 15–34).
5. Ibid., p. 18.
6. Tanya Krzywinska, *Sex and the Cinema* (London: Wallflower Press, 2006), p. 139.
7. Osborn, 'Luminous and Liminal', p. 15.
8. Bruno Bettelheim, *The Uses of Enchantment: The Meaning and Importance of Fairy Tales* (Harmondsworth: Penguin, 1975), p. 167.
9. Ibid., p. 168.
10. See for example Will Lawrence's review in *Empire Online* of the first film. Here he associates the sexual abstinence apparent in the film with Meyer's Mormon faith: 'Meyer is a devout Mormon, her tale a metaphor for carnal abstinence, allowing young girls to splash around in a pool of obsessive love without having to swim in the turbulent waters of scary teenage sex' ('Review of *Twilight*', *Empire Online*, 14 October 2011, http://www.empireonline.com/reviews/reviewcomplete.asp?FID=135600 (accessed 14 October 2011)).

11. Sarah Schwartzman, 'Is *Twilight* Mormon?', in Clarke and Osborn, *The* Twilight *Mystique*, pp. 121–36, pp. 128–32.

12. I do not wish to be contentious here – abstinence in a young woman can clearly be a sign of strength, and possibly a refusal to submit to patriarchal hypocrisy. Yet Bella does not resist as such: abstinence is enforced upon her by Edward – she makes several attempts to have sex with Edward in the texts but it is Edward who does the resisting.

13. Jack Zipes, *Fairy Tales and the Art of Subversion: The Classical Genre for Children and the Process of Civilization* (New York: Routledge, 1983), p. 18.

14. See Kohlenberger's chapter in this collection.

15. See Marina Warner, *From the Beast to the Blonde: On Fairy Tales and Their Tellers* (London: Chatto & Windus, 1994).

16. Schwartzman, 'Is *Twilight* Mormon?', p. 129.

17. Yvonne Tasker, *Working Girls: Gender and Sexuality in Popular Cinema* (London and New York: Routledge, 1998), p. 139.

18. Zipes, *Fairy Tales and the Art of Subversion*, p. 46.

19. Ibid.

20. Angela Carter, 'The Company of Wolves', in Angela Carter, *The Bloody Chamber* (1979; London: Vintage, 2006).

21. Peter Hutchings, *The Horror Film* (Harlow: Pearson Longman, 2004), pp. 10–1.

22. Lori Branch, 'Carlisle's Cross: Locating the Post-Secular Gothic', in Clarke and Osborn, *The* Twilight *Mystique*, pp. 60–79, p. 60.

23. Emma McElroy and James McElroy, 'Eco-Gothics for the Twenty-First Century', in Clarke and Osborn, *The* Twilight *Mystique*, pp. 80–91, p. 80.

24. Ewan Kirkland argues in this collection that the binary of culture and nature is symbolic of 'whiteness' in the series; the Scandinavian style and architecture of the Cullens' residence, and the symbols of Western culture embodied in objects such as graduation caps and the piano, further this notion.

25. Warner, *From the Beast to the Blonde*, p. xvii.

26. Branch, 'Carlisle's Cross', p. 61.

27. Angela Carter, 'The Bloody Chamber', in Carter, *The Bloody Chamber*.

28. Kathleen E. B. Manley, 'The Woman in Process in Angela Carter's "The Bloody Chamber"', in Danielle Marie Roemer and Cristina Bacchilega (eds), *Angela Carter and the Fairy Tale* (Michigan: Wayne University Press, 2001), pp. 83–93, p. 83.

29. See Kirkland in this collection.

7

'WHERE HAVE ALL THE MONSTERS GONE? LONG TIME PASSING': THE AESTHETICS OF ABSENCE AND GENERIC SUBVERSION IN *NEW MOON*

Wickham Clayton

As a mainstream Hollywood film sequel, *The Twilight Saga: New Moon* (2009, dir. Chris Weitz) has failed. As a genre picture[1] and a sequel, *New Moon* automatically comes with a set of expectations which are established for the viewer with a familiarity of the first cinematic instalment, *Twilight* (2008, dir. Catherine Hardwicke).[2] Vera Dika, writing about the form and function of genre sequels,[3] asserts:

> ...the replication of material while supplying a suitable level of variation serves two purposes for the film-viewing audience. It facilitates the film's game by supplying the known ground rules, while the innovations supply the film's interest and shocks. This technique allows the viewer to feel secure in his knowledge of the formula, distanced by the formulaic predictability of the events, while none the less excited by the surprises and variations![4]

While Dika's analysis appears true for a large number of genre films and sequels, *New Moon* refuses to fully satisfy these expectations. There are, however, other film sequels that have proved successful because of their refusal to, as Dika says, facilitate 'the film's game'.

The disappointing sequel

Todd Berliner, in an essay about *The Godfather Part II* (1974, dir. Francis Ford Coppola), argues that sequels attempt to recreate the viewing experience of the original film – and in some cases promise to better their predecessors – but ultimately disappoint the viewer. He writes:

> The almost inescapable failure of sequels results from the fact that, at the same time a sequel calls to mind the charismatic original, it also recalls its absence, fostering a futile, nostalgic desire to reexperience the original nostalgic moment as though it had never happened. Hence, the experience of a sequel differs fundamentally from that of rewatching a beloved movie.[5]

By explicating the almost unavoidable disappointment that results from viewing a film sequel, Berliner is then able to theorise about the reasoning behind generic sequel design. He later states, '[t]o compensate for the sequel's inherent sense of absence and loss, the maker of a movie sequel tends to supply excessive amounts of whatever audiences seemed to have liked most about the first movie.'[6] These statements provide the analytical median for Berliner's central argument: 'As with most sequels, *Godfather II* disappoints its audience, but it does so in a particularly extravagant way. The film's conspicuous refusal to satisfy paradoxically serves as a source of audience pleasure.'[7] While I would argue that *New Moon* does not do this as intricately or fully as *The Godfather Part II*, a large segment of the film does underwhelm on a narrative and aesthetic level, making it – perhaps conversely against academic tradition – worthy of interest and analysis.

Twenty-five minutes into the film's 130-minute runtime,[8] Edward, the male lead from *Twilight* and the first part of *New Moon*, wilfully leaves to protect Bella, the female lead, from any harm he could cause her as a vampire. The tension created through a romantic relationship between a male vampire and a female human is the primary element that drives the plot of the first film. His disappearance removes this tension, leaving *New Moon* without its driving narrative thread, and until Laurent, a vampire introduced in the previous film, reappears and fights with four giant wolves exactly an hour into the film, the dynamic created through the interaction between humans and monsters is lost from the series. Here, the film revives in altered form the foundational generic elements of supernatural horror. Approximately the second quarter of the second film in a series *about* monsters *lacks* monsters, and is therefore a literal narrative representation of the sequel's inherent sense of absence and loss.[9]

Even though the vampires in *Twilight* do not make their true nature known until approximately 50 minutes into the film, there still exists an anticipatory element to the narrative development, whereas the disappearance of Edward in *New Moon* leaves the plot to develop almost aimlessly, a point generally noted, sometimes peripherally, by critics.

The reception of absence

Genevieve Koski writes, ' ... in the fallout of a nasty paper-cut incident, Pattinson skips town with the rest of his clan, leaving Stewart to explore her range of mopey expressions alone.'[10] Koski's review, only addressing this period in basic narrative terms, overlooks the experience of viewing this segment, a fallacy that is repeated across other critical reviews. For instance, Michael Phillips writes, 'With the boy with the fwoopy hair off to sunny Italy to deal with the Volturi ... Bella pines and pines again, and retreats into herself. Then she is pulled out of her funk – halfway, anyway; it's a big funk – by her pal Jacob, who is sweet and hunky ... '[11] Roger Ebert also summarises this period in brief:

> Edward leaves, because Bella was not meant to be with him. Although he's a vegetarian vampire, when she gets a paper cut at her birthday party one of his pals leaps on her like a shark on a tuna fish. In his absence she's befriended by Jake (Taylor Lautner), that nice American Indian boy.[12]

Another critical approach has been to address the period of absence as a negative experience, with reviewers highlighting it as a point of contention with the film. Mick LaSalle writes of what he sees as the toll this takes on the pace:

> Edward knows that associating with a human exposes her to too much danger, even from his own family. So he abandons her, thinking it's for the best. But Bella mopes around for months ... There's mopey and then there's torpid, and 'New Moon' is about as sluggish a teen movie you can find ... With Meyer's story leaving Edward largely out of the picture, Pattinson can't add any intrigue to this non-starter of a love triangle.[13]

LaSalle highlights what he sees as both a deficiency in pacing and in narrative tension; based on this review, it is, in effect, a slow film where nothing happens. A similar criticism is made by Claudia Puig, who writes,

> Pattinson isn't given much to do in this installment [sic] since he removes himself from Bella for her own protection. Bella spends an inordinate amount of time pining away. Unless it's a [sic] Ingmar Bergman film, watching an expressionless person stare out a window or trudge around alone in the woods is simply a drag.[14]

Puig's review is particularly of interest, as it engages with the experiential aspect of this absence in terms of 'worth'. Bergman, who significantly created films about absence, specifically the absence of a god,[15] in films such as *The Seventh Seal* (1957), does incorporate shots such as the ones Puig describes in his film *Persona* (1966), among others. Puig's statement makes the implicit assumption that Ingmar Bergman's films are worthy, and perhaps enhanced by including protracted sequences of people staring out windows, without anticipating the argument that the same thing could be said of *New Moon*. The absence of Edward from the film's narrative does, in fact, enhance not only *New Moon* but also the whole of *The Twilight Saga*, as an analysis of the film's form and narrative shows.

Visualising absence

New Moon assumes a visual design that echoes the preceding *Twilight* and informs the succeeding *The Twilight Saga: Eclipse* (2010, dir. David Slade). However, *New Moon* makes significant variations, usually overlooked to create its own unique visual identity. Within *New Moon*'s overall visual aesthetic, this period of absence is created to both smoothly integrate into the overarching design as well as stand out with regard to its narrative significance.

The most obvious visual element that sets *New Moon* apart from *Twilight* or *Eclipse* is the use of colour. Where both *Twilight* and *Eclipse* opt for a colder visual, desaturating the reds and yellows except during key shots,[16] which results in frequent appearances of blue, white, black and grey in the *mise-en-scène*, *New Moon*'s colour design is based upon earth tones, highlighting browns and deep greens. The regular use of red and yellow in the colour palette can be seen from the outset of the film. The opening sequence, foreshadowing the climax of *New Moon*, shows Bella in Italy running through a sea of people in bright red cloaks. This contrasts distinctly with the opening of *Twilight*, in which a deer is shown

in the forest drinking water, then running away from a predator. In the latter
sequence, the only colour that is particularly striking is the occasional flash of a
bright green plant, which stands in contrast against the washed-out colouring
of the rest of the shots.

Although the use of earth tones predominates throughout the film, the
period of absence is visually demarcated by using muted forms of the colours.
This can be seen most succinctly during the sequences involving Bella and
Jacob in the workshop repairing the motorcycle. This segment of the film contains frequent uses of red, but the colour is not as sharp and brilliant as the
earlier sequences in the film, such as Bella's birthday gathering. Despite the
occasional expressionistic uses of this bright red – Bella's blanket as she wakes
up from a nightmare, for instance – the washed-out colouring dominates the
bulk of the compositions. The contrast in presence/absence colouring is highlighted within the film during Bella's dream of lying in a field, talking with
Edward. This scene breaks up the period of absence, as a distinct visual counterpoint by using bright light and a range of brilliant colours. When the dream
is over, the film returns to the muted colouring seen earlier, but richness of the
colour palette begins to return during the confrontation between Bella and
Laurent. Although the clearing in which they meet is barren of vegetation, the
yellow of the ground and the green of the trees are more saturated, accompanying the physical appearance of a vampire with increased richness of the visual
template. The colours become gradually more saturated until the climax of the
film in Italy, which contains the aforementioned red cloaks, the red eyes of the
Volturi, the bright yellow sports car driven by Alice and a light blue sky. It is
apparent that the brightness of the colours accompanies Bella's increased physical proximity to Edward.

The editing also plays a heavy role in the pace and experience of Bella's time
without monsters. Within this period, the more action-oriented sequences in
New Moon contain an editing pace similar to those that are more moderately
paced in both *Twilight* and *Eclipse*. Aside from those, the filmmakers take great
pains to create long single takes, and make each sequence feel deliberate and
slow. Again, this allows the visual aesthetic to echo Bella's sense of time passing gradually. Some of the longer takes in this period involve technologically
intensive methods to retain the illusion of a single take. After Edward leaves,
Bella is shown sitting in her room looking out of her picture window. She sits
in place as the camera moves smoothly around her in 360 degrees, and every
time the window comes into frame, the changing of the seasons can be seen,
accompanied by inter-titles revealing that it is October as the plants outside are
still green, which passes into November, the trees barren and the grass brown,

which then turns into December and the snow-covered ground. In total, the shot lasts one minute and 15 seconds. In his commentary, Chris Weitz describes the shot as follows:

> ... this very complicated CG sequence which involves first shooting the element of Bella with a Steadicam, but having markers on the set so that we could match exactly the move that Dave Crohn did with the Steadicam, with a robotic camera, which would move precisely the way that he did, so we could do multiple passes, and that every time we looked out the window we would see a new month.[17]

Another scene with a nearly identical shot design occurs as Jacob repairs the motorcycle with Bella's help. In a single take, the viewer is shown the work at different stages, as the camera moves around the shed. This shot lasts 48 seconds in total, and Weitz again reveals that this was acquired through the use of motion-controlled camerawork. This indicates a specific and wilful aesthetic design that is unique to *New Moon*, and the period of absence draws out the aesthetic elements that slow the pace and mute the visuals. This places Bella and her conflict centrally to the film, and shows thought and intent behind what LaSalle dismisses as 'torpid' and 'sluggish'.

The aurality and narrativity of absence

In order to understand the significance of *New Moon* within the aesthetic and narrative development of *The Twilight Saga*, it helps to return to the first instalment for comparison. *Twilight* opens with Bella's voice-over, ruminating upon dying for someone she loves, and informing the viewer that she left Phoenix, Arizona to live with her father in Forks, Washington. Later, her narration periodically reappears in the film to give brief insights. So, within *Twilight*, Bella's voice is subject to the narrative flow, only explaining points of plot development.

New Moon, however, begins with Bella's voice-over quoting from *Romeo and Juliet*, which is one of the diegetic themes of the film. This voice-over does not appear again until Edward leaves, in which, during the changing of the months, we hear Bella's voice dictating an e-mail to Alice. This is heard over the music used to accompany the montage, which includes Bella waking up screaming in the middle of the night, sitting alone in the school cafeteria, writing the message we hear her dictating and looking at her e-mail inbox full of undelivered messages to Alice. The music takes initial priority; however, the central aural focus is later replaced by Bella's voice-over. Both of these in turn are drowned out by Bella's screams in her sleep, and aside from this all that is heard are muted ambient noises, and at one point Charlie's voice can be faintly heard calling her name when he runs into her room to comfort her. Therefore, Bella's emotions, attempts at communication and pain become the dominant force within the film's sound space. Bella's internal focus not only takes preference within the sound design of the film, but also becomes the narrative driving force of *New Moon*, which is a reflection of the primary function of the film.

With regard to the narrative of *The Twilight Saga*, Edward's role in the life of Bella drives the plot forward because he, as well as the other vampires with whom he is affiliated, frequently provide an action to which Bella is required to respond. Essentially, in *Twilight* and at the beginning of *New Moon*, Bella only takes action when forced to by outside circumstances. Even in *Twilight*'s climax, when she escapes from Alice and Jasper, Bella is acting under direct orders from James, and failure to act would result, she believes, in her mother's death. Likewise, in the opening of *New Moon*, all of her actions are dictated by the characters surrounding her. Edward and Alice plan her birthday party even though she doesn't want one, an accidental paper cut forces her to submit to the protection of the Cullens as Jasper attacks, and even Edward's decision to leave is an event that happens *to* her.

Once Edward leaves and Bella is rescued from the forest, the dynamic between plot and character realises a shift. From this point, Bella's inertia comes at the cost of plot stagnation. The montages of Bella sitting as seasons change, her recurring nightmares and her sitting alone in the school cafeteria exist in order to demonstrate the passage of time, and to create an understanding of her character's perspective and emotional state, without any plot development. Although Charlie talks to her about her behaviour, it is Bella's idea to go to a movie with Jessica, to ride on a stranger's motorcycle, to buy her own motorcycle and to approach Jacob to repair it. Despite the fact that her motivation is to appear adjusted enough so that Charlie will not ask her to leave, and to do something dangerous enough that will cause Edward to appear to her, the specific decisions are not derived from a detailed ultimatum, such as the one presented by James. She has a defined motivation, but the manifestation of her decisions comes from the defining elements of her character. Bella's own characteristics and decisions become the impetus for the narrative, instead of the latter dictating her actions.

Although *Eclipse* largely demonstrates a return to Bella as a reactive character, there are a few significant changes. She discovers a way to outsmart Edward in order to spend time with Jacob, and despite the fact that the battle against the newborns is occurring against her will, she insists on Edward staying with her away from the action. In these situations, she makes decisions that dictate the development of the action. Although *New Moon* appears an anomaly to the franchise in its character/plot dynamic, the events of the film inform Bella's character, and therefore alter Bella's relationship to the events that threaten to entirely dictate her actions in the succeeding film.

Conclusion

The narrative positioning of *New Moon* most concisely points to the way in which its period of absent monsters not only stands out as a unique section of the film series, but as necessary to the development of the serial narrative of *The Twilight Saga*. This is enhanced by an analysis of the aesthetic design of the segment, and therefore has significant implications for the overall development of the series. Does it function as a satisfying sequel? No. Nor does it fully satisfy as a supernatural horror film, as it lacks monsters for a significant amount of time. It fails even to fully function as a romance, with romantic tension punctuating few sections of this two-hour-plus film. *New Moon* subverts generic categorisation and underwhelms the viewer on many counts. However, this is the very reason it proves fascinating and suggests that there may be more to *The Twilight Saga* than Bella smooching monsters.

Notes

1. The work done by Judith Kohlenberger in this collection is dedicated to this argument of *Twilight's* generic affiliation. I am thus writing of the series with the awareness that it shares both horror and romance genre tropes.
2. This raises the question of the film's literary roots. However, I am reading the film solely as a cinematic viewing experience, as the very nature of adaptation from written word to filmic representation demands variation.
3. Dika writes specifically of the slasher sub-genre of horror, but I would argue her statement addresses the essence of genre sequelisation as a whole (Vera Dika, *Games of Terror: Halloween, Friday the 13th and the Films of the Stalker Cycle* (London: Associated University Press, 1990)).
4. Ibid., p. 84. This statement is a specific reference to the function of *Friday the 13th Part 2* (1981, dir. Steve Miner), but the financial success of that film can arguably be attributed to the very thing Dika is discussing.
5. Todd Berliner, 'The Pleasures of Disappointment: Sequels and *The Godfather, Part II*', *The Journal of Film and Video* 53/2–3 (Summer/Fall 2001), pp. 107–23, p. 109.
6. Ibid.
7. Ibid., p. 108.
8. The times used here have been based upon the US NTSC DVD release (2010).

9. Ewan Kirkland, in this collection, writes of the overarching sense of loss and absence in the series' central romance, by appropriating and arguing the theory of the 'sexlessness of racial white identity'. The narrative is certainly subtly imbued with this sense of loss and absence, but my concern is with the overt expression of it in my chosen segment of *New Moon*.

10. Genevieve Koski, 'Review: *The Twilight Saga: New Moon*', *The AV Club*, 2009, http://www.avclub.com/articles/the-twilight-saga-new-moon,35588/?_r=true (accessed 5 May 2012).

11. Michael Phillips, 'Review, *The Twilight Saga: New Moon*', *Chicago Tribune* – Talking Pictures Blog, 2009, http://featuresblogs.chicagotribune.com/talking_pictures/2009/11/the-twilight-saga-new-moon-x-stars.html (accessed 5 May 2012).

12. Roger Ebert, 'Review, *The Twilight Saga: New Moon*', rogerebert.com, 2009, http://rogerebert.suntimes.com/apps/pbcs.dll/article?AID=/20091118/REVIEWS/911199998 (accessed 5 May 2012).

13. Mick LaSalle, 'Review: *The Twilight Saga: New Moon*', *SFGate*, 2009, http://www.sfgate.com/cgi-bin/article.cgi?f=/c/a/2009/11/19/DDOO1AN7L9.DTL (accessed 5 May 2012) (link no longer working).

14. Claudia Puig, 'Werewolves Inject Life into *New Moon* but the Sequel Still Splutters', *USA Today*, 2009, http://www.usatoday.com/life/movies/reviews/2009–11-19-twilight-new-moon_N.htm (accessed 5 May 2012).

15. An observation also made by Woody Allen through the character of Mary in *Manhattan* (1979, dir. Woody Allen).

16. Edward catching Bella's dropped apple in *Twilight* and the frequent use of bright red/orange for Victoria's hair in *Eclipse* are two apparent examples.

17. Weitz, 2009 *New Moon* DVD Audio Commentary.

PART 3

ROMANCING THE TOMB: SEXUAL DYSFUNCTION AND SEXUALITY

8

'MY DISTASTE FOR FORKS': *TWILIGHT*, ORAL GRATIFICATION AND SELF-DENIAL

Ruth O'Donnell

Twilight is a story preoccupied with self-denial, a theme that plays out in the love affair of the heroine Bella and the vampire Edward, but that I argue is ultimately a reflection of Bella's relationship and unresolved issues with her mother. Employing a psychoanalytic methodology to examine the novel[1] and film (2008, dir. Catherine Hardwicke), this chapter examines how the subject of maternal abandonment is represented and finds a form of resolution in this fantastical narrative.

Introduction: towards a psychoanalytic reading of *Twilight*

The use of psychoanalytic methodology in the study of film has a long history, with each discipline finding commonalities in their shared preoccupation with dreams, fantasy and striving towards psychological meaning. In its application to the horror genre, psychoanalysis has provided one 'explanation' for the pleasures that this form of cinema affords. Psychoanalytic methodology appears uniquely placed to make sense of the fantastical narrative elements of the horror film that may otherwise appear baffling, interpreting them as an attempt to deal with repressed material on the part of the spectator. Mark Jancovich, writing on horror, suggests that:

> fantasy tries to deal with the very materials that rational 'realist' discourse exists to repress, and it therefore offers a potentially subversive critique of the social world. The unconscious desires that erupt in dreams and the horror are the product of social repression, and in giving expression to these desires, horror therefore implies a critique of the social world that represses them.[2]

However, such an approach to the film text is not without its limitations, and the use of psychoanalytic methodology within film studies has been criticised for its ahistorical (and Western-culture-biased) approach and grand theorising. In his account of this debate, Steven Jay Schneider admits that 'Whether Freudianism, or any other species of psychoanalytic thought, can successfully shed light on filmic horror's textual processes ... remains an open question'[3] and may partly depend on the reader buying into the 'project' of psychoanalysis, both at the level of the individual and cultural product. Nevertheless, the writer concedes that many films in the horror genre 'have been interpreted as thematising, narrativising, and embodying ideas and constructs similar to those found in orthodox psychoanalytic theory and its revisions,'[4] and for this reason psychoanalysis remains a useful tool for the interpretation of moving image artefacts, perhaps in particular those with fantasy elements. While *Twilight* cannot be considered a horror film in the strictest generic terms, its fantastical elements and privileging of the vampire, one of horror's most popular symbols, suggest that the text may be 'open' to a psychoanalytic reading. The figure of the vampire, and its associated themes of orality, such as sucking, drinking, biting and insatiable oral craving, lends itself to an interpretation within a classical Freudian schema that explores developmental preoccupations and anxieties. None more so than the oral stage, which is characterised by the infant's preoccupation with feeding, and by extension, the mother, involving a host of developmental anxieties around the issue of oral satiation and frustration. As *Twilight* is a story preoccupied by (oral) self-denial, both on the part of its vampire and human characters, psychoanalysis as a theoretical framework seems wholly appropriate, and will be used to here to consider how issues of orality and maternal neglect are explored and 'worked through' by the narrative.

Twilight begins with an act of rejection by the mother; the story that follows can be read as an exploration of the child's experience of this abandonment and anger towards the maternal figure. The narrative presents what Freud termed a 'compromise-formation', describing this phenomenon as the outcome of the conflict between an unconscious desire that seeks fulfilment and an opposing trend governed by the conscious ego, which is disapproving of such a want. In the compromise-formation, expressed through psychological symptom or dream, 'both trends have found an incomplete expression'.[5] In the case of Bella (Kristen Stewart), she is allowed both the denial and gratification of her dependency needs: claiming both independence and dependence. This is expressed through the oral themes that are given their most literal form in the figure of the vampire, as well as through more general motifs of eating and nurturance. Extending this further, Bella's oral self-denial can be interpreted as symptomatic of an eating disorder. The implications of this will be considered in relation to the maternal neglect that Bella suffers.

Psychoanalyst and film scholar Glen O. Gabbard suggests that popular films capture 'common developmental crises', while providing 'wish fulfilling solutions to human dilemmas'.[6] Freud's own analysis of literature reveals similar mechanisms at play.[7] As a popular narrative, the *Twilight* books and films indeed work through certain psychodynamic issues and provide solutions to these 'crises'. In this reading of *Twilight* Freud's model of psychosexual stages is employed to argue that regression to the 'oral stage' is made at the expense of mature (i.e. genital) sexuality. Freud's concept of 'projection' can be applied to Bella's narrative, in which internal perceptions are projected onto the external world and other people. *Twilight* can be understood as an exploration of the mother–daughter bond and its pre-Oedipal conflicts, in particular the psychical struggles surrounding the meeting of oral needs in infancy. The relationship between Bella and her mother Renee (Sarah Clarke) is projected onto the romantic dyad of Bella and Edward (Robert Pattinson). The narrative offers a portrait of a distorted mother–child relationship, based on 'insecure attachment' patterns,[8] using the fantasy figure of the vampire to explore this dynamic. The vampire is an appropriate figure for the exploration of such themes: he rejects the consumption of flesh for blood, which in its liquid form is reminiscent of mother's milk. The erotic qualities associated with the vampire are based on oral eroticism at the expense of genital sexuality, a blurring of the categories of masculine and feminine in favour of a more polymorphic sexuality.[9] This includes a rejection of the reproductive capacities of the body, as well as the decay and death characteristic of the living organism. Bella, in her oral fixation, also denies the body and seeks to transcend its limits.

Edward as love object and ego ideal

The heroine of *Twilight* is a symbolic neglected child, casually overlooked by an immature mother who is preoccupied by her romantic life. Bella displays symptoms of 'disorganised attachment',[10] a result of having intermittent or unreliable nurturing in the early period of childhood, as well as exhibiting behaviour indicative of an eating disorder, such as a tendency to skip meals. The neglect she suffers leads Bella to project her feelings of dependency onto others, expressed through her attempts to meet other people's needs and the conscious denial of her own. Her fantasising therefore takes the form of a figure that is able to meet all of her unconscious dependency needs: Edward. He displays an ambivalent attitude towards Bella, which echoes the unpredictable parenting she experienced from Renee. It is also expressive of the 'splitting' of the maternal figure by the infant, whose needs must inevitably at times be denied by the mother. The young child's developing ego cannot integrate its mixed feelings towards an object – in this case the maternal breast – and splits it into 'bad' and 'good'.[11] Edward's erratic behaviour towards Bella in *Twilight* is suggestive of a non-integrated attitude towards the love object, which is typical at the oral stage of development. Edward is also preoccupied by oral self-denial in his refusal to drink human blood and so parallels Bella's own oral fixation. He expresses Bella's compromise formation in his ability to meet her dependency needs and his simultaneous self-denial. Thus, Edward embodies Bella's ego ideal. This is reflected by the film's *mise-en-scène*, which visually pairs the couple, through shot composition, wardrobe and lighting. Kristen Stewart and Robert Pattinson, who play the film's protagonists, share similar shaped features, dark eyes and hair.[12] Stewart's Bella is almost as pale as the Cullen vampires, and she jokes with classmate Jessica (Anna Kendrick) that she was kicked out of Arizona for being too pale. In this context, paleness is linked to social marginalisation and aligns her with the Cullen siblings, who choose to separate themselves from their peers.[13]

The visual matching of Bella and Edward supports the apparent inevitability of the couple's love relationship (not an uncommon sentiment of romantic fiction). This is apparent from the film scene showing Bella's first sighting of Edward. Watching as he and his siblings walk through the school cafeteria and take their seats at a table, she turns to look over her shoulder to catch a further glance of Edward. She is framed in a medium close-up, her face in a three-quarter profile. Edward, who glares back, is positioned in a similar profile shot. Both appear anxious at the other's presence. Another example of visual alignment is offered in the science class scene in which they first talk to each other. Both are dressed in light colours: he in a grey t-shirt, she in an off-white long-sleeved top. A medium shot positions them side by side, sitting at the workbench, turned to each other, with a microscope dividing the frame in two. Close-ups of Bella and Edward provide a further mirroring effect of the couple. This is exaggerated by the performance styles of the pair: each one wrinkles his or her brow in confusion at the other's enquiries, answering the questions put to them in hesitant, awkward replies, often preceded by a sharp exhalation of breath. The overall effect is a sense of visual and auditory mimicry, one that continues in the performances and *mise-en-scène* throughout the film.

Another scene in which visual pairing is apparent is the 'meadow' scene. The couple are again dressed in similar colours: Edward in a blue shirt and grey jacket; Bella in a grey t-shirt and hooded top. Their clothing reflects the 'cold' colour palette evident in this woodland scene and repeated elsewhere in the film: the greens of the forest foliage appear almost blue and the skin tones of Bella and Edward have a similar cold hue (this colour scheme is disturbed when sunlight breaks through and hits Edward's skin, causing it to sparkle). A high-angle shot frames the couple lying side by side in the meadow. Accompanying close-ups of Edward and Bella's faces, their heads resting in the grass, mirror each other as they look into the other's eyes. Thus the *mise-en-scène* conveys the twinning of Edward and Bella, which is suggestive of psychological projection on the part of the heroine and the fantastical meeting of her hitherto neglected needs.

Maternal neglect and the denial of self

Such visual matching is also an indicator of the inevitability of Bella's association with the Cullen family and their function in expressing her own psychological preoccupations. For if Edward is the embodiment of Bella's ego ideal, it is only because he so perfectly reproduces the heroine's existing relationship dynamics – especially in regard to her mother. The self-denial that characterises Bella finds its most extreme expression in the act of sacrifice she makes to rescue Renee from the vampire James (Cam Gigandet). The film *Twilight* opens with Bella's voice-over stating 'I'd never given much thought to how I'd die,' accompanied by images of a deer being stalked through the undergrowth.[14] Thus, she is aligned with this object of prey. As the deer flees and is finally caught, the image fades to white as Bella continues, 'But dying in the place of someone I love seems a good way to go.' Only later do we learn that this person is her mother, signalling an inversion of the mother–child relationship. The voice-over transverses images of Bella leaving her home in

Phoenix, Arizona, 'So I can't bring myself to regret the decision that brought me here to die … the decision to leave home.' Death and loss of the maternal home are thus explicitly correlated; abandonment by the mother is equated with annihilation of the self. Bella's later attempt to rescue her mother from James is the inevitable conclusion of the self-sacrifice which structures her relationship with Renee. The story begins with an act of abandonment by the mother, who is going on tour with her husband Phil (Matt Bushell), a minor league baseball player.[15] Bella is to live with her father Charlie (Billy Burke) in smalltown Forks, Washington, a fate for which she has volunteered, to spare her mother the pain of separation from Phil. In going along with her daughter, Renee effectively chooses her husband over her teenage child. She is depicted as, at the very least, unreliable, with Bella admitting, 'I would miss my loving, erratic, harebrained mother.' When she explains to Edward that she chose to leave Arizona for her mother's sake, he replies by asking, 'And now you're unhappy?' It appears that her own emotional well-being is something to which she has given little thought. His observation is also an early indication that Edward will be more attentive to Bella's needs than her mother. Renee is disorganised and irresponsible, traits that it is implied extend to her mothering. In one scene from the film, ringing her daughter from a payphone, she says, 'Don't laugh, I didn't lose my power cord, it ran away. Screaming. I literally repel technology.' Talking to her daughter, one of her first questions is whether there are any cute guys in the school. Renee appears to style herself more as an older sister than mother, and so fails to provide the emotional support her daughter needs. Rejected by Renee, Bella can be thought of as a neglected child, demonstrating symptoms characteristic of parental negligence. She projects her own unmet needs onto her mother and becomes a premature caregiver, caring for herself – the abandoned child – and Renee at the same time. In the book, when asked by Edward what her mother is like, she replies, 'She's irresponsible and slightly eccentric, and she's a very unpredictable cook. She's my best friend.'[16] Bella's use of such terms indicates Renee's immaturity, unpredictability and failure to meet her daughter's needs. She is positioned as a friend rather than a mother. The comment about her cooking is especially revealing, as dependence needs are often expressed orally.

Bella's 'insecure attachment': risk-seeking and rescue fantasy

Bella can be described as demonstrating disorganised attachment tendencies, one of three forms of infantile 'insecure attachment' patterns defined by psychologists,[17] as the consequences of neglectful parenting. Studies by Carlson and Putnam[18] indicate that this classification in infancy has childhood out-comes such as 'internalizing problems and dissociation symptoms ('confused, seems to be in a fog', 'strange behaviour', 'gets hurt a lot, accident prone', 'delib-erately harms self or attempts suicide') during the high school years, and psy-chopathology at 17 years'.[19] Such symptoms seem to characterise the heroine's own behaviour. Bella is not comfortable in her own body. She is depicted as accident-prone in the film: she slips and falls on a patch of ice walking down the driveway, telling her father as he helps her up, 'Ice doesn't help the uncoordi-nated.' On a school trip, Edward catches Bella as she slips on a walkway, angrily demanding, 'Could you at least watch where you walk?' She avoids most forms of physical activity: her attempts at volleyball end in hitting schoolmate Mike (Michael Welch) on the back of the head with the ball. She refuses his request to accompany him to the school dance, telling him, 'Prom. Dancing. Not such a good idea for me.'[20]

Her physical clumsiness is accompanied by a tendency to put herself in harm's way, demonstrating an inability to read dangerous situations. On a day trip to Port Angeles with her friends, leaving a bookstore, she wanders down a deserted alley and is attacked by a gang – Edward rescues her just in time to escape assault. Overt recklessness on the part of Bella becomes apparent in *The Twilight Saga: New Moon* (2009, dir. Chris Weitz). Abandoned by Edward, she engages in a number of risky activities. She tries to ride a motorbike and crashes it; she takes a joy-ride on the back of a stranger's bike; she dives off a high cliff into the ocean. Each instance is justified by Bella's attempt to see Edward's face: as she embarks on the activity he appears to her in a hallucination, pleading with her to stop. High-risk behaviour is one symptom of disorganised attach-ment observed by psychologists Leiberman and Zeanah[21] The child also dem-onstrates what is termed 'parentified' behaviour,[22] which reflects the distorted nature of the parent–child relationship and is characteristic of Bella's relation-ship with Renee. Her emotional response to others taking care of her is, there-fore, extreme. When Bella observes that her father has put snow-chains on her tyres she notes: 'My throat suddenly felt tight. I wasn't used to being taken care of, and Charlie's unspoken concern caught me by surprise.'[23] It is significant that this admission comes moments before Edward's first rescue of Bella in the book's narrative. (The connection is muddied by the film, which separates these two points by a couple of scenes.) As she stands in the school car park checking her tyres, a van skids on the ice and hurtles towards her – Edward pulls her out of the way just before she is crushed, stopping the van with his hand. This epi-sode is the key to understanding the controlling dynamic of Bella and Edward's relationship, for Bella's deepest desire is to be looked after. After the episode in

Port Angeles, over dinner, Edward confesses that 'I feel very protective towards you' and it signals the beginning of their relationship. She is preoccupied by having her dependency needs met, much more so than the fulfilment of adult sexual desires: the couple only kiss in *Twilight*, and don't have sex until much later in the series. This rejection of adult sexuality is projected onto Edward, who prohibits them from having premarital sex; the net effect, however, is the same. Her failed genital sexuality is indicative of Bella's inability to progress past oral dependency. Her sexual longings always have a strong aspect of oral regression – as do Edward's.

The projection of oral needs onto others is also clear in Bella's care-giving attitude towards her father, typically taking the form of cooking. In the book he must remind her, 'Bells, I fed myself for seventeen years before you got here.'[24] And although she frequently describes cooking for her father it remains unclear if she joins him in eating at meal times. This remains vague in the film adaptation, which shows Bella and Charlie eating together in the local diner. Edward expresses an interest in feeding Bella and on a number of occasions when they are together he asks if she is hungry. In the book, when she joins him for lunch in the cafeteria, he fills a tray with enough food for both of them and tells her to eat. He, of course, eats nothing. Following his rescue of her in Port Angeles, he takes her for dinner and insists that she eats something. In this way, Edward takes care of her, both feeding her and protecting her from physical danger – from the skidding van on the ice in the schoolyard, the gang in Port Angeles and finally the threat of vampires James and Victoria (Rachelle Lefevre). The protective dynamic of their relationship is visually expressed in the publicity poster for the film: Pattinson's Edward hovers over Stewart's physically diminished Bella, as if shielding her from danger. There is no lovers' embrace, no lingering eye contact between the pair.

Yet, although Edward is her rescuer, their relationship is characterised by ambivalence. This is evident from the film's depiction of Bella's first day at school. She enters a class and glances over at Edward, who immediately tenses in his seat, clutches his hand to his mouth and glares at her furiously. In the diegesis, his response is explained by his struggle to control his appetite, yet his facial expressions are indicative of disgust. Two disgust-based responses are the defining features of anorexia: towards food and towards the body.[25] The vampire represents a solution to the anorexic's rejection of the body and simultaneous oral-fixation. He has transcended corporeality and escaped mortality. At the same time, he is preoccupied by oral demands and, in the case of Edward and the Cullens, in the denial of these urges. Edward can be seen as a fantastical compromise formation of the anorexic.

'Fright without solution': Edward as protector-persecutor

Edward's initial disgust-based response to Bella is soon displaced by rather different behaviour: the next time they meet in class he is charming and attentive. This strange, alternating conduct continues as their relationship progresses with a frustrated Bella telling Edward in the film that, 'Your mood swings are giving me whiplash.' In addition, she later confronts him over his superhuman rescue of her in the car park, which provokes an angry response from him. Bella then confesses in the voice-over, 'That was the first night I dreamt of Edward Cullen,' an indication that her attraction is based on his contradictory behaviour. This ambivalence can be understood in terms of the mother's unpredictable behaviour towards the child in cases of maltreatment. Researchers have found that if an infant is placed in a situation of 'fright without solution', this will account for a disorientated response. The attachment figure is both the cause of the alarm and its solution, creating an irresolvable 'approach–flight paradox'.[26] This is what Bella faces: Edward is both her rescuer and a threat to her life. Early in the film, Edward warns her, 'If you were smart, you would stay away from me.' Bella responds with, 'Let's say for argument's sake that I'm not smart.' Throughout the film, Edward warns that he is a danger to her but Bella steadfastly refuses to heed his warnings (indeed, he is indirectly responsible for Bella's exposure to James and the consequent problems with the Volturi vampires).

Hesse and Main[27] give examples of parental frightening behaviour predicted to provoke infant alarm, such as 'indices of entrance into a dissociative state' including 'parent suddenly "freezes" with eyes unmoving, half-lidded'; 'threatening behaviour inexplicable in form', such as in non-play situations the 'stiff-legged "stalking" of the infant on all-fours, exposure of canine tooth, hissing or deep growls directed at infant'; 'frightened behavior patterns inexplicable in origin' including 'sudden frightened look (fear mouth, exposure of whites of eyes)' in absence of environmental change; also 'frightened retreat from the infant or approaching infant apprehensively as though a potentially dangerous object'.[28] Some of these descriptions are certainly suggestive of Bella's and Edward's own interactions. He responds in peculiar fashion to her expression of desire: 'I smelled his cool breath in my face. Sweet, delicious, the scent made my mouth water ... I leaned closer, inhaling. And he was gone, his hand ripped from mine. In the time it took for my eyes to focus, he was twenty feet away.'[29] Note that Bella's desire is stated in oral terms: 'delicious' and 'made my mouth water'. In the film, a short-lived make-out session in Bella's bedroom ends when Edward rips himself away from their embrace, slamming himself against the wall, an anguished look on his face, as he tells her, 'I'm stronger than I thought,' suggesting he is able to control his appetite, even if Bella cannot. Such unpredictable reactions (as well as the animal mannerisms demonstrated elsewhere in the narrative by Edward) suggest that alarm characterises many of Bella's responses to Edward and that their relationship reflects a distorted parent–child dynamic.

The behaviours that correlate with a 'disorganised attachment' diagnosis in infancy also predict child attitudes towards her parents of: hostility (persecutor), helplessness (victim) and compulsive care-giving (rescuer).[30] These attitudes are demonstrated by Bella and Edward towards each other, she typically playing the role of victim and he oscillating between persecutor and rescuer. In studies of the disorganised attachment subject:

> the child may represent both the self and the attachment figure as help-less victims of a mysterious, invisible source of danger. Finally, because contact with the child may have comforted the distressed caregiver, the implicit memories of DA may also convey the possibility of construing the self as the powerful rescuer of a fragile adult.[31]

This model resonates with the dramatic denouement of *Twilight*. Enjoying a game of baseball in the forest, the Cullen family and Bella are discovered by three roaming vampires. The tracker vampire James and his partner Victoria begin a chase of Bella which ends in Phoenix. Edward's adoptive siblings Alice (Ashley Greene) and Jasper (Jackson Rathbone) take Bella to a hotel while the other Cullens try to outwit the pair, but a phone call from James claiming he has Renee prompts Bella to sneak past her carers to stage a rescue attempt. However, when she reaches her childhood ballet school to rendezvous with James, she finds herself alone with him. This is the moment the opening voice-over refers to, when she imagines herself dying in the place of her mother. When Edward and the Cullens finally reach her, she has already been bitten by James and is bleeding to death; here, Edward's ultimate act of self-denial is in sucking the venom from Bella's bloodstream without killing her. The final displacement of Bella's own dependency needs – at their most basic, to stay alive – in favour of her mother's reveals that her existence is structured by self-denial. Edward is a figure of fantasy wish-fulfilment who does everything to protect her and gratify her needs. He is a projection of Bella, with the notion of oral self-denial repeated in him: Edward's own life is driven by hunger, the constant denial of his wish to feed – and the placing of Bella's needs before his own, which is made most apparent by this scene.

The episode between Bella, James and Victoria, and the latter's pursuit of the heroine throughout the remainder of the *Twilight* series, hints at one reading of

Bella's self-sacrifice. Her initial choice to live in Forks can be interpreted as an attempt to avoid provoking her mother's anger. In the narrative of the *Twilight* series, Bella spends her energies evading the rage of Victoria, who can be read as a projection of her mother Renee. Victoria seeks to avenge the loss of her mate James; had Bella insisted that her mother stay with her in her home town of Phoenix, Renee would also have been separated from her husband Phil. Bella chooses the move to Forks to avoid this enforced split and the anger that she (unconsciously) fears her mother would direct towards her. The casting choices of the film *Twilight* support this interpretation: both Renee and Victoria have red curly hair, so the two are visually paralleled. The alignment of Victoria/Renee (and by extension James/Phil) is stressed by narrative elements. James and Victoria are transient, always on the move, seeking out the next kill. This echoes the travelling life that Phil leads on tour as a minor league baseball player and one that Renee adopts to be with him. As Phil makes his living playing baseball, his image is associated with games. In the film, Edward tells Bella that James is a tracker, adding that his own defensive posture towards her 'made this his most exciting game ever'; James himself claims that Edward's 'rage will make for more interesting sport than his feeble attempt to defend you'. Finally, this association is borne out through James and Victoria's discovering Bella while the Cullens are playing baseball – the sport that Phil plays and that Renee follows him around the country for (indirectly, the reason for Bella's abandonment). The two couples, and in particular Renee and Victoria, are thus thematically linked. In short, *Twilight* can be read as an exploration of Bella's unconscious fear of maternal anger and the disturbed defence mechanisms which she has adopted to avoid it.

The devouring mother and the anorexic daughter

Fear of maternal anger has various interpretations. The child fears that she will be abandoned as a consequence of her mother's rage. As it happens, the act of abandonment in Bella's case happens first sequentially.[32] But maternal rage can also be interpreted as a projection of the child's own rage at the mother. At the oral stage, the infant's anger at being frustrated or deprived of its basic needs is experienced as persecutory. These emotions are so intolerable that, psychoanalyst Melanie Klein argues, they are expelled onto the mother so that it feels to the infant as if it is the mother who is attacking her – and this persecution often takes the form of devouring and engulfment. As the infant develops, she introjects (internalises) the mother as an identity figure; this forms the basis of the super-ego. Typically, 'introjection of the good object is also used as a defence against anxiety'.[33] However, there is also the possibility that introjection may include the incorporation of a 'bad object'

– this internal persecutory object will be experienced as an attack from within. The bad internal object is linked psychoanalytically to disturbed eating, and, as alluded to above, Bella's distorted relationship with her mother, as well as her general behaviour, indicates that she may be suffering from an eating disorder.[34] Edward, and more broadly the Cullen family, presents for Bella an ideal version of her own self. Refusal to eat and denial of hunger is linked to the beauty of the Cullen siblings, which is evident from passages in the book. On her first day in the cafeteria, she notes that the Cullen family 'weren't eating, though they each had a tray of untouched food in front of them'. As well as their pale beauty, she notes that 'they also had dark shadows under their eyes – purplish, bruise-like shadows'.[35] The next few times she sees the Cullens in the cafeteria she won't eat anything, claiming to her friends she feels ill. In refusing to eat, Bella emulates the Cullens. The Cullens' behaviour noted in the cafeteria is replicated when Bella visits Edward at home: the family is finally cooking in the kitchen that up until now has remained unused. The Cullens' cooking for Bella also echoes Edward's attempts to make her eat and their protective behaviour towards her. Bella turns down the meal they are preparing, claiming she has already eaten – typical behaviour of someone displaying disturbed eating patterns. Supporting this claim is that the film shows no visual evidence for Bella having had a meal – we do not see her eat prior to visiting the family. The Cullens make a show of being human – of eating – but their full plates of food and empty kitchen betray that they are 'passing' – just like the sufferers of eating disorders who try to disguise their condition.

Bella's refusal to eat is symptomatic of regression. Psychoanalysts such as Helmut Thomae[36] indicate that anorexia is a regression from adolescent genitality to infantile orality. The anorexic, starved of food, is both dependent on the mother and at the same time rejects the mother and seeks independence. Also, through starving, the developing adolescent's body appears to return to its prepubescent state and defy ageing. Bella is preoccupied by her own ageing in relation to the ever-youthful Edward. Unconscious ambivalence towards the mother is exaggerated at adolescence, especially as the bodily changes of nascent womanhood threaten to render the girl more like the mother. Other analysts, such as Hilde Bruch,[37] argue that anorexia is the consequence of real infant neglect. Discussing Bruch's work, writer Janet Sayers suggests that in cases of child mistreatment 'the mother in effect abused and seduced the daughter into compliance with her needs, her daughter accordingly becoming obsessed with sensing out what the other wants, thereby losing sight of what she wants. 'The resulting lack of sense of self, writes Bruch, is aggravated by adolescence with its demands on the individual to develop an identity separate from the parents'.[38] The above description of the anorexic is resonant of the dynamic between Bella and her mother.

Anorexia has a close correlation with the types of dissociative behaviour that Bella demonstrates. Such anorexic patients 'display a disturbing lack of anxiety about their own life-threatening behaviour, yet are preoccupied by death and anxiety about annihilation'.[39] Bella's fantasy of becoming a vampire is in line with the compromise formation that those suffering from eating disorders entertain: a disavowal of death and simultaneous rejection of life – for the vampire is neither dead nor alive. Psychologists indicate that such patients demonstrate a preoccupation with death, 'an unspoken anxiety of being annihilated at the hands of a predator or of being annihilated for predatory acts of harm towards another'.[40] Such behaviours, 'fueled by a preoccupation with death, lack of signal anxiety and dissociation, are a potentially lethal mix that becomes even more lethal when a significant depression or impulsiveness are added'.[41] In such situations 'the destructive behaviour is physically directed at his or her body, in an excited, perverse addiction to near death in which there is a felt need to know and have the satisfaction of seeing oneself destroyed'.[42] Bella demonstrates a remarkable lack of concern over her own safety, both in the high-risk behaviours she engages in following Edward's departure in *New Moon*,[43] but also in her attempts to take on James single-handedly in *Twilight*. A preoccupation with death is exhibited by some anorexics alongside identification with sharp-toothed carnivorous animals, whilst harbouring 'dissociated murderous wishes to prey on others'.[44] Thus Bella's fantasy of Edward is a projection of her own dissociated imaginings. Farber et al[45] indicate that some anorexics' vegetarianism and refusal to eat meat represents a reaction formation.[46] It should be noted that the Cullens consider themselves 'vegetarian' vampires as they drink animal blood rather than the human equivalent.

In conclusion

This chapter has argued that *Twilight* explores the psychological consequences of Bella's maternal abandonment, giving expression to the unconscious rage that she feels towards her mother. The narrative of *Twilight* presents a fantastical 'solution' to the psychological crisis experienced by the heroine; Bella exhibits symptoms of disorganised attachment, which can be traced to Renee's neglectful parenting. This has consequences for how she relates to her parents and explains Edward's particular appeal as an attachment figure. She denies her own needs to meet those of others, while simultaneously fantasising that she will be looked after by a superhuman figure that can save her from all danger. Disorganised attachment has various symptoms of psychopathology, including dissociation and the inability to read dangerous situations. Bella demonstrates self-harming behaviour to gain the attention of her mother or mother substitute, Edward. This is made apparent from Renee's visit to her daughter in hospital at *Twilight*'s close, in which she finally reassures Bella that, having settled in Jacksonville with Phil, Bella can come to live with them once again, an offer that is promptly rejected. As indicated elsewhere in the chapter, this tendency is equally clear following Edward's abandonment of Bella in *New Moon*, when she throws herself into risky behaviours such as motorbike riding and cliff diving. She fails to read signs of danger nor does she appear to value her life, seeking sustenance in fantasies depicting her own devouring. Part of this is signalled by her relationship with Edward, flagged as an altogether dangerous proposition. His ambivalent demeanour and inconsistent behaviour towards Bella echoes the neglectful parenting she has experienced with Renee. However, although their dyad recreates the mother–child dynamic, her relationship with Edward also indicates growing independence and a rejection of her family – especially in her wish to become a vampire. This is significant, as it indicates her wish to separate from her parents, the fulfilment of which the mother's distorted relationship with her daughter has effectively prohibited.

I have suggested that Edward is a projection of Bella's own wish to have her oral needs simultaneously denied and satiated. He is both self-denying, refusing to drink the blood of humans, while meeting Bella's desperate craving for protection. Finally, Bella's fantasy of Edward can be understood as the compromise formation of an anorexic. She can identify with a carnivorous predator, who in his 'vegetarian' ways embodies a reaction formation. In her relationship with Victoria, she can experience persecutory maternal rage and her own rage towards the mother, which she cannot quite bring herself to acknowledge consciously. If Victoria symbolises Renee, it should be remembered that she is finally defeated and killed in the fourth book of the *Twilight* series. The adventures of Bella can be understood as the wish-fulfilment of an angry abandoned girl who, in fantasy at least, exacts her revenge upon her rejecting mother.

Notes

1. Stephenie Meyer, *Twilight* (London: Atom Books, 2006).
2. Mark Jancovich (ed.), 'Introduction', in *Horror, The Film Reader* (London and New York: Routledge, 2002), pp. 21–25, p. 21.
3. Steven Jay Schneider (ed.), *Horror Film and Psychoanalysis: Freud's Worst Nightmare* (Cambridge: Cambridge University Press, 2004), p. 8.
4. Ibid.
5. Sigmund Freud, 'Two Encyclopaedia Articles: Psycho-analysis and the Libido Theory', in *The Standard Edition of the Complete Psychological Works of Sigmund Freud*, Vol. 18 (1920–22): *Beyond the Pleasure Principle, Group Psychology and Other Works* (1920; London: Hogarth Press, 1957), pp. 233–59, p. 242.

6. Glen O. Gabbard, *Psychoanalysis and Film* (London: Karnac Books, 2001), p. 5.

7. Freud looks at the role of the creative writer in fulfilling her own fantasies as well as those of the reader in 'Creative Writers and Day-Dreaming'. He suggests that all unmet wishes are ambitious or erotic in nature, the latter more unpalatable of the two typically being given expression within dreams (as opposed to day-dreams). The author must take pains to disguise the fantasies that she depicts, to make them more palatable to the reader, which if left unaltered would 'repel us or leave us cold' (Sigmund Freud, 'Creative Writers and Day-Dreaming', in *The Standard Edition*, vol. 9 (1906–08): *Jensen's 'Gradiva' and Other Works* (1908; London: The Hogarth Press, 1957), pp. 141–54, p. 152). The successful writer thus provides wish-fulfilment that is sufficiently disguised: 'our actual enjoyment of an imaginative work proceeds from a liberation of tensions in our minds ... not a little of this effect is due to the writer's enabling us thenceforward to enjoy our own day-dreams without self-reproach or shame' (ibid., p. 153).

8. Mary D. Salter Ainsworth, Mary C. Blehar, Everett Waters and Sally Wall, *Patterns of Attachment* (Hillsdale, NJ: Erlbaum, 1978).

9. Christopher Craft makes the link between blood, milk and semen in *Dracula* (Bram Stoker, *Dracula* (Westminster: Constable & Co, 1897)). Discussing the initiation scene between the count and Mina Harker, in which she drinks from a cut vein in his chest, Craft suggests 'We are at the Count's breast, encouraged once again to substitute white for red, as blood becomes milk: the attitude of the two had a terrible resemblance to a child forcing a kitten's nose into a saucer of milk. Such fluidity of substitution and displacement entails a confusion of Dracula's sexual identity, or an interfusion of masculine and feminine functions, as Dracula here becomes a lurid mother offering not a breast but an open and bleeding wound' (Christopher Craft, ' "Kiss Me with Those Red Lips": Gender and Inversion in Bram Stoker's *Dracula*', *Representations* 8 (Autumn 1984), p. 125). Alternatively, in his frenzied feeding Dracula – and the vampire in general – can be thought of as a greedy infant. Barbara R. Almond argues, 'My view of the vampire fantasy as a condensation of mother–child bonding gone wrong begins, in a sense, with the blood that first nourishes the foetus through the placenta. That blood later becomes another warm, isotonic fluid – milk – that nourishes the infant who wakes at night and feeds. And the infant's urgent feeding may be experienced as ruthless, particularly if exhaustion and inner conflict increase maternal ambivalence. Dracula, viewed as a monster baby, never moves beyond the stage of infantile ruthlessness' (Barbara R. Almond, 'Monstrous Infants and Vampyric Mothers in Bram Stoker's *Dracula*', *International Journal of Psychoanalysis* 88/1 (2007), p. 221).

10. Mary Main and Judith Solomon, 'Discovery of an Insecure Disoriented Attachment Pattern: Procedures, Findings and Implications for the Classification of Behavior', in T. Berry Brazelton and Michael Youngman (eds), *Affective Development in Infancy* (Norwood, NJ: Ablex, 1986), pp. 95–124.

11. Melanie Klein, 'The Development of a Child', *International Journal of Psychoanalysis* 4 (1923), pp. 419–74.

12. Actress Kristen Stewart, whose eyes are green, had to wear coloured contact lenses for the role.

13. Ewan Kirkland's chapter in this collection considers the racial whiteness of the Cullen family and the hegemonic superiority that it implies. Kirkland suggests that whiteness's association with death and alienation from the body resonates with the themes of *Twilight*, finding particular expression in Bella's relationship with Edward.

14. The next sequence set in the forest occurs when Bella confronts Edward about his true nature as a vampire, further aligning Bella with the position of hunted and Edward as hunter.

15. Baseball is an occupation that resonates with the career fantasies of childhood. Note also that Phil is only a minor league player. The fact that he has failed in his ambition as a major league player is suggestive of a continuation of this childish fantasy.

16. Meyer, *Twilight*, p. 90.

17. Ainsworth et al., *Patterns of Attachment*.

18. Eve Bernstein Carlson and Frank W. Putnam, 'Further Validation of the Dissociative Experiences Scale Paper', presented at the annual meeting of the American Psychological Association 1988, quoted in Sharne A. Rolfe, *Rethinking Attachment in Early Childhood Practice: Promoting Security, Autonomy and Resilience in Young Children* (Sydney: Allen & Unwin, 2005).

19. Ibid.

20. In the unpublished partial draft of *Midnight Sun* (Stephenie Meyer, *Midnight Sun*, 2008, www.stepheniemeyer.com/midnightsun.html (last accessed 24 May 2011)), Edward's father Carlisle, Forks' hospital surgeon, is struck by the number of Bella's old injuries: 'Look at all the healed contusions! How many times did her mother drop her?' In the book *Twilight* Bella alludes to dissociation from her own trauma, noting, 'I do a good job of blocking painful, unnecessary things from my memory' (ibid., p. 6), though we are never given details of what such painful memories may comprise.

21. Alicia F. Lieberman and Charles H. Zeanah, 'Disorders of Attachment in Infancy', *Child and Adolescent Psychiatric Clinics of North America* 4/3 (2005), pp. 571–87.

22. Iván Boszormenyi-Nagy and Spark, Geraldine M., *Invisible Loyalties* (New York: Harper and Row, 1973).

23. Meyer, *Twilight*, p. 47.

24. Ibid., p. 129.

25. Jean Mitchell and Helen McCarthy, 'Eating Disorders', in Lorna Champion and Michael Power (eds), *Adult Psychological Problems: An Introduction*, 2nd edn (Hove: Psychology Press, 2000), pp. 103–30.

26. Mary Main and Erik Hesse, 'Parents' Unresolved Traumatic Experiences Are Related to Infant Disorganized Attachment Status: Is Frightened and/or Frightening Parental Behavior the Linking Mechanism?', in Mark T. Greenberg, Dante Cicchetti and E. Mark Cummings, *Attachment During the Preschool Years: Theory, Research and Intervention* (Chicago: University of Chicago Press, 1990), p. 163.

27. Erik Hesse and Mary Main, 'Special Section: Frightened, Threatening, and Dissociative Parental Behavior: Theory and Associations with Parental Adult Attachment Interview Status and Infant Disorganization', *Development and Psychopathology* 18 (2006), pp. 309–43.

28. Hesse and Main, 'Special Section', p. 320.
29. Meyer, *Twilight*, p. 230.
30. Main and Solomon, 'Discovery of an Insecure Disoriented Attachment Pattern'.
31. Anne P. De Prince and Lisa D. Cromer, *Exploring Dissociation: Definitions, Development and Cognitive Correlatives* (Binghamton, NY: Haworth Medical Press, 2006), p. 60.
32. The order of these events does not matter at an unconscious level; the fact that maternal anger and abandonment are linked is sufficient).
33. Melanie Klein, 'Notes on Some Schizoid Mechanisms' (1946), in *Envy and Gratitude and Other Works 1946–1963* (London: Hogarth Press and Institute of Psycho-Analysis, 1975), p. 6.
34. In what may be an authorial in-joke, early in the book Bella mentions her 'distaste for Forks' (Meyer, *Twilight*, p. 5).
35. Ibid., p. 16.
36. Helmut Thomae, 'Some Psychoanalytic Observations on Anorexia', *British Journal of Medical Psychology*, 36 (1963), pp. 237–48.
37. Hilde Bruch, *Eating Disorders; Obesity, Anorexia Nervosa, and the Person Within* (New York: Basic Books, 1973).
38. Janet Sayers, 'Anorexia, Psychoanalysis, and Feminism: Fantasy and Reality', *Journal of Adolescence* 11 (1988), p. 366.
39. Sharon K. Farber, Craig C. Jackson, Johanna K. Tabin and Eytan Bachar, 'Death and Annihilation Anxieties in Anorexia Nervosa, Bulimia, and Self-mutilation', *Psychoanalytic Psychoanalysis*, 24/2 (2007), p. 289.
40. Farber et al., 'Death and Annihilation Anxieties', p. 290.
41. Ibid., p. 291.
42. Ibid., citing research by Betty Joseph, 'Addiction to Near-death', *International Journal of Psychoanalysis* 63 (1982), pp. 449–56.
43. Stephenie Meyer, *New Moon* (London: Atom Books, 2007).
44. Farber et al., 'Death and Annihilation Anxieties', p. 291.
45. Ibid.
46. This is a defence mechanism whereby the 'unacceptable' impulse in question is replaced by a strongly opposing tendency. Freud first mentions the reaction formation in *Three Essays on the Theory of Sexuality* (Sigmund Freud, 'Three Essays on the Theory of Sexuality', in *The Standard Edition of the Complete Psychological Works of Sigmund Freud*, vol. 7 (1901–05): 'A Case of Hysteria', 'Three Essays on Sexuality' and Other Works (1957; London: Hogarth Press, 1905), pp. 136–243). Bella's desire to become a vampire can be read as an attack on the mother within, and a simultaneous disavowal of death and rejection of life. The vampire neither ages, nor reproduces; her rejection of corporeality is very much a rejection of the feminine body. However, this is complicated by the later films *The Twilight Saga: Breaking Dawn – Part 1* (2011 dir. Bill Condon), and *The Twilight Saga: Breaking Dawn – Part 2* (2012, dir. Bill Condon) in which Bella gives birth.

9

OF MASOCHISTIC LIONS AND STUPID LAMBS: THE AMBIGUOUS NATURE OF SEXUALITY AND SEXUAL AWAKENING IN *TWILIGHT*

Marion Rana

Twilight is primarily a tale of sexual awakening. The saga's superficial endorsement of the value of sexual abstinence cannot conceal its true appeal, the deeply erotic and sensual tension so central to the plot, the novels being dubbed 'abstinence porn' for a good reason.[1] At the same time, the films reflect deep societal and individual ambiguities about sexuality and the sexual roles of (young) women in particular. The danger Bella's pregnancy puts her into, the risk she is playing with whenever she engages sexually with Edward – a risk that she embraces with masochistic delight – thus underline societal assumptions on the dangers of sexuality for young women. In comparison, as a male vampire, Edward has nothing to fear from his sexual encounters with Bella. He can neither become pregnant nor can Bella physically harm him. As Carrie Anne Platt accurately points out in relation to the portrayal of male and female sexuality in the book series: 'We worry about the life-altering consequences of sex for teenage girls far more often than we worry about teenage boys, seeing the loss of female innocence as a greater social tragedy.'[2] In the films, the portrayal of sexuality is thus ambiguous: on the one hand, it is shown as a welcome step in the development both of a conscious and emancipated self and of a maturing relationship, while on the other hand it is seen as a dangerous pitfall, especially for young women. Similarly, female sexual agency is both celebrated (in the morally good characters of, for instance, Bella or Alice) and condemned (in the morally ambivalent or bad characters such as Maria and Victoria). This chapter will thus highlight the different layers of ambiguity in *Twilight* and draw attention both to the sexual deviance alternately embraced and condemned in the films and the gender roles conjured up through the use of sexuality.

'I'm not even sure that's legal': sexual angst and sexual danger

The first film of the saga, *Twilight* (2008, dir. Catherine Hardwicke), in particular is characterised by the disapproval of Bella's awakening sexuality. Bella's father Charlie is deeply uncomfortable about his daughter's romantic stirrings: the first shot after she and Edward have spent their first (chaste) night together shows Charlie handling a weapon – more than a hint at his unease with Bella's new relationship. His disapproval of this sexual awakening is illustrated even more clearly when he snaps the shot-gun shut after asking Bella to bring Edward in and thus comically confirms his misgivings. Ironically, however, Charlie's over-anxiousness about Bella's sexuality has the opposite effect on her – Bella's resolve to have sex with Edward seems to have been brought on by her father's insistence that she 'be safe' and his relief about finding out that she is still a virgin. Thus, it is directly after her conversation with Charlie that Bella tries to seduce Edward (in *The Twilight Saga: Eclipse*, 2010, dir. David Slade).

Not only Bella's father – who by virtue of his role alone is predestined to disapprove of his daughter's sexuality – but also Bella's friends show clear signs of discomfort both with the Cullens' obvious sexual maturity and, later, with Edward and Bella's display of affection, the blatant eroticism of their relationship and the (deviant) sexual attraction between the Cullens. Thus, when Jessica shares with Bella her knowledge of the Cullens' familial and romantic relationships, she explains: 'The blonde girl, that's Rosalie, and the big dark-haired guy, Emmet, they're a thing. I'm not even sure that's legal.' To her friend Angela's reminder that 'they're not actually related', Jessica simply shrugs and reaffirms her misgivings: 'Yeah, but they live together – it's weird.' Similarly, Mike's confrontation with Bella about his discomfort around her romance with Edward is disarmingly honest, while at the same time ironically striking much further home than he expects: 'So, you and Cullen, eh? That's ... I don't like it. I mean, you know – he just looks at you as if you're something to eat.' Mike's statement is quite obviously motivated by jealousy, but it is also rooted in his and the other teenagers' sexual angst, sparked by the apparent sexual tension between Edward and Bella.

Bella herself rejects both Jess's and Mike's warnings and, 'dismissing abstinence as a petty repression of human sexuality reflective of rural mores ... views herself as liberated from outmoded moral codes'.[3] Yet, when Edward forces abstinence on her, 'she chafes against its restrictions on her burgeoning sexuality yet also exploits it to heighten the masochistic interplay of pleasure and pain'.[4] We will come to talk about the masochistic characteristics of Bella and Edward's relationship later in this chapter.

The dangers of Bella's awakening sexuality are symbolised in the ominous and erratic hunting scene at the beginning of the first film: the innocent deer, a symbol of the virginal Bella, is hunted down and ultimately, presumably, devoured by – we later realise – Edward. Since Edward and his family have devoted themselves to not killing humans and living on animal blood instead, the deer hunt signals Edward's taming of his wild and uncivilised nature and the control he exerts over both his body and his mind. At the same time, however, the association of the physical and sexual danger for Bella is clear: even though the audience may not yet be aware of the fact that it is he whose hunt we are witnessing, the contrary civility of the hunt aside, Edward is none the less introduced as a wild and merciless hunter.

Edward's dangerous streak is also highlighted during his first appearance (that the audience is aware of): when the Cullens show up at the school cafeteria, they all wear different shades of white[5] – apart from Edward, who is dressed completely in black and grey. While the white epitomises the innocence and inherent ease and peace of the relationship between the two couples, Edward's black signals his danger as a single but attractive male. Contrastingly, this suggestion is countered by the angelic association when the camera turns to Edward in the biology room and the white wings of the owl behind him seem to be attached to his back. This ambiguity is in line with his capturing the deer from the opening scene with his hands rather than for instance biting its neck, which, considering the alternatives, underlines his comparatively tamed and civilised, yet predatory nature.[6] His simultaneously shadowy and angelic appearance makes up part of the ambiguity surrounding Edward.

'Take control. You're a strong, independent woman': ambiguous gender roles

Feminist scholarship concerned with a deconstruction of the *Twilight* narrative has so far mainly been occupied with pointing out the anti-feminist and misogynistic messages and the traditional, conforming gender roles in both the novels and the films.[7] The relationship between Bella and Edward has thus been interpreted as 'borderline abusive',[8] with Edward being over-protective of Bella, exhibiting the obsessive behaviour of a stalker, and Bella submitting (however grudgingly) to his constant monitoring, controlling behaviour and (emotional and physical) trespassing: 'Over the course of the series,[9] Edward's protective impulses cross the line into behavior that would be considered controlling and frightening in any other relationship.'[10] Within the narrative frame, Edward's behaviour is justified through the assertion that Bella is vulnerable, constantly putting herself in danger and thus needing constant surveillance and help: a damsel in distress in need of a strong, loving and resourceful hero.

In line with these arguments, most scholars define Bella as weak: 'In spite of the bravery and emotional strength that she exhibits at various points in the series, Bella's dominant characteristics are her physical weakness and need to be protected from danger all of the time.'[11] The idealisation of this over-protection 'perpetuates the idea that young women are objects to be possessed, cherished, and defended from every danger by the men in their lives'.[12] Tison Pugh confirms this interpretation by explaining that '[i]ndications of abuse circulate throughout Bella and Edward's love affair, yet readers are encouraged not to criticize but to admire their rapturous affection for each other, and in this manner Edward's cruelty is re-signified to indicate his heartfelt devotion to Bella.'[13]

The more critical aspects of Edward's stalking behaviour have been removed from the film adaptations, however, and Bella's depiction as emancipated is fore-grounded within the action. Thus, Edward lets Bella climb about in a treetop high above the ground without holding on to her – a seemingly un-noteworthy event but one which Meyer's Edward would never have allowed. Further, the depth of Bella's obsession with Edward is at least questioned in the films, giving Bella a hint of ironic disapproval when she shakes her head after having finished her litany about loving him irrevocably. Moreover, Bella acts as a disseminator of feminist thought when she verbosely disapproves of unwanted male attention[14] and when she encourages Angela to take control of her emotional and sexual life. Brushing aside Angela's worries that Eric will not ask her to the prom, Bella advises: '*You* should ask him. Take control. You're a strong, independent woman.' She thus actively encourages a gender non-conformative pattern of sexual behaviour. It is also noteworthy that Bella calls Angela a 'woman' rather than the more common 'girl', emphasising Angela's independence, maturity and position of power.

Looking at the critical discourse surrounding both the *Twilight* films and novels, the characters' sexuality, in particular, has become the object of much critical examination. Platt argues that in the novels, female sexuality is portrayed as a threatening force that 'must be controlled at all times'[15] and that sexuality is quite literally equated and associated with death since Bella is fatally injured during childbirth. Furthermore, the fact that the consequences of sexual intercourse severely endanger Bella but have virtually no (physical) effect on Edward highlights the sexual double standard which perceives girls at a much higher risk through sexual interaction than boys. Most importantly, however, Platt argues that far from being sexually empowered, Bella has virtually no sexual agency: she cannot act on her sexual desire

> because Edward prevents her, but she also seems incapable of making a conscious decision to not act on it, because she loses all control in the face of her desires. The relationship remains chaste only so long as Edward chooses to impose his moral code and physical strength on Bella.[16]

In a similar vein, Danielle Dick McGeough points out that 'Bella's inability to control her intense sexual urges implies that the adolescent female body lacks control at both the physical and rational level.'[17] Even though the series does have the potential to fill the gap in representations of female sexual desire and agency, McGeough's argument contends that, 'rather than celebrate and embrace Bella's sexual desires, the novels treat her sexual longing as excessive.'[18]

In the films, traditional gender stereotypes surrounding sexuality are reproduced in several instances: primarily, Edward's being completely overwhelmed by Bella's scent and his struggle to keep his desires in check play with biological assumptions according to which men are ruled by their hormones and can barely control themselves once sufficiently aroused. Thus, we learn that he nearly killed Bella in an outburst of sanguine lust when they first met and that every moment with her is a struggle to remain in control of his physical urges. Further, traditional concepts around male protection over help-seeking females are strengthened through Edward's over-protectiveness of Bella and, most importantly, through the consistent quarrel between Jacob and Edward over their claim on (one might also say: possession of) Bella. Jacob's conversation with Bella before the prom – at the end of *Twilight* – thus provokes a strong territorial reaction from Edward: by coming to Bella's side, putting his arm around her shoulder, blocking her path to Jacob and effectively ending their conversation, Edward makes it very clear that he regards Bella as his property and is laying claim to her.

The combination of her father's inability to protect her and her last-minute rescue by Edward in *Twilight* officially mark the passing of responsibility and authority for Bella from Charlie to Edward: Bella is not able to defend herself with the pepper spray her father gave to her. When her father's symbolic presence fails to protect her, however, Edward does. In *Eclipse*, then, Charlie's inability to protect Bella is a given, and instead, Bella is passed back and forth between Jacob and Edward for protection. The implication of both the passing over of responsibility from Charlie to Edward and the protection and/or love triangle between Jacob, Edward and Bella is clear: there is always a male at Bella's side who looks after and is responsible for her. Bella taking care of herself is at no point part of the master plan.

Apart from the kiss he forces upon Bella in *Eclipse*, Jacob frequently tests, but ultimately accepts Edward's claim on and possession of Bella: when she lies freezing in her hilltop tent in *Eclipse*, he waits for Edward's permission to lie next to her and warm her up with his body heat.[19] Again, Bella is not an active part of the decision-making process: the boys instead negotiate their territorial claims on her over her innate, and for all intents and purposes, uncaring body.

The gender roles in the films, however, also allow for alternative, more subversive readings. Far from being simply misogynistic and conservative, they are full of ambiguities and ambivalences. For instance, critics of the seemingly regressive sexuality and conservative morals of the text generally see the authorial ambivalence on Edward and his sexual and moral values. Indeed, his commitment to what he himself calls 'old-fashioned' beliefs is what stands in the way of pre-marital sex between himself and Bella. Arguing that he wants to save Bella's soul, Edward is very firm about not wanting to engage in any sexual activities before they are married. If we follow Bella's train of thought, however, we get a more progressive picture of sexuality. Even though she concedes that she would not have sex with a partner whom she does not truly love, she sees no reason to wait for sexual intercourse with Edward, impatient and desiring even when there is a very concrete danger for her. Rather than submit to his valuation of the sacredness of marriage and marital sexuality only, Bella uses the ceremony as a means to an end. She agrees to marry Edward in order to have sex with and be transformed into a vampire by him. The link between her desire to have sex with Edward and her putting up with marrying him is even stronger in the films than in the novels: in the former, her acceptance of his proposal comes straight after the sexual frustration of his rejection and the confirmation that he will not have sex with her if they are not married. Bella's motive for marrying Edward thus could hardly be clearer.

'I won't give in. I know what I want':
female sexuality and empowerment

Stereotypically, it is men who are expected to be more promiscuous and less in control of their sexual urges and desires. Within this traditional ideological construction, it is women's responsibility to keep the sexual tension from escalating for as long as possible. Rather than living out her own sexual desires, the woman is required to keep the man at bay and protect both his but most importantly her innocence. Instead of acting out her own sexual agency, therefore, the sexual act is characterised by the woman giving up her defence and allowing the man to engage with her sexually.[20] This, however, is in direct contrast to the portrayal of Edward and Bella's relationship. 'I won't give in. I know what I want,' Bella narrates at the end of the first film. While in this instance she is talking about her desire to be turned into a vampire, she displays the same determination in attaining her sexual goals. This is already apparent when Edward and Bella's relationship is still marked by an overwhelming sexual innocence: in the meadow scene after Edward's coming-out as a vampire, they lie next to each other without even touching, both on their backs with just their heads tilted to each other. Bella's body, however, is notably turned towards Edward's while his is firmly fixed to the ground.

Edward finds it hard to cope with Bella's demands of physical contact and proximity which seem to be enhanced by the sense of danger that he never fails to verbalise in a titillating play of risks. He explains to her:

Edward: I wanted to kill you. I've never wanted a human's blood so
          much in my life.
Bella: I trust you.
Edward: Don't.
Bella: I'm here, I trust you.
(When she moves in to kiss him, he flees.)

As their relationship and the implicit eroticism deepens, Bella's sexual urges become more intense and more difficult to control. Thus, when they kiss for the first time Bella tries to escalate the situation, kissing him more urgently, pressingly. It is not quite obvious whether she is pulling him onto the bed or whether he is pushing her – the escalation of sexual action looks mutual. However, when Edward feels himself lose control, he jumps back and shouts, 'Stop!', casting Bella as the aggressor. Bella's apology affirms this attribution of her as the driving force behind the escalation. Other scenes further confirm

Bella's depiction as sexually dominant, for example, her desire to keep kissing Edward despite his reminder that they 'have to go to class', or her initiating their first kiss after they are reunited in *The Twilight Saga: New Moon* (dir. Chris Weitz) – even though this depiction is not as strong in the films as in the novels.[21] Indeed, it could be argued that the female gaze that pervades the films further signals Bella's sexual agency.[22]

Other female characters confirm the depiction of women as sexually empowered. For instance, it is Bella's mother who left Charlie and it is she who has remarried (while he has remained single and seemingly sexually inactive). Similarly, Jessica very clearly tries to woo Mike, and Angela seeks a relationship with Eric. Looking to the vampire couples, Alice is very overtly sexual when she is around her boyfriend Jasper, toying with him during the training session, moving seductively, kissing him and winning the physical fight against him. Rosalie openly shows her sexual attraction through her appreciation of Emmet's physical power and agility, as when he half-climbs, half-jumps up at a tree in order to catch a ball, she says appreciatively: 'My monkey-man.' The sexual allusion is clear, and again, it is the female vampire who brings sexuality into the equation in a competitive and semi-aggressive situation.

Female sexuality is thus portrayed as empowering. The associations with it cease to be positive, however, when the sexually empowered woman in question is depicted as morally bad. While there are a few hints at Victoria's sexual nature in *Twilight*, the main storyline of sexually manipulative female vampires enfolds in *Eclipse*, both through Victoria, James' partner, and the figure of Maria, Jasper's sire. Maria's flashback portrayal casts her and her friends as seductive and insatiable sirens ('I can never stop once I've started'), invoking female sexuality as threatening. After having turned Jasper, Maria controls him through romantic and sexual means, as he concedes: 'I thought what Maria and I had was love. But I was her puppet. She pulled the strings.'[23] Maria's behaviour towards Jasper is mirrored by Victoria's control over Riley. Just as Maria in Jasper, Victoria has no real interest in Riley and simply uses him for revenge, as Edward explains:

> She only created you and this army to avenge her true mate, James. That's the only thing she cares about. Not you... You're from Forks. You know the area. That's the only reason she chose you. She doesn't love you.

Victoria proves Edward right when she lets Riley be killed without coming to his rescue.

'What a sick, masochistic lion': sadomasochist tendencies in Edward and Bella's relationship[24]

As Pugh points out, Bella and Edward's dominant emotion, love, is overshadowed by the pain they draw from their relationship.[25] Love and sexual longing are described as uncontrollable needs rather than desires and the characters consequently have little power to resist them: whenever he is around Bella, Edward has to endure physical pain because his longing for her blood is so strong. Bella's sexual desire for Edward is similarly strong but her masochistic experience is mainly fed by the danger which their proximity creates for her, for he could lose control at any second and kill her. Instead of shying away from this possibility, however, Bella routinely tries to escalate the situation and thus, willingly or not, heightens the danger to her life. The erotic tensions that arise from this interplay of danger and seduction are most clear when Edward explains his vampiric existence to Bella in the wood scene. And even though she claims not to be afraid, she very clearly is – both partners, however, are just as clearly enjoying the sadomasochistic prolonging of the conversation and the detailed and visual description. When Edward thus explains to Bella that '[y]our scent – it's like a drug to me. You're like my own personal brand of heroin,' the camera angle tilts so that we view Bella from above and Edward from below, mirroring their positions of power and thus heightening the atmosphere of immediate danger. The following scene illustrates Bella's tendency to escalate any danger she is in: to Edward's confession that 'I still don't know if I can control myself,' she replies: 'I know you can,' and proceeds to climb up the tree, forcing him to either retreat or come physically closer to her. As Pugh explains: 'When her sexual desires metamorphose into needs and thus become implicated and intermeshed with incessant torment, Bella sacrifices romantic pleasures for masochistic pains, which tortuously lead her back to pleasure.'[26] Thus, '[w]ithin the mutually masochistic dynamics of the *Twilight* books, sexuality is less a matter of individual choice than a painful addiction in which Bella and Edward seek pleasure with each other as all-powerful yet ultimately self-negating partners.'[27]

This is undoubtedly evident in the films. Bella, positioned as the 'silly lamb' within the quote from which this chapter takes its title, thus acts as enticing and willing prey, leading Edward away from school and the safety of the fellow students' audience into the dark woods to discuss his secret with him, then stands with her unprotected back towards him. In her apperception, this is a sign of trust, but it could certainly be interpreted as desire for a masochistic thrill.

In *Twilight*'s pivotal scene of Edward's 'coming-out' in the woods, the oft-quoted biblical analogy of the wolf/lion and the lamb is drawn:

Edward: And so the lion fell in love with the lamb.
Bella: What a stupid lamb.
Edward: What a sick, masochistic lion.

This scene is most interesting because, as a matter of fact, Bella is clearly not the lamb. Despite all the concentration on her supposed physical and emotional inferiority to Jacob and Edward, which Pugh calls the 'fiction of her inferiority',[28] it is Bella who calls the shots in both relationships. Furthermore, if one of the partners is cast as masochistic, it should be Bella – after all, it is she whose very life is in danger, yet she keeps returning to the masochistic thrill of experiencing and heightening this danger. The exchange between Edward and Bella, however, illustrates well the ambivalence of sexual desire and masochistic pleasure both partners draw from their relationship: Bella coyly pretends to be the innocent lamb when it is in truth she who tries to escalate their (sexual) relationship for her own masochistic thrill. Edward, on the other hand, draws apparent pleasure in presenting himself as the Byronic hero who is dominated both by his bodily urges and the sexual temptation acted out by Bella. Pugh's analysis of the analogy as presented in the novels supports the same thesis:

One might expect for the lion to act the role of aggressor/sadist and for the lamb to play the role of victim/masochist within Bella and Edward's analogy, but from Edward's perspective, his love for her casts him as the suffering masochist unable to preserve himself from a cruel 'lamb'. It could be posited that Bella's description of herself as a 'stupid lamb' does not explicitly reveal masochistic tendencies, but it is this lamb's willingness to die at the hands of her leonine lover for which she upbraids herself while nonetheless pursuing a love affair that she herself realizes she is not likely to survive.[29]

The sadomasochistic streak of Bella and Edward's relationship finds its culmination in the biting scene near the end of *Twilight*. Having been bitten by the vampire James, Bella needs her blood purified and the venom sucked out in order not to be turned into a vampire herself. Reluctantly, since he is not sure whether he will be able to stop drinking Bella's blood and thus fearing he may kill her, Edward starts sucking out the venom. The resulting biting scene could hardly be more sexual: Edward's obvious arousal, Bella's panting, his inability to stop, her obvious enjoyment, even the roaring fire in the background all illustrate that what we are perceiving is a substitute for sexual action from which both partners draw masochistic delight.[30]

Interpretation of the gender aspects in Bella's sadomasochism hinges on the definition of sadomasochism as empowering or disempowering. If we consider sadomasochistic desire to be rooted in a (personal) history of sexual violence and/or physical and mental abuse, we would have to agree with Sheila Jeffreys that '[s]adomasochism and other forms of self-harm can ... be seen as the result of oppressive forces such as sexual abuse, bullying, physical violence, hatred and contempt rather than celebrated as "transgressive" or "agentic".'[31] As Jeffreys points out, however, sadomasochistic practices can also be employed in a conscious act of sexual border crossing and transgression,[32] as attempts to break up traditional norms of gender behaviour: rather than merely being a passive object of sexual desire and recipient of pleasure, the sadomasochistic woman enters willingly into an unrestrained, orgy-like scenario that revolves around the unambiguous taboo of enjoying suffering and pain. Arguably, therefore, Bella's embracing of her and Edward's sadomasochistic experimenting can be read as another instance of Bella trying to deconstruct and rethink traditional norms of female sexuality.

The *Twilight* narrative, as we have seen, revolves around sexuality – be it the lack thereof, the desire for, or its vampiric substitute: the drawing of blood. Even without any explicit sexual intercourse taking place, therefore, the films are highly sexually charged. It is this ambivalence – the absence of sexuality and simultaneous presence of sexual tensions implicit in nearly every encounter between not only Edward and Bella, but most other couples – that lays the ground for all the other sexual ambiguities the films present: sexual empowerment as a feminist goal and achievement, as a feminist celebration of lust and power versus female sexuality as a threatening force; sexual awakening as a time of angst and inhibitions versus as a welcome step of maturation; the desire to be 'safe' and the purity and chasteness of the young love affair versus the masochistic tendencies of Bella and Edward's relationship. The films continuously move within and play with the societal ambiguities around teenage sexuality and the sexual role of teenage girls. It is not surprising therefore, that both critics of traditional gender and sexual roles and their defendants can find fault with the presentation of sexuality in the films: the *Twilight* film saga caters to all sides of the sexual debate, and this may well go some way to aid in understanding its criticised reception.

Notes

1. See Christine Seifert, 'Bite Me! (Or Don't!)', http://bitchmagazine.org/article/bite-me-or-dont, 2008 (accessed 5 May 2011).

2. Carrie Anne Platt, 'Cullen Family Values: Gender and Sexual Politics in the *Twilight* Series', in Melissa Click, Jennifer Stevens Aubrey and Lissa Behm-Morawitz (eds), *Bitten By Twilight: Youth Culture, Media and the Vampire Franchise* (New York: Peter Lang, 2010), p. 80.

3. Tison Pugh, *Innocence, Heterosexuality and the Queerness of Children's Literature* (New York: Routledge, 2011), p. 148.

4. Ibid.

5. Turn to Ewan Kirkland's 'Racial Whiteness and *Twilight*' in this volume for an analysis of this scene as a reinforcement of 'whiteness' and racial symbolism.

6. At the same time, the angelic wings allude to the figure of the angel of death. Following this line of interpretation, the wings accentuate the menace emanating from Edward. However, in both the medieval Christian and the Islamic tradition, the angel of death is not a dangerous and ill-meaning being in himself. Rather, he watches over the dying, separates their souls from their bodies and guides them to the afterlife. This is in line with both Edward's and Bella's tendency to disattribute responsibility for their actions (such as Edward conceding that he is not strong enough to stay away from Bella, and the emphasis on their relationship as fate throughout the films).

7. See e.g. Platt, 'Cullen Family Values' and Danielle Dick McGeough, '*Twilight* and Transformations of Flesh: Reading the Body in Contemporary Youth Culture', in Melissa Click et al., *Bitten By Twilight,* pp. 87–102.

8. Platt, 'Cullen Family Values', p. 71.

9. Platt's analysis is concerned with the book series but in most parts can be unproblematically applied to the films.

10. Platt, 'Cullen Family Values', pp. 81–82.

11. Ibid., p. 81.

12. Ibid., p. 72.

13. Pugh, *Innocence, Heterosexuality and the Queerness of Children's Literature*, p. 147.

14. As demonstrated when Angela and Jess are dress shopping and a few boys knock on the shop window, shouting 'Nice!' and leering at them; Bella mumbles, 'Oh, that's disgusting.'

15. Platt, 'Cullen Family Values', p. 83.

16. Ibid., p. 84.

17. McGeough, '*Twilight* and Transformations of Flesh', p. 90.

18. Ibid.

19. As a vampire, Edward has no innate body heat and would thus draw heat from Bella rather than warm her up. The werewolf Jacob, however, has an unnaturally high body temperature.

20. See e.g. Michael S.Kimmel, *The Gendered Society* (New York: Oxford University Press, 2000), pp. 222–30.

21. In the novels, Bella's insistence on having intercourse with Edward is highlighted and thematised much more vigorously. The following scene, taken from Meyer's *Eclipse*, is a good example of how Bella tries to pressure Edward into having sex with her, fully taking on the traditionally more masculine role: 'I pulled myself against him and crushed my mouth to his snow-cold lips. "Careful now, love," he murmured under my urgent kiss. "No," I growled. He gently pushed my face a few inches back. "You don't have to prove anything to me." "I'm not trying to prove something. You said I could have any part of you I wanted. I want this part. I want every part." I wrapped my arms around his neck and strained to reach his lips. He bent his head to kiss me back, but his cold mouth was hesitant as my impatience grew more pronounced. My body was making my intentions clear, giving me away. Inevitably, his hands moved to restrain me. "Perhaps this isn't the best moment for that," he suggested, too calm for my liking' (Stephenie Meyer, *Eclipse* (London: Atom, 2009), pp. 474–5.

22. Traditionally, most films present a male gaze, i.e. the audience assumes the perspective of a heterosexual man. The camera might thus, for example, focus on women's bodies, trying to excite the assumed heterosexual male audience. Different critics have argued that the *Twilight* novels and films both employ a female gaze, showing itself for instance in the camera angles in the second biology lesson, when Bella's gaze (and with it that of the audience) lingers on Edward's eyes, his hands and his mouth. This may be considered further evidence of the fetishisation of Jacob's physique, though perhaps, not unproblematic (for we might consider this to be more a 'queered' gaze).

23. This image of an abulic and heteronomous Jasper is reproduced by Bella in a nightmare in which Maria murmurs seductively into Jasper's ear, obviously urging him on to kill Bella.

24. Writing for a collection of essays has many advantages and one main flaw: there is never enough room to fit in all aspects of one topic. So instead of forcing too many different strands of argument into this chapter, I have decided to concentrate on the sadomasochistic tendencies of Edward and Bella's relationship. Allow me, however, to briefly draw your attention to other aspects surrounding the topic of sexuality and violence which the films touch upon: the connection between love and violence (as exemplified, for example, in Sam's disfigurement of Emily); the contradictory portrayal of sexual violence as peccadillo (as in Jacob's forced kiss on Bella) or severe crime (as in Rosalie's rape); and the abusive tendencies of Edward and Bella's relationship (such as his bodily refusal to let her visit Jacob, or the physical violence Edward unwittingly exerts during the couple's honeymoon).

25. Pugh, *Innocence, Heterosexuality and the Queerness of Children's Literature*, pp. 140–2.

26. Ibid., p. 141.

27. Ibid., p. 149.

28. Ibid., p. 150.

29. Ibid., p. 157.

30. Interestingly, biting scenes in the films are portrayed sexually allusively only when conducted with partners of the opposite sex. In the flashback of Carlisle biting Edward, Edward is very clearly in pain while the same scene with Esme is quite different, her mouth opening slightly, and she seems to moan. The picture is slightly blurred,

creating a sort of low-lit bedroom atmosphere in which the scene appears as if a semi-transparent veil shifts across the lens. The desire to avoid any homoerotic allusions is very clear. At the same time, however, both James's attack on Bella and Jacob's flirtations with her are also (in James' case mainly) directed at Edward. Both James and Jacob thus lock eyes with Edward when they bite or embrace Bella. The female body appears as the site of metaphorical homosexual intercourse. In the novels, this interplay comes to a climax when Edward and Jacob work together over Bella's dead body, trying to resurrect her. The sexual allusions (Edward's tongue flicking over Bella's skin, his repeated penetration etc.) create a virtual sexual triangle between Bella, Edward and Jacob (which has, of course, been implicitly alluded to from the start). It will be interesting to see how *The Twilight Saga: Breaking Dawn – Part 1* and *Part 2* together will visualise this triangle in the film and whether the sexual allusions will remain as obvious – or will perhaps be foregrounded, as was the case with the aforementioned biting scenes.

31. Sheila Jeffreys, 'Body Modification as Self-Mutilation by Proxy', in Viv Burr and Jeff Hearn (eds), *Sex, Violence and the Body: The Erotics of Self-wounding* (Basingstoke: Palgrave Macmillan, 2008), p. 24.

32. Ibid., pp. 23–4.

10

'VENUS IN FANGS': NEGOTIATING MASOCHISM IN *TWILIGHT*

Mark Richard Adams

Edward: And so the lion fell in love with the lamb.
Bella: What a stupid lamb.
Edward: What a sick, masochistic lion.

Twilight (2008, dir. Catherine Hardwicke)

A key complaint directed at *The Twilight Saga* criticises the relationship of Edward and Bella as being predominantly based on violence and submission. However, too often, these critiques fail to explore these issues further, or fail to engage with specific evidence within the text, instead repeating arguments surrounding acceptable teenage sexuality.[1] Initially perhaps, *Twilight* uses the conventions of teen romance and horror in ways that are often interpreted to be both sexist and disempowering, reinforcing conservative ideology linked with the horror genre. However, horror itself is known to open up spaces for the possible exploration of and engagement with alternative definitions of sexuality. By highlighting blood-letting, bodily de[con]struction, and ultimately death as key themes, the teenage horror drama appears a particularly appropriate platform for the investigation of masochistic ideology and the utilisation of sadomasochistic relationships.

An alternative perspective then, based upon a queer textual reading[2] and understanding of the vicissitudes of masochism rather than violence and abuse per se, may open up the possibility of a more empowering reading and, in turn, open up a deeper dynamic at work in *The Twilight Saga* franchise. In the previous chapter, Rana engaged with the idea of sadomasochism in discussing sexual power and agency within *Twilight*. This chapter will aim to delve into these issues using an psychoanalytic framework to explore a sexuality beyond heteronormative understandings of romance. Positioning the Bella and Edward relationship in a masochistic context uncovers the possibility for understanding their sexuality in terms of a desired suffering. With this as a starting point, *Twilight*, and its literary counterpart, can be shown to reveal some interesting, and at times conflicting, potential spaces for female masochistic desire.

Psychoanalysis and masochism

There is no clear, fixed understanding of masochism and, often alongside sadism, its definition and attributes have repeatedly been debated amongst psychoanalysts and philosophers. This discussion will begin by briefly drawing upon these debates to examine the difficulties in defining masochism, highlighting theories key to *The Twilight Saga*.

Alongside sadism, Freud judged masochism to be 'the most common and the most significant of all the perversions'; the connections between them render both relevant to this discussion.[3] At one stage he viewed the 'coupling of activity with masculinity and of passivity with femininity'[4] as a biological fact, and, in turn, he associated this with sadism and masochism respectively. Thus, in his earlier work Freud emphasised clear gendered divides and characterised passivity as being aligned with submissiveness. He believed that male sexuality contained 'an element of *aggressiveness*'[5] and a 'desire to subjugate'[6] which he proposed was biologically linked to the need to overcome 'the resistance of the sexual object'.[7] This analogous aggressive male sexuality is clearly highlighted in *Twilight* through Edward's desire to feed on Bella, a violent act that seemingly underpins their initial encounters and the beginning of their relationship. Freud also argued that often 'masochism is nothing more than an extension of sadism turned round upon the subject's own self,'[8] that is to say, pleasure is derived by an individual subjecting himself to suffering, applicable to Edward when he positions himself within Bella's presence. Bella is complicit in this relationship wherein she places herself in a supposedly weaker and dependent position in relation to Edward. Annie Reich later discussed masochistic female patients demonstrating extreme attachment to potentially abusive partners, noting 'the self-esteem of the submissive woman falls to a strikingly low level when she is away from her lover. The man, on the other hand, is overrated; he is considered to be very important, a genius. He is the only man worthy of love.'[9]

It takes little effort to relate this description to the events of *Twilight* and to even suggest that the narrative more fully endorses this masochistic viewpoint by making Edward 'perfect'.

These approaches to masochism have therefore highlighted positions of power and submission, and seem to repeat deeply problematic conservative attitudes towards gender, sexual power and male dominance. These ideas would seem to support the negative critical arguments against the *Twilight* films, in which Edward is presented as a dominating force and Bella as the meek dependent victim, replicating these early psychoanalytic frameworks of masochism; activity/passivity, sadism/masochism and masculinity/femininity. However, the relationship between the two characters can be best understood by widening our understanding of sadomasochism.

The masochistic contract

Victor N. Smirnoff's 'The Masochistic Contract' suggests that 'the satisfied masochist seems to enjoy a situation in which pain and humiliation would be the expected reaction', thus placing him or herself into scenarios orchestrated to provoke and/or obtain this desired suffering.[10] The suffering masochists experience is, in turn, a source of pleasure or comfort to them, as it is within the apparent *displeasure* that they find their actual *pleasure*. This progression of logic threatens to expose the inherent contradictory nature of masochistic behaviour, disturbing the presumed binary of pain and pleasure. Additionally, Smirnoff suggests that the sadist 'aims at the ultimate destruction of the victim, and tries to mutilate and annihilate him'.[11] While this might initially appear to be what Edward desires, his more developed want is *not to* feed from Bella,[12] thus causing her 'annihilation', but instead to *not* feed off her; for him *to suffer by being with her.* Edward's pleasure therefore derides from a masochistic obsession with disallowing or overriding his compulsion to drink her blood. Smirnoff's definition defuses the overt potential sadism that previous psychoanalytic theories would place onto Edward, opening up space instead for his masochistic pleasure to co-exist alongside Bella's. An initial reading of Bella and Edward's relationship would seem to position her in a dominated, dependent state, whereas the masochistic contract can instead offer a new perspective on the character's own abilities to control her situation. This is because Edward's desire to feed is weaker than and suppressed by his desire to suffer, the latter being more receptive to Bella herself. Smirnoff makes it clear that 'the essential phenomena of masochism may well be not in the suffering but in the position of the masochist in the masochistic relationship'.[13] Edward's own masochistic pleasure can be understood despite his more dominant position, as pain and suffering does not necessarily lie solely with the submissive. Rather than focus on aggression and sadism, the emphasis must be on the masochistic pleasure itself and how suffering is utilised and, more importantly, encouraged by the masochist. This also calls into question the previously discussed notions of a passive masochist and active sadist, suggesting at least a more provocative and controlling position for the former and a less deliberate attempt to incite displeasure by the latter.

Central to Smirnoff's argument, then, is that 'there can be no possible sadistic-masochistic meeting: the sadist only accepts to be the tormentor of an innocent and protesting victim; the masochist can only be the victim of a reluctant executioner *malgre lui*.'[14] The masochistic contract thus is both the agreement between the masochistic supplicant[15] and the supposedly dominant 'executioner', but also an illumination of the paradoxical nature of sadomasochistic relationships. Those perceived as masochists are also capable of sadism, yet the masochistic contract ultimately means that the hierarchical power rests with the presumed submissive. It is the submissive partner in the relationship who must grant permission (and therefore the illusion of power) to the partner who is performing the role of the sadist. In light of this understanding of masochism then, the characters' relationship can be considered potentially transgressive through their oscillating occupation of multiple active and passive, gendered masochistic positions. In order to further understand the radical (or indeed perhaps conventional) nature of this construction with regard to generic conventions, it must be considered in the historical context of the teenage sexuality on screen.

Teen horror and textual analysis

Twilight follows an established tradition of supernatural teenage drama, as well as influential horror texts that deal with teenage, and in particular female, sexuality.[16] These films allow 'the eruption of violence and sexuality into the domestic sphere through supernatural forces that invade the family home or render its inhabitants monstrous'.[17] *Twilight* clearly takes its lead from these collisions of teenage school life and the supernatural, and therefore it would be remiss not to mention the influence of the hugely successful *Buffy the Vampire Slayer* television series (WB 1997–2001; UPN 2001–2003), which also featured a 'tortured' relationship between a human and a vampire against the backdrop of teenage angst and domestic issues. The horror genre, with its conflation of sex and death and use of penetrating phallic weaponry (including vampire fangs), may be seen as a vehicle for conservative attitudes and moralistic punishment.[18]

Whilst there is a history of masochistic interpretations of female sexual desire within cinema, this does not preclude the inclusion of more productive, transgressive and forward-thinking ideals within the horror genre. The presumed heterosexual, 'normal' definition of sexuality can be potentially displaced by other sexual practices that have been, over time, judged by society as 'deviant' or a 'perversion'. Yet these are ultimately still part of 'a natural continuum of human sexual behaviour to which we all belong'.[19] An alternative reading can thus be forged for Bella, whereby her sexuality is not understood in conventional heteronormative terms, but as a deeply complicated, masochistic force engaging in a sadomasochistic game with the object of her affections.

Introduced in the novel as seemingly defined by her suffering, Bella willingly brings herself back to the small community of Forks which she clearly despises, adding that she is 'really more kind of the "suffer in silence" type'. *Twilight* therefore tells its story against a backdrop of self-imposed suffering that serves to mark Bella out as different and as an individual who embraces her need to suffer. Complementing this emotional pain is a consistent and near constant state of physical instability. In the opening half hour of the film, Bella is hit by a ball, slips on ice, trips over walking and notably is almost crushed by an out of control vehicle; she exists in a state of emotional and physical turmoil, a position of continual 'near-death' experiences. This correlates with what Betty Joseph[20] termed masochistic 'addiction to near-death', primarily found in Bella's commitment to the 'killer', Edward. Joseph observed that masochistic patients 'get more and more absorbed into hopelessness and involved in activities that seem destined to destroy them physically as well as mentally'.[21] The more Edward pulls away, and the more he emphasises the danger he represents, the closer Bella appears to be drawn to him, with little regard for her own safety. Bella does not display relief at her own survival but instead attempts to understand Edward and his apparent regret at saving her life, demanding to know why he did not let her die. Further, her description of Edward's mood swings as giving her 'whiplash' alludes both to the car accident and the rhetoric of emotional pain manifest as physical injury. The potential physical pain of the car accident is now transplanted into the emotional-physical pain of her relationship with Edward; a partnership defined by the masochistic suffering and pain they cause, and demand from, each other.

Bella's attraction to Edward is initially based on the intrigue and mystery of the outsider, and soon evolves to include the potential for danger. The potential for suffering is clear, and this seems to drive them forward; as mentioned, Bella is seemingly dominated by the powerful vampire who could kill her in seconds, and he in turn suffers in trying to repress his blood lust.

When Bella realises his vampiric nature the two confront each other in the isolated woodland; 'I've killed people before,' confesses Edward but Bella simply responds that 'It doesn't matter.' This would seem to feed into both the notion of the dependent woman who sees the violent partner as perfect [22] and further, wherein the masochist, in this case Edward, 'go[es] over and over their unhappiness, failures, things they feel they ought to feel guilty about'.[23] In this key confrontation, Edward explains his attraction to Bella: 'I wanted to kill you. I never wanted a human's blood so much in my life ... it's like a drug to me. You're like my own personal brand of heroin.' Despite Edward's open admissions of wanting to drain her, thus killing her, Bella's only fear is that he will leave her.

The danger presented by Edward allows Bella to act out more easily her masochistic desires, whereby he can play the sadistic role, allowing her to externalise the source of her suffering. Sacher-Masoch's literary *Venus in Furs*,[24] utilised by Smirnoff as a means to illustrate his argument, can be just as easily applied to the cinematic *Twilight* saga. In *Venus in Furs*, the central character, Severin, is eventually beaten by 'The Greek', a true sadist, and this removes the control of the victim found in masochistic contracts; 'the sadist aims at the ultimate destruction of the victim, and tries to mutilate and annihilate him. The masochist is not seeking to be killed or destroyed, but to be branded. Not by the absolute power of the other, but by the fictitious power that he himself has bestowed on the executioner.'[25] The closest parallels with Bella's situation can be drawn from the character of James, a tracker whose solitary desire is to hunt, kill and feed off her, in a twisted reflection of Edward's own obsession. James can thus potentially fill the position of The Greek, the true sadist who will not obey the rules, finding genuine delight in causing Bella to suffer, outside of her own control, and thus without pleasure. Whilst James' actions do not 'cure' Bella, as happens between The Greek and Severin, it should also be noted that James' sadistic game is not fully enacted due to Edward's rescue and the gradual return of control to Bella. As with the conclusion of *Venus in Furs* (as discussed by Smirnoff), James' violence is simply an act of suffering for Bella, whilst conversely Edward's own bite is 'allowed', and even desired, thus reaffirming their masochistic contract, and saving her from annihilation. Bella's need for suffering, therefore, must be dictated by her own terms, and unlike the truly sadistic James at the film's climax, Edward's sadistic desire must be negotiated and ultimately controlled.

After James' attack Bella awakens in hospital. She is instantly resistant to his attempts to separate them, the intensity of her protests highlighting her belief that Edward's drinking of her blood consummated their relationship. Yet for

Edward, the feeding was too sadistic, his suffering lessened by the culmination of his desire to taste her. For Bella, this was the ultimate act of masochistic submission – as defined in the masochistic contract – in a situation where the choice was hers (a crucial point to which we will return). She actively draws him to her even as he resists, pulling away to avoid his own suffering despite overtly claiming to be the 'masochistic lion'. Smirnoff indeed states that the masochist 'does not appear as the victimised accomplice to a sadistic executioner, but as his educator – just as the sadist is the pedagogue of his reluctant victim'.[26] Bella educates Edward in her choice of suffering, her desire to live on the edge of the threat that he poses, offering her neck to him only to receive kisses rather than the bites she so desires.

Conclusion

The Twilight Saga is presented initially as a traditional tale of romance but, as has been demonstrated, it depicts far more controversial and alternate, transgressive depictions of sexuality. Bella and Edward are drawn together because both desire danger and suffering, the offering of danger and the unknown for the other. Thus what seems at first to be painted as a traditional romance is in fact based on a masochistic and highly sexualised sense of dependency.

W hat must now be asked then is whether masochism is being used to suggest an incomplete or failed sexual development,[27] therefore supporting the cycle of punishment that surrounds teenage romance and horror. Smirnoff's masochistic contract has gone some way towards disputing this, emphasising the possible positions of power that Bella may in fact occupy within the relationship. Yet, feminist scholar Bat-Ami Bar On asserts that 'there is no true liberation where there is abuse, humiliation and exploitation, not even when they occur in a context that is voluntary, chosen and of mutual interest.'[28] Thus Edward and Bella's mutually desired masochistic relationship stands accused of repeating the ideology of patriarchal oppression. John Stoltenberg elaborates further, stating that a 'woman's compliance or acquiescence in sadomasochism is therefore entirely delusional and utterly meaningless.'[29] Accordingly he renders 'consent' as meaningful only between two persons 'who are equally enfranchised by culture to act wilfully and without constraint ... that is, who are genital males'.[30] In addition, it has further been argued that sadomasochists 'have internalised the eroticisation of cruelty and power imbalance that allegedly structures heterosexual relations',[31] which would see Bella positioned as a victim of society rather than seeking to break free of its conventional confines.

If Bella's relationship with Edward is to be understood as potentially trans-gressive, then any progressive potential lies in how an individual interprets the possibility of a masochistic contract. If accepted as a liberating position, ena-bling the masochist to gain control of their own power and desire, then Bella perhaps stands as a strong female in control of her own sexuality. However, if her consent is impossible, then Bella merely reaffirms patriarchal values which insist on submissive female roles. The reality perhaps lies somewhere in between. What *The Twilight Saga* indisputably does do, however, is open up a space in which this may be debated, and presents at least the *possibil-ity* of a transgressive romantic desire beyond culturally normalised acceptable sexuality. By offering up an arena in which variant perspectives and ideas can be contemplated, the characters' masochism problematises the more simplistic readings of the *Twilight* films and obliges a reassessment of its themes and mes-sages in such critiques which characterise much of the films' opposition. *The Twilight Saga* thus creates a space in which masochism can be understood as a possible component of teenage sexuality, offering up the potential for a more positive, less reactionary view of both the films and their impact on teenage audiences and popular culture at large.

Notes

1. See for instance Talashira, 'The 10 Worst Things About *Twilight*', http://www.squidoo. com/10-worst-things-about-twilight, 2008 (last accessed 7 June 2012).
2. For a further approach to queering *The Twilight Saga*, see R. Justin Hunt's work on scent, elsewhere in this collection.
3. Sigmund Freud, 'Three Essays on the Theory of Sexuality (An Excerpt)' (1905), in Margaret Ann Fitzpatrick Hanly (ed.), *Essential Papers on Masochism* (London: New York University Press, 1995), p. 86.
4. Sigmund Freud, 'Instincts and their Vicissitudes (An Excerpt)' (1915), in Hanly, *Essential Papers on Masochism*, p. 97.
5. Freud, 'Three Essays', p. 86. Emphasis in the original.
6. Ibid.
7. Ibid.
8. Ibid.
9. Annie Reich, 'Extreme Submissiveness in Women' (1939), in Hanly, *Essential Papers on Masochism*, p. 424. This quotation might remind us of *Twilight*'s sequel, *New Moon* (2009, dir. Chris Weitz).
10. Victor N. Smirnoff, 'The Masochistic Contract' (1969), in Hanly, *Essential Papers on Masochism*, p. 63.
11. Ibid., p. 69.

12. Edward's desire to feed is explored in further detail by Ruth O'Donnell in her chapter in this collection, ' "My Distaste for Forks": *Twilight*, Oral Gratification and Self-denial'.

13. Smirnoff, 'The Masochistic Contract', p. 62.

14. Ibid., p. 68.

15. Whilst the use of the word 'supplicant' can connote passivity, as Smirnoff's theory will show, this is entirely an act; a form of controlled submission which only *presents* the image of the masochist as a supplicant.

16. Examples of teenage horror linked with sexuality include *Teen Wolf* (1985, dir. Rod Daniel), *Carrie* (1976, dir. Brian De Palma), *Ginger Snaps* (2000, dir. John Fawcett), *Halloween* (1978, dir. John Carpenter), *Scream* (1996, dir. Wes Craven).

17. Shelley Stamp Lindsey, 'Horror, Femininity, and Carrie's Monstrous Puberty', in Barry Keith Grant (ed.), *The Dread of Difference: Gender and the Horror Film* (Austin: University of Texas Press, 1996), p. 279.

18. See Laura Mulvey, 'Visual Pleasure and Narrative Cinema', *Screen* 16/3 (Autumn 1975), pp. 6–18.

19. Harry Benshoff, *Monsters in the Closet: Homosexuality and the Horror Film* (Manchester: Manchester University Press, 1997), p. 39.

20. Betty Joseph, 'Addiction to Near-death' (1981), in Hanly, *Essential Papers on Masochism*, pp. 511–525.

21. Ibid., p. 511.

22. Reich, 'Extreme Submissiveness in Women'.

23. Joseph, 'Addiction to Near-death', p. 515.

24. Leopold von Sacher-Masoch, *Venus in Furs* (1870; London: Zone Books, 1989).

25. Smirnoff, 'The Masochistic Contract', p. 69.

26. Ibid., p. 72.

27. Again, see O'Donnell in this collection.

28. Bat-Ami Bar On, 'Feminism and Sadomasochism: Self-Critical Notes', in Robin Ruth Linden, Darlene R. Pagano, Diana E. H. Russell and Susan Leigh Star (eds), *Against Sadomasochism: A Radical Feminist Analysis* (East Palo Alto, CA: Frog in the Well, 1982), p. 80.

29. John Stoltenberg, 'Sadomasochism: Eroticized Violence, Eroticized Powerlessness', in Linden et al., *Against Sadomasochism*, p. 128.

30. Ibid.

31. Annamarie Jagose, *Queer Theory: An Introduction* (New York: New York University Press, 1996), p. 65.

PART 4

THE POLITICS OF PALLOR: POST-COLONIALISM AND RACIAL WHITENESS, QUEERED?

11

THE CULLENS: FAMILY, MIMICRY AND THE POST-COLONIAL VAMPIRE

Simon Bacon

Bella:	How old are you?
Edward:	Seventeen.
Bella:	How long have you been seventeen?
Edward:	A while.

Twilight (2008, dir. Catherine Hardwicke)

It has been said that imitation is the greatest form of flattery, and yet when viewed through a post-colonial context it takes on a much more sinister and subversive character. Here, the act of what Homi Bhabha terms mimicry[1] points out the inherent flaws and contradictions within the object that is being copied. Situated within a very particular hierarchy of power, the mimicry of dominant or colonial oppressors by those subjugated, enacts a ploy of resistance through the act of mirroring. The function of such mimicry not only takes part in an ever-evolving post-colonial rehabilitation, but also highlights the inherent defects of homeland ideological and political discourse. As such, 'minority' figures within popular culture come to portray, or mirror, the face of dominant and normalised society to reveal and critique both its contradictions and systems of oppression.

In Catherine Hardwicke's film version of *Twilight* (2008, dir. Catherine Hardwicke), the vampire clan of the Cullens *appear* to embody the popular image of the 'all-American family', and indeed they are the only representation of this kind in Forks. To emphasise this point, in the first film we see them playing what Edward describes as 'the American pastime', baseball. Yet on closer inspection this 'perfectness' takes on an unnatural patina, a strategically feigned response to the culture they find themselves in. In doing so, they do not manifest but rather mimic the qualities most desired by the dominant white American (human) community around them.[2] It is the level of what could be called pre-meditation within their actions that reveals the darkness floating just beneath the *sparkling* white surface of the modern revenant. This mimicking, or enactment, of familial perfection opens up a space for an oppositional reading of the 'conservative' contemporary vampire family in which their normalisation actually emphasises not only their own 'otherness' but also the inherent 'otherness' of the society which would exclude them.

The vampire family album

Traditionally configured as a solitary figure within Western folklore, the notion of a vampire belonging to a family has been largely absent until relatively recently.[3] From folklore, and specifically that of Northern and Eastern Europe, the vampire's relation to family was via a 'familial larder' returned to for both food and company, and even sexual relations, but rarely associating or 'bonding' with its own kind.[4] The vampire's predatory nature meant that, like the big cats to which it is sometimes equated, it was loath to share its food source and was not even compelled by biological necessity to join with others of its kind to reproduce. It was not until Anne Rice's novel *Interview with the Vampire*[5] that vampires were seen to be not only gathering together, but also forming family units. Here Rice's interpretation of the vampire breaks the earlier mould of the Byronic vampire, as seen in John Polidori's *The Vampyre*[6] and continued in the figure of Bram Stoker's *Dracula*[7] and arguably in many of the cinematic manifestations of The Vampire King since. Not only do Ricean vampires long to be around humans, but they also desire to form similar social bonds and groups. Consequently, we see in the novel and in Neil Jordan's 1994 cinematic version of *interview with the Vampire* the main vampire characters Lestat and Louis choosing to create and live in the intimacy of a smaller, or what one would call family, unit when they give 'birth' to the vampire child Claudia.

The inherent perverseness of the vampire family created by choice, rather than biology, was further compounded in the teen-vamp films of the 1980s, where it formed a dark reflection in comparison to the human families shown. The teen-vamp films of the 1980s consisted of six mainstream Hollywood releases between 1985 and 1989 all featuring a teenage male protagonist struggling against the monstrousness of his burgeoning sexuality made manifest through the figure of the vampire.[8] Although the films have been cited for holding ultimately Reaganite conservative plots that promote a return to American family values,[9] the most well-known of this series, *The Lost Boys* and *Near Dark* (both released in 1987, dirs Joel Schumacher and Kathryn Bigelow respectively), utilise the vampire family as a foil to the 'normal' human, or American middle-class, family.[10] Both films present the human family as broken or dysfunctional (not unlike Bella's family, and those that live in and around Forks) but it is ultimately down to the eldest male child to *choose* to repair the family unit. In both cases, however, he is asked to choose between the vampire family and his own.[11] In *Near Dark*, the vampire family – lead by Jessie, the 'father', and Diamondback, the 'mother' – is a gang of fugitives travelling the roads of America in search of food and excitement. As Ken Gelder notes in his book *Reading the Vampire*: 'The film juxtaposes the lawlessness of the vampire gang – they can do "anything we want" – with the law-abiding world of the father and his family.'[12] The hero of the story, Caleb, has little or no difficulty choosing between the two, not least because his father manages to convert his vampire girlfriend Mae back into a human. In *The Lost Boys*, however, the vampire family infiltrates the human family in a two-pronged – or perhaps fanged – attack as Rob Latham observes:

> This villain turns out to be Max, who not only has been insinuating himself into Lucy's good graces but also has been secretly stage-managing David's efforts to draw Michael into his own undead 'family' – his ultimate goal being to secure a mother for his footloose brood of bloodsuckers.[13]

In both cases the vampire family is ultimately rejected because they are unnatural, their familial bonds are not formed through normal biological reproduction and consequently they do not live by the rules set out by society; indeed on the contrary, the vampire makes no attempt to do so.

In the twenty-first century this situation has changed dramatically, and not just with the example set by the Cullen family, as will be discussed shortly. Films such as the Butcher brothers' *The Hamiltons* (2006) and the novel *The Radleys* by Matt Haig[14] show non-oppositional vampire families doing their best to assimilate and cope with the stresses and strains of everyday life. Though gifted with superhuman powers, they simply crave acceptance and to be left alone to enjoy a – very – long and happy life.[15] The Cullens, however, differ from these other modern vampire families, for their enactment of family life is not just a contemporary concern of the here and now, but rather their performing of 'the family thing' has been perfected over decades – in fact too perfectly.

The perfect family?

Within the town of Forks, Washington State, the Cullens are just too damn perfect. They embody all that the human families in the area are not. They are totally devoted to each other, as Elizabeth Baird Hardy comments in *Twilight and History*: 'They are willing to die for one another, because protecting the family is, to them, far more important than individual survival.'[16] Carlisle, as a doctor, spends hours at the local hospital saving lives, whilst Esme dutifully stays home to tend the house, and all the children attend Forks High School wearing the latest fashions and driving new cars. All of them are considered good looking, if aloof, and are the envy of all the other pupils. Their considerable wealth is on obvious and constant display. Although Kat Burkhart states: '[t]he primary goal of the Cullen family is to remain inconspicuous, to blend in with the local human population, and to act appropriately for the circumstances and the decade',[17] this is exactly what they do not achieve. They do not blend in but stand out as different, or indeed perhaps better or even ideal, in everything they do.

This idealisation is very evident in the films, which foreground this difference through aesthetics, particularly in the first instalment *Twilight* (2008), in which the vampires are so white they almost shine – or indeed *sparkle* – which of course they actually do in sunlight, becoming a marble statue of human perfection in the manner of Michelangelo's David or Praxiteles' Apollo.[18] This flawless perfection, on the level of a work of art, would seem to establish that the Cullens' mimesis of humanity is not just an attempt to copy the everyday, but to represent an ideal of humanity. This is seen in many of the things they do, from the house that they live in, to their constant academic success and perpetual cyclical matriculation. This again points to how determined, and indeed, *pre-determined* their performance of humanity is. Burkhart further observes that:

> In different locations and at different time periods, the roles changed as a result for each of the Cullens; and as teenage vampires, their experiences – including the family roles they played, whether as 'siblings' or openly

married couples – would have reflected changes in the lives of American teenagers throughout the twentieth century.[19]

One would expect their constant observation of the changing nature of society and its expectations over time would reveal how average and mundane humanity is, and yet they specifically aim for the ideal and not the real. This level of intent on their part suggests that they do not want to just blend in and remain unnoticed but actually want to critique the societal roles and functions that they are enacting; that their performance is a knowing one and therefore hides a far darker intent on their part.

Will the real vampire family please stand up?

The menace of mimicry is its double vision which in disclosing the ambivalence of colonial discourse also disrupts its authority.[20]

It can be argued then that it is the Cullen family's shared level of intent to be more human than human that as a whole binds them together. This can be read as a subterfuge and a hiding of their true natures, the camouflaging of their true intent to allow the 'lion' to lie down with the 'lamb', as Edward described to Bella in the first film. This is most clearly observed in what is termed as their 'vegetarianism'. Whilst specifically configured to appeal to human sensibilities, inferring an ethical even holistic lifestyle, it means something very different to vampires, who cannot live on vegetable matter. Edward himself indeed reveals the more knowing level of this behaviour when in the first film he tells Bella:

> My family, we think of ourselves as vegetarians, right, 'cause we only survive on the blood of animals ... but it's like a human only living on tofu: it keeps you strong but you're never fully satisfied.

As such, their abstinence can be seen as a matter of masking or deception so as not to transgress one of the deeper-held taboos of humanity, that of cannibalism. This is a recurring problem within the films, for the Cullens must be seen as human on some level for Bella and Edward's relationship to work. Subsequently cannibalism is used to distinguish the good 'human' Cullens from the 'non-human', bad vampires, the Volturi, trackers and Newborns, who all consume human blood.[21] The fact that this constantly bubbles away under the surface of their human veneer is revealed by Edward when he tells Bella of the effect she had, and still has, upon him. Remembering their first encounter at school he recalls, 'I wanted to kill you ... I've never wanted a human's blood so much in my life ... but it's you, your scent it's like a drug to me. You're like my own personal brand of heroin.' These lines are visually emphasised in the film as we see Bella's hair being blown by a fan wafting her scent towards Edward as he grimaces, clutching his hand to his mouth to restrain himself.

That this desire is not limited to Edward alone, but in fact affects the whole Cullen family, penetrating their facade, is made clear at Bella's birthday celebrations at their home in *New Moon* (2009, dir. Chris Weitz). Whilst opening a gift she cuts her finger on a piece of wrapping paper, and Jasper attacks. Edward pushes her away to protect her and in the process she cuts herself more severely on a broken vase.

This ends with Bella finding herself faced with nearly the entire family hungering for her blood. Only Carlisle manages to restrain himself but the rest of the family are revealed for the performers they truly are. His calm and restraint are, as he explains, attributed to 'Centuries of experience in the emergency room' but are actually due to the amount of practice he has had in enacting this role. Indeed in the cinematic version he tells Bella whilst tending to her wounds that he is not affected by her blood due to 'years and years of practice'. Thus it is the long-established nature of their continual (re-)enactment which finally uncovers the premeditation of their vampiric mimesis.

Carlisle himself has been a vampire since the mid-seventeenth century, but the children are relatively new, having only held this identity since the beginning of the twentieth. That said, they have enacted their youth over and over again. This point is made overt in the first film when Bella notices the art in the Cullens' home, which is formed from over 100 graduation caps, of which Edward explains, 'We matriculate a lot.' Their performance of American youth is not one born of spontaneity but of experience, as Kyra Glass von der Osten in *Twilight and History* points out: 'Ultimately the Cullens' family life is a pastiche of the history of the American family, incorporating attributes that are contemporary, colonial, or just plain unusual, at least among European Americans.'[22] However, the term pastiche possibly does not connote the sinister nature of this imitation in which the knowing lions imitate lambs, for Edward repeatedly refers to himself as a monster. But possibly more sinister than cosying up to what might be their next meal, they also reveal the cracks and absurdities in the system they are mirroring – if monsters can be more human than humans, then we must question whether to be human means we may well all be monsters.

The post-colonial vampire

He is the effect of a flawed colonial mimesis, in which to be Anglicized is *emphatically* not to be English.[23]

Homi Bhabha's *The Location of Culture* views mimicry as a focus of anxiety, both in the construction of identity in the one who mimics but also in that of the one being imitated.[24] The mimic could be considered totally unaware of his own attempts at imitation – the more he tries to be something he is not, the more he just reveals himself as increasingly Other. This is not unlike the situation of Louis in *Interview with the Vampire*, unbeknownst to himself. His continuing attempts to be human, or return to the humanity that he has lost, reveal him to be monstrous and distinctly inhuman.[25] The Cullens on the other hand, are well aware of how inhuman they are, and are not. Subsequently, their performance of mimicry is what would be termed 'strategic', in that it does not affect their own identity but instead destabilises the object they reflect.

As mentioned above, the vampires do not choose to copy the average American family but rather the affluent 'fashion model' family that the rest of us can only fantasise about being. In fact, they are *the model family* – gorgeous, talented, wealthy, healthy and ethically committed, but ultimately posed, self-manufactured. Their sense of Otherness comes not from their sparkling whiteness – Bella is often shown as being even whiter than Edward – nor from their aversion to bright sunlight, but from the fact they are too human: a copy which is more perfect than the original.[26] Consequently, it can be argued, that it is not conceived as a way to blend in with the society around them but to show how absurd and inhuman its forms of exclusion and inclusion are. This is noted by Bhabha when he says: 'mimicry rearticulates presence in terms of its "otherness", that which it disavows.'[27] The Cullens, who are actually the Other that normal human society rejects, become the perfect model of what that same society aspires to, resultantly becoming more than human. In so doing, the 'normal' humans become disavowed by the perfect humans who are, in fact, not human at all. Bhabha further observes that:

Mimicry does not merely destroy narcissistic authority through the repetitious slippage of difference and desire. It is the process of the *fixation* of the colonial as a form of cross-classificatory, discriminatory knowledge within an interdictory discourse, and therefore necessarily raises the question of the *authorisation* of colonial representations.[28]

The Cullens show the absurdity of what human society considers human, and the more convincing their performance becomes and is accepted, the less authority the ideologies of normalised human society holds. In being represented as non-human – that is, beyond human categorisation – the Cullens extend the importance of this realisation to all groups considered Other by normal society; their performance of extreme 'whiteness', both visually and ideologically, shows how absurd all ethnic and racial discrimination is. Thus *Twilight* utilises the legacy of the colonial mindset and applies it to contemporary American, and Western, society. Subsequently this highlights both the ubiquity and the absurdity of using 'whiteness', in its ideological representation, as a benchmark of idealised identity, at the start of the twenty-first century.[29]

Conclusion: white as the new black

In *Our Vampires, Ourselves*, Nina Auerbach argues contemporary 'domestication' of the vampire as a diminution of its former powers. Her view of the role of the family in 1980s teen-vamp films was that 'the purified family is all we need to see: the ramifications of vampirism have shrunk from the political arena into the snug domestic unit.'[30] Undoubtedly the political construction of the idealised American family has been continually utilised – not only within these narratives – as an indicator of the nation's moral health as a whole (the President as Father of the Nation, for example), but further reinforced in its media and popular-culture portrayals. Through this a framework is constructed of the perfect family against which all others are implicitly or explicitly judged, and in which the ideology of the contemporary capitalist American dream is upheld and embraced. In this scenario, there is no doubt that it is the Cullens who very much embody what is termed in *The Lost Boys* as the 'blood-sucking Brady Bunch'. This family, made up of unrelated members, enacts a totally believable performance of an imagined perfection, the ultimate capitalist media family dream. As mentioned above, it is the sinister knowingness within this performance that unbalances the ideological structure of the system that it mimics. Their performance of the perfect family has been honed down over repeated, and repeating, (re-)enactments. This purposeful act simultaneously takes them to the heart of the society that excludes them, and reveals how meaningless that particular society's construction of identity really is.

The family as the fundamental ideological foundation of nationhood and its attendant signification of inclusion and belonging becomes subverted and destabilised by finding its most aspirational expression in the body that is seen as monstrous and abject. To reinterpret Bhabha's earlier example wherein to be 'Anglicized' is most definitely not to be English, the Cullens' mimicry of humanity or American society[31] shows them not only as *emphatically* not-human, but questions whether such a term even exists. Or rather that the very things that define what it is to be human, as defined by contemporary America, are such artificial constructions that they can only be successfully enacted, or played, by actors. The vampire here becomes the perfect performer, whose outsider position enables him to view the spectacle of society for what it is and thus reproduce it with the flawless execution of the practised recitalist. That this mimicry is undertaken by an Othered group, in this case, and particularly the non-human, collapses any and all credibility within socially constructed categories of exclusion. Within the milieu of modern day America this connects the Cullens not only to immigrant groups within the USA but also wider implications for homeland security and American foreign policy.[32]

Ultimately the Cullens' mimicry works by reflecting society: it reveals not only its defects but also the superficiality behind its own system of how its features should be arranged. However, this superficiality also shows how easy it is to rearrange this construction and reconfigure the parameters of exclusion and inclusion, and that belonging does not mean the convincing performance of 'whiteness', or the ideologically normative, but is unstable, enunciative and continually negotiable.

Notes

1. Homi K. Bhabha, *The Location of Culture* (London: Routledge, 2004), pp. 121–31.

2. Somewhat curiously they stand apart from the other 'minority' group within the film and novels, the Native American Indian tribe of the Quileutes who, in contrast to the Cullens, make very little attempt to integrate into the general community and largely live apart from the townspeople. This simultaneously points to the ways that minority groups within contemporary America do not necessarily unite in their shared subjugation and social exclusion and a certain antipathy between those that seemingly choose to integrate and those that do not.

3. Nancy Schumann points out that this notion has always been more complicated for the female vampire, or those in 'covens' (*Take a Bite: Female Vampires in Anglo-American Literature and Folklore* (London: CallioSoph, 2011).

4. See Paul Barber, *Vampires, Burial, and Death: Folklore and Reality* (New Haven: Yale University Press, 1988); Erik Butler, *Metamorphoses of the Vampire in Literature and Film: Cultural Transformations in Europe, 1732–1933* (Rochester: Camden House, 2010); Bruce A. McClelland, *Slayers and their Vampire: A Cultural History of Killing the Dead* (Michigan: University of Michigan Press, 2006); and James B. Twitchell, *The Living Dead: A Study of the Vampire in Romantic Literature* (Durham: Duke University Press, 1981).

5. Anne Rice, *Interview with the Vampire* (London: Sphere, 1976).

6. John Polidori, *The Vampyre; A Tale* (London: Sherwood, Neely, and Jones, 1819).

7. Bram Stoker, *Dracula* (Westminster: Constable & Co, 1897).

8. Whilst there have been other series of vampire films, the Hammer productions of the late 1950s to the early 1970s are probably the most famous, boasting nine films featuring Dracula, beginning with *The Horror of Dracula* in 1958 and ending with *Seven Golden Vampires* in 1974 (seven of these starred Christopher Lee). These, however, took place over a much longer time frame and had much smaller budgets than the teenage vampire features mentioned here. Also the films mentioned all feature teenage protagonists. However, there were also a few other mainstream vampire releases during this period that were explicitly aimed at a more 'grown-up' audience, such as *The Hunger* by Tony Scott (1983), *Lifeforce* by Tobe Hooper (1985) and *Vampire's Kiss* by Robert Bierman (1989).

9. See Nina Auerbach, *Our Vampires, Ourselves* (Chicago: University of Chicago, 1996); and Sorcha Ní Fhlainn ' "It's Morning in America": The Rhetoric of Religion in the Music of *The Lost Boys* and the Deserved Death of the 1980s Vampire', in Niall Scott (ed.), *The Role of the Monster: Myths and Metaphors of Enduring Evil* (Oxford: Inter-Disciplinary Press, 2009), pp. 147–56.

10. See Auerbach, *Our Vampires, Ourselves*; Ní Fhlainn, 'It's Morning in America'; and Robin Wood, *Hollywood from Vietnam to Reagan – and Beyond* (New York: Columbia University Press, 2003). Wood in particular discusses 'the family' in relation to American film and politics, both as an abstract notion of an ideological ideal but also as an inherently monstrous construction because of that; see especially pp. xxvi, 65, 76–7 and 152.

11. In what could be considered an interesting gender deviation, *Breaking Dawn – Part 1* (2011, dir. Bill Condon) and *Breaking Dawn – Part 2* (2012, dir. Bill Condon) continue to see Bella succeeding in retaining both.

12. Ken Gelder, *Reading the Vampire* (London: Routledge, 1994), p. 104.

13. Rob Latham, *Consuming Youth: Vampires, Cyborgs, and the Culture of Consumption* (Chicago: University of Chicago Press, 2002), p. 62.

14. Matt Haig, *The Radleys* (Edinburgh: Canongate, 2010).

15. Curiously, in both *The Hamiltons* and *The Radleys*, the vampires age at a comparative rate to the humans around them, and in *The Radleys* even suffer from early male baldness and beer-bellies, though this is often remedied by the ingestion of human blood.

16. Elizabeth Baird Hardy, 'Jasper Hale, the Oldest Living Confederate Veteran', in Nancy R. Reagin (ed.), *Twilight and History* (Hoboken: John Wiley & Sons, Inc., 2010), p. 125.

17. Kat Burkhart, 'Getting Younger Every Decade: Being a Teen Vampire during the Twentieth Century', in Reagin, *Twilight and History*, p. 249.

18. Though it is important to note that the mimicry of humanity enacted by the Cullens, which can also be read as 'American-ness', not only examples them as other through their being 'white' as post-colonial allegory to 'black', but also to 'red', 'yellow', female and 'gay'. However, Ewan Kirkland adds an interesting discussion to this meaning of whiteness in post-colonial discourses in his chapter in this collection.

19. Burkhart, 'Getting Younger Every Decade', p. 246.

20. Bhabha, *The Location of Culture*, p. 126.
21. Cannibalism plays an ambivalent role in this configuration. Whilst often used as a way to create Otherness and abjection, particularly within colonial discourse (see Francis Barker, Peter Hulme and Margaret Iversen (eds), *Cannibalism and the Colonial World* (Cambridge: Cambridge University Press, 1998) and M. Daphne Kutzer, *Empire's Children: Empire and Imperialism in Classic British Children's Books* (New York: Garland Publishing, 2000)), it was also posited by Freud as an act of identification (see Barbara Creed, 'Freud's Worst Nightmare: Dining with Dr Hannibal Lecter', in Steven Jay Schneider (ed.), *Horror Film and Psychoanalysis: Freud's Worst Nightmare* (Cambridge: Cambridge University Press, 2004)). Equally, Wood (*Hollywood from Vietnam to Reagan*) sees cannibalism of indicative of the monstrosity of the non-normative family but also of the consuming nature of the idealised family that is ideologically imposed by contemporary American politics.
22. Kyra Glass von der Osten, 'Like Other American Families, Only Not: The Cullens and the "Ideal" Family in American History', in Reagin, *Twilight and History*, p. 201.
23. Bhabha, *The Location of Culture*, p. 125.
24. The equating of the place of the vampire in human society with that of the colonised subject may seem a spurious one in that post-colonial discourse is largely predicated upon the notion of a more powerful group subjugating a less powerful one, and so mimicry in this configuration offers one of the few options of dissent or resistance. Vampires, whilst being in the minority, within *The Twilight Saga*, are shown as being greatly more powerful than the human population. However, as is the colonial subject, they can be shown to be dependent upon the society that controls them, or that they rely on for food. As such the vampire can be seen as a colonised subject but one who chooses to be subjugated. This positioning of a feigned weakness through power allows their acts of mimicry to read not as points of resistance but as social critique.
25. As an interesting predecessor to the Cullens, he only drinks the blood of rodents or other small animals. However, Louis is made clear as a guilty tortured soul, whereas for the Cullens their motivation is more ambiguous: do they truly share this ethic or is this a means by which not to be observed as the Other they seek to hide in themselves?
26. For a different reading of this effect see Ewan Kirkland's chapter in this collection.
27. Bhabha, *The Location of Culture*, p. 130.
28. Ibid., p. 129.
29. There is an interesting equivalence here with the 'whiteness' performed by the character of Batty in Ridley Scott's film, *Blade Runner* (1982). The cloned being, Batty, is played by Rutger Hauer, a perfect example of Aryan whiteness, and yet in being a slave to humankind he is also identified as African American; see Kaja Silverman, 'Back to the Future', *Camera Obscura* 9/3 27 (1991), pp. 134–47.
30. Auerbach, *Our Vampires, Ourselves*, p. 168.
31. There is a sense here, and within the narratives themselves, that being human and American are synonymous. This is further exampled by the Quileute Indians, who are not seen as 'American', and so are configured as monstrous shape-shifters and,

resultantly, not human. No doubt this is a post-colonial legacy of portraying other cultures as 'savages', much closer to the animal world.

32. For examples of this see Stanley A. Renshon, *National Security in the Obama Administration: Reassessing the Bush Doctrine* (New York: Routledge, 2010); Marc A. Thiessen, *Courting Disaster: How the CIA Kept America Safe and How Barack Obama is Inviting the Next Attack* (Washington: Regnery Publishing Inc., 2010); and Michael Otterman, *American Torture: From the Cold War to Abu Ghraib and Beyond* (Melbourne: Melbourne University Publishing Ltd, 2007).

12

RACIAL WHITENESS AND *TWILIGHT*

Ewan Kirkland

Whiteness and the vampire

Vampires are very white, and the vampires of *Twilight* are no exception. One of the aspects which distinguishes vampires from humans is the pale white skin which marks them as Other. Yet race has never been solely a matter of skin tone, and many further aspects of traditional vampires associated with white ethnicity – a problematic relationship to sunlight, noble or upper-class heritage, a preference for European high culture – also feature across *The Twilight Saga*. The discourse of light whereby vampires' skin sparkles when touched by sunlight, the Cullens' privileged lifestyle of fast cars and stock-market manipulation, the sexual abstinence and brooding melancholy which characterises the series' central romance, can further be related to cultural representations and conceptions of whiteness. The blanched fluid which rushes through Bella's body, transforming her physical constitution in the closing scene of *Breaking Dawn – Part 1* (2011, dir. Bill Condon), suggests that a visual whiteness informs screen depictions of the state of vampirehood, bearing associations of death, coldness and emptiness as well as physical perfection, noncorporeality and bodily transcendence. The Cullens' Caucasian persuasion is most evident in their juxtaposition with the Quileute tribe of werewolves, a supernatural group more visibly ethnicised, who function to throw the racial aspects of their 'paleface' nemeses into relief.

Despite the evident pallor of its skin, few writers engage with the whiteness of the vampire, traditionally understood as a monstrous figure who comes from the outside, to threaten the normativity of white bourgeois society. As detailed by Ken Gelder,[1] many interpretations and articulations of the vampire identify him as a distinctly Jewish figure. Stoker's tall, thin Dracula for instance, with 'beaky' nose, black moustache and beard, is seen as reflecting historically specific Victorian anxieties concerning the influx of Eastern European immigrants into 1890s London. In his financial affairs, Dracula reproduces anti-Semitic stereotypes as a gold-hoarding nomad whose trade and wealth cross national boundaries, the drain of capital inherent in Jewish international business practices symbolised by the vampire's drain of blood from the healthy indigenous population.

J. Halberstam also discusses the novel *Dracula*[2] as entrenched in nineteenth-century discourses which increasingly construct Jewishness as a racial identity, noting parallels between the Count and heavily racialised figures such as Svengali, Fagin and Shylock.[3] The ghettoised 'vampire nests' which feature across the *Buffy* (Twentieth Century Fox Television, 1997–2003) and *Angel* (Twentieth Century Fox Television, 1999–2004) series, typically occupying dilapidated buildings in run-down urban districts, perpetuate the construction of the vampire as a degenerate race, although contemporary film and television vampires are as likely to reside in palatial mansions, high-tech Gothic castles, or decadent nightclubs. Referring to the staking of Lucy Westenra, Milly Williamson further associates the vampire with women of colour who were Othered and objectified by the Victorian medical establishment in their efforts to construct female expressions of sexuality as a descent from civilisation into primitive savagery.[4] Contemporary vampires continue to mark the boundaries between the normal and the perverse, exemplifying the depravity of an inhuman subject free from the guilt, soul or civil responsibility necessary to restrain more antisocial impulses and desires. Yet the privileged, powerful, fair-skinned vampires of recent popular culture frequently remind audiences that uncivilised behaviour is not limited to non-white cultures and races. In a study of more recent vampire fiction, Dale Hudson writes of 'Vampires of Colour' in the context of a 'multicultural whiteness'. Vampire films are described by Hudson in a familiar manner as 'stories of thwarted immigration and failed assimilation',[5] featuring monsters that 'disrupt national and racial certainty' while 'threatening to destabilize the fantasy of national and racial purity'.[6] The multiracial vampire gang of *Blade* (1998, dir. Stephen Norrington) and the Eastern European horde spreading the Reaper strain in the film's sequel (2002, dir. Guillermo del Toro) similarly bespeak the horrors of vampire hybridity, while

True Blood (HBO, 2008–present), explicitly locating the species within contemporary multicultural America, draws parallels between vampires and various minorities Othered along lines of sexuality, race and class. Notwithstanding, the vampire gangs of *Blade* are headed by the heavily Caucasian Deacon Frost, the Reapers are uniformly white in complexion and the minority status of *True Blood*'s vampire community does not seem to impact upon the immense power and privilege enjoyed by the majority of its members.

At the same time as detailing the manner in which the figure has been interpreted racially, Gelder's overview underlines the significatory richness of the vampire.[7] Williamson's study illustrates notable transformations in vampire representations since the publication of Stoker's novel;[8] while Halberstam's exploration of the Gothic monster – a figure that informs much contemporary horror film and television – emphasises its polymorphous nature.[9] Many accounts which read the vampire as a Semitic figure are founded upon specifically historico-political interpretations of *Dracula*, relating the novel's content to anxieties at the time of publication, and signifiers of Semitism (and anti-Semitism) which subsequent screen undeads inherit do not necessarily carry the same meaning as their ancestors. Many of the activities that originally defined the vampire might instead be more associated with a dominant Caucasian identity. Vampires continue to be associated with the sense of invisible sinister figures manipulating events from behind the scenes. But in line with recent conspiracy theories, these are as likely to circulate the machinations of establishment figures who are not Jewish, but profoundly white, Anglo-Saxon and Protestant. The idea of reverse colonisation, predicated on the lack of concrete identity, allowing the vampire to disperse across European national boundaries, has much in common with the figure of the white Western tourist whose globetrotting emerges from a sense of entitlement, racial non-particularity and imperial heritage. The hoarding of capital, lack of national allegiance and financial mobility which circulated Jewish representations, now seems more to define twenty-first-century capitalism, an enterprise characterised by 'stupid white men' who outsource labour, evade taxation and propagate a form of global corporate capitalism, one effect of which is the erasure of national cultural difference.

Clearly, not all of these features are evident in all contemporary vampire narratives, or indeed the *Twilight* films. Nevertheless, many recent screen vampires can be understood as articulating, capitalising upon, and – in many respects – deconstructing the meanings circulating white racial and ethnic identity through the white vampire. While whiteness is in many ways characterised by its invisibility, one consequence of current screen vampires, particularly those placed in contemporary multicultural and multiracial settings, is the rendering of whiteness visible, be it expressed through skin colour, characterisation, cultural preference, or association with the mythic symbols of white identity. In common with many others, the *Twilight* films play on the whiteness of the vampire, consciously or unconsciously, in a manner which suggests the continuing hold of such mythologies, or else the extent to which whiteness is now being understood as a specific identity, rather than a normative position, and a fantastically constructed one at that.

Twilight and the *mise-en-scène* of whiteness

Richard Dyer, in his influential study *White*, considers the vampire as characterising the whiteness of Western horror.[10] In this context, Hudson's claim that changes in the context of the Lugosian tradition led to 'the "whitening" makeup signalling a clown more than a corpse'[11] appears over-dismissive of the racial significance carried by this cosmetic trope. While by no means reducible to physical appearance, skin colour is situated as the primary marker of racial difference – and sameness – and in the context of the *Twilight* series it is hard to ignore just how pale Edward's skin is. Throughout the films, and in publicity stills accompanying their release, Edward's pallor is either devoid of tone, given a bluish tinge or carries an ethereal sheen. In pictures where both Pattinson and Stewart are depicted, his always appears the paler skin. This aesthetic reverses the tradition, expressive of the intersection of visual representations of race with gender, where depictions of heterosexual couples always construct women as fairer in skin colour than men.[12] One paradox of white identity sees the presentation of whiteness as both an unmarked, non-particular, mundane identity, and a special state distinguishing certain people as better than others. In *Twilight*, this contradiction is evident in the pairing of Bella Swan – who jokes that she was kicked out of Arizona for not being tanned enough, and whose name suggests traditional feminine whiteness – and Edward Cullen. Hers is the seemingly unremarkable, grounded, slightly awkward one-bathroom whiteness, in contrast to the whiteness of Edward, a man whose skin sparkles when it comes into contact with sunlight.

One of *Twilight*'s major revisions of horror film mythology is that vampires do not 'dust' when touched by sunlight – a pivotal component of the cinematic vampire's undead ontology – but rather become lit up from within. The moment Edward reveals himself as this angelic glistening figure can be understood in the context of the ongoing synonymous relationship between cinema and the vampire,[13] cinema's 'lighting for whiteness'[14] and affinities between racial whiteness and contemporary vampire film and television such as

Underworld (2003, dir. Len Wiseman), *Daybreakers* (2009, dir. Michael Spierig and Peter Spierig) and *Being Human* (BBC 2008–present).[15] While Edward's sparkling skin represents an extreme example of the visual depiction of whiteness, a more habitual yet no less racialised strategy for representing white characters circulates Edward's adopted vampire family, the Cullens. A notable example of the '*mise en scène* of whiteness'[16] occurs in the scene set in the Forks High School cafeteria, in which the family are first introduced. In this moment the camera moves from Bella and her multicultural group of friends to the five Cullens, a shift that entails a distinct lightening of the palette. First sighted through the white slats of the window blinds, once they enter, against the pale blue of the cafeteria walls and floor, their bleached skin is extenuated by the surroundings and further by their clothing. Emmett, dressed in white trousers, sweater and t-shirt; Rosalie, whose white scarf follows the line of her tumbling blonde hair; Alice, wearing a white cardigan over a white blouse set off by a dark waistcoat; and Jasper, sporting a pale starched shirt with collar up to his chin underneath a white sweater – are all clad in a manner which foregrounds their racial identity as white people. Evident of the slippage between white as a visual presence on the screen, white as a term used to distinguish a racialised group of people and white as a symbol connoting, amongst other things, purity, virtue, transcendence,[17] the lighting, makeup, costumes, cinematography, all resonate a whiteness which serves to associate the Cullens with the tone's racial and symbolic connotations. Jessica's voice which plays over these images casually underlines such meanings while introducing the Cullens to Bella and the audience. Their Alaskan roots, and their preference to keep to themselves – a tendency with clear sexual implications – resonate with mythologies locating Caucasian origins in harsh mountainous territories alongside genealogical narratives constructing the Aryan people as the purest expression of mankind's racial origins.[18] Whiteness is presented as both desirable and superior, Becky remarking of Edward: 'He's totally gorgeous, obviously, but apparently, nobody here's good enough for him.' And whiteness is also strange, a recurring theme of Jessica's narration and an overriding consequence of the ethereal blanched quality of the scene, the manner in which the Cullens are singled out over the other Forks High School students, and the implied incestuousness which this racialised form of 'purity' requires. In the context of white stardom Sean Redmond also discusses a *mise-en-scène* of whiteness, suggesting that in comparable moments, whiteness becomes visible as a paradox of extraordinary/ordinariness, a performance entailing considerable personal or industrial labour or as an entity which entails, amongst other things, 'glow, halo light, and glitter'. Here, 'whiteness "outs" itself as a racial category "made up" in culture' and as a consequence 'potentially opens it up to contestation and critique'.[19] While one aspect of *Twilight*'s disposition towards the whiteness of its characters is a celebration of white beauty and specialness, another consequence of its Caucasian vampires' overdetermined association with whiteness is to make the race strange, one political intention of the critical study of whiteness in popular culture.[20]

Twilight and white privilege

Although white beauty is celebrated across the *Twilight* films in a manner reinforcing ideas of white superiority, the saga also reflects in a fairly uncritical manner, notions of white privilege. This is most clearly evident in the things the Cullens own. Their house is a luxurious abode, contrasting again with the down-to-earth residence of the series' heroine. While subverting the traditional construction of the vampire lair as a dark, underground, malodorous place, Castle Cullen is no less extravagant or palatial. The house's location and Scandinavian aesthetic, full of white walls and well-lit white space, once more connect the Cullens with accounts associating white origins with mountainous Iceland-esque regions of the globe. At the same time, the light that the heroine observes as characterising the Cullens' home continues associations between the vampire family and Dyer's 'culture of light'.[21] Each Cullen owns an expensive car – compared with Bella's clutch-sensitive truck and homemade motorbike – which, in what might be understood as an expression of privileged disregard for speeding laws and the safety of lesser folk, they drive way too fast. The image of Alice motoring through Italy in a convertible, wearing headscarf and dark glasses, recalls a 1950s white glamour synonymous with Monacan royalty, Hitchcockian platinum-blonde heroines and neo-noir ice queens. The Cullens' lifestyle is funded by astute stock market decisions based on Alice's predictions. A kind of supernatural insider trading founded on the privileged information afforded special individuals while denied others, the Cullens exploit this with no evident regard for those who implicitly lose money as a consequence of their informed speculation. In this respect the Cullens are not dissimilar to the capitalist-coded vampires of earlier fiction, Gelder repeatedly referencing Marx's famous reflection on the parasitic nature of capitalism to underline this connection.[22] Indicative of the series' disposition towards its privileged white family, the exploitation of their powers in this manner is represented as an act of smug legitimised superiority.

As Nicholas Michaud notes, the Cullens of *Twilight* – in common with many fictional vampires – are indeed depicted as vastly superior to humans.[23] They are immortal and do not age. They have heightened senses. They are gifted with abilities which allow them to read thoughts, manipulate emotions, predict the future. Edward is 'impossibly fast and strong', a quality possessed by all vampires but particularly pronounced in this one, giving him the impression of being able to fly. The Cullens are able to move through space at remarkable speed, something facilitated by both supernatural abilities and their considerable capital. The ease whereby the Cullens can abandon their mountain-top pad at a moment's notice, jet off to Europe or race through the forest at a breakneck pace has distinct racial and ethnic dimensions. Bella and Edward's honeymoon journey, pausing momentarily to sample with an appreciative yet detached tourist's gaze the generic multiracial colour of Rio nightlife before settling in the family's colonial mansion, underlines the ethnic dimensions of this unparalleled mobility. The vampires' 'exhilaratingly expansive relationship to the environment'[24] can be directly connected with white culture's imperialist history. Expressed in American popular culture in the form of the Western,[25] it is not without reason that infringement of territory so frequently represents the point of conflict between Cullens and Quileute werewolves. Such 'ontological expansiveness', identified by Shannon Sullivan[26] as a habit of white privilege, expresses the sense in which 'white people tend to act and think as if all spaces – whether geographical, physical, linguistic, economic, spiritual, bodily, or otherwise – should be available for them to move in and out of as they wish.'[27] The scene, breathtaking as it is, where Edward leaps through the trees with Bella clinging to his back, might be understood as a pure expression of this impulse. Edward soars triumphantly through the branches towards the sunlight, unhampered by human limitations, environmental consequences or the land rights of others. The sequence culminates in a beautiful panoramic view of the landscape, devoid of humans or the signs of civilisation, a wilderness solely surveyed and claimed by the superior white man and his chosen mate. The scene then transitions to show Edward, at the piano, implying his mastery over the audio as well as the visual elements of the film. Edward's virtuosity as a pianist, like his preference for Debussy, like the Gothic paintings and historical etchings which decorate the Cullens' home, expresses the kinds of cultural capital which contribute to the invisible and weightless knapsack of white privilege.

The association between Edward's skin colour, his status, and the manner in which he is treated within the *Twilight* texts is also suggested by Rebecca Housel. In a spirited defence of Jacob over the vampire rival to Bella's affections, Housel observes: 'Edward is given undeserved consideration; similar to other beautiful "sparkly" people in society, like celebrities, he is forgiven for his transgressions, even rewarded for them.'[28] While the overdetermination of the vampires' white-ness may have the effect of foregrounding, denaturalising and destabilising this usually unmarked identity, the series is largely supportive of the entitle-ment whiteness bestows. The films' clearest justification of white privilege and authority resides in the characterisation of Dr Carlisle Cullen. Introduced in the hospital scene immediately following Bella's rescue by her pale-faced suitor – nearly crushed to death by a big black car driven by a big black student – Carlisle's depiction constitutes another remarkable example of the whitening of the Cullen clan. Like his adopted family, the whiteness of Carlisle's pale skin and blond slicked-back hair are extenuated by his costume and surroundings. The white doctor's coat and hospital walls are, more clearly than the casual clothing and high school cafeteria of his children, aligned with white science, power and authority. The benevolent white patriarch is positioned as natural wielder of that authority, and shown to exercise it with absolute benignity. As such, Dr Cullen represents an expression of the extent to which 'white science is highly prized and, more often than not, valorised, especially if it is combined with humanist tendencies', absent from which are the counter-discourses which posit a hyper-white science as a destructive force within fantasy cinema.[29]

Such hyper-whiteness is reserved for the Volturi, who, audiences are informed, have no respect for human life, only art, science and the law. A ritual-bound aristocratic organisation, in contrast with the relaxed modern democracy of the Cullen household, the hierarchical vampire elders represent an older, more elitist class-based notion of whiteness, pre-dating the racialisation of the term and its expansion to the newly enfranchised, newly enbourgeoisied citizens of colonising nations. Within the *Twilight* universe, the Volturi serve to distin-guish the Cullens' supposed benign exercise of power from the self-serving cruelty, corruption and violence which is the dark heritage and foundation of white privilege.

Twilight and absence, denial, death

While whiteness is an identity repeatedly associated with positive qualities such as virtue, cleanliness, health and innocence, Dyer also notes the darker side of whiteness connoting 'emptiness, absence, denial or even a kind of death'.[30] *Twilight*, as many commentators have observed, is an abstinence tale, its teen characters perpetually repressing their carnal desires to consume one another, sexually or bodily, and this has particular pertinence to academic understand-ings of racial whiteness. As Dyer observes, a fundamental aspect of white identity – evident in religious, genealogical and imperial discourses – is the requirement to control, suppress and sublimate one's physical desires in an attempt to 'master and transcend the white body'[31] and thereby rise above more physically bounded baser races. George A. Dunn's observation that Edward's first encounter with Bella tests 'that gentlemanly self-restraint he's worked so long and hard to cultivate'[32] suggests the extent to which her physical proximity challenges codes of male behaviour embedded in particular formations of white heterosexual masculinity, requiring a flight to Alaska, a cold, mountainous region where Edward can restore his glacial sense of white manhood. The inhuman effort required to resist Bella's body is repeatedly emphasised: in Edward's reference to Bella as his own personal brand of heroin, an analogy which implies the deadly nature of their interaction while connoting a physical addiction necessitating considerable mental resolve to overcome; in the perseverance with which she is perused first by James, then by Victoria, then by the entire Newborn Army; in the actions of Jasper, driven to a frenzy by the smell of her paper cut. Audiences are told of the phenomenal self-control exercised by Carlisle – the exemplary representative of white masculinity – in turning Edward rather than drinking him dry, and such knowledge underlines the extent to which the younger vampire controls his baser instincts and urges.

The heterosexual romance of *The Twilight Saga* frequently evokes the fairytale whiteness Chrys Ingraham[33] observes in wedding culture, captured in the scene beneath the illuminated gazebo where the couple dance at Bella's Monte Carlo-themed prom, in images of the couple lying together in meadows filled with pale flowers, in the snow-covered mountain where Bella and Edward camp in anticipation of the approaching vampire army, in the moonlit water where the couple finally come together. 'Old school' Edward's insistence on marriage as the culmination of their relationship is indicative of his investment in certain romantic conventions, exemplified in the virginal white bride in her white bridal gown surrounded by the white imagery which pervades the wedding industry. The couple's wedding is characterised by the aesthetic of whiteness which has defined their courtship: Bella's white shoes and white dress, white fairy lights and white cake, surround and racially define the white couple at the centre. At the same time the contradictory sexlessness of white racial identity[34] suffuses the series' romance with yearning, angst and anxiety, accompanied by a sense of loss and absence. Whiteness as absence is discussed by Garner[35] – as a racial identity unmarked as racial, as a presence rendered invisible through saturation, in white hegemony's eradicating process of naturalisation, through the evaporation of white identity in discourses of individualism. The theme of absence echoes throughout the series. Following their first meeting, Edward is unaccountably absent for days, and when they are together, their relationship is notable for the lack of what defines a heterosexual coupling. For much of the second film Edward only registers as a ghostly vapour, his absence so profoundly felt it makes Bella wake up screaming. The melancholy heroine sitting immobile by the window as the months pass by and Lykke Li sings 'all that I had was all I'm gon' get' suggests – in addition to a form of white femininity founded on passivity[36] – a mode of white heterosexuality rooted in immobility, non-corporeality and unsatisfied desires. This white disposition towards sexuality even inflects upon Jacob's relationship with Bella and those of the werewolf pack, the contrasting dangers of losing control evident in the scarred face of Sam's girl-friend Emily. As Dyer suggests, whiteness can characterise a text in terms of its formal arrangement and perspective towards its subject matter,[37] and here the whiteness of *The Twilight Saga* – not as a series of stereotypes, but rather 'narrative structural positions, rhetorical tropes and habits of perception'[38] – extends beyond the ethnicity of its Caucasian cast, incorporating non-white characters and relationships, just as it informs the films' pale aesthetic, cold mountainous locations and indie rock soundtrack.

Unsurprising for a vampire narrative, death is also a recurring theme of the *Twilight* films. Death is foregrounded in the opening line of the first film where Bella muses about dying for someone she loves, in Bella's dream at the beginning of the second, where she misrecognises her grandmother in her own aged reflection and in the Robert Frost poem which opens the third, weighing up the options of dying by either ice or fire. Not only are the vampires dead, but their immortality emphasises for Bella the fact that she is herself dying, the solution being for her to die at Edward's hand and become undead like him. Deadly pallor is a central visual component of the cinematic vampire, and associations between Edward's body and that of a corpse are evident in repeated reference to his skin as 'pale white and ice cold'. Edward's own self-hating description of his skin as 'the skin of a killer' recalls Dyer's observations about white people as both dead and the agents of death to others.[39] Bella soliloquises that death is what brought her to Edward, and later finds that bouts of 'life-threatening idiocy' – motorbike racing, cliff diving – serve briefly to return him to her, even in a ghostly disembodied form. Death is never far from Edward and Bella's relationship, evident in the zombie worms discussed in the biology class where they first meet, the story of *Romeo and Juliet* which frames the second movie and foreshadows the death of the romantic couple, averted with only seconds to spare, and in the spectre of Bella's turning, which hangs over part three like a pall, the 'darkness' of which is spurned in favour of remaining in the 'light'. As Redmond discusses in relation to another fantasy film adaptation, the white light which characterises white identity can also have an eradicating quality.[40] The purity of whiteness, its triumph over the body, at its extreme, constitutes a kind of physical annihilation evident in the scene where Edward threatens to expose himself at the San Marcos Day celebration before a crowd of anti-vampire festival goers. Assuming a Christ-like pose, the sunlight against his skin threatens to destroy him as surely as it would within a more traditional vampire narrative.

Such ambivalent images illustrate the extent to which negative dimensions of whiteness – as a racial identity, as a tone, as a polysemic symbol – encroach even upon texts which largely celebrate racial whiteness and much of what it signifies. The paradoxical association between whiteness and heterosexual romance and whiteness and death is most clearly underlined in Rosalie's rape revenge narrative, which culminates in her 'melodramatic' arrival to murder her rapist ringleader, dressed in full bridal gown. Bella's pre-wedding anxiety dream reveals a similar slippage between these two aspects of whiteness. A parody of the white wedding, in which not just the bride but every guest is dressed in unreal white, the scene shifts dramatically in tone as the camera pulls back to reveal bride and groom stood on a pile of bloodstained white bodies. Something of white sex as queer sex[41] – a consequence of white identity's problematic relationship with the body, sense of reproductive inadequacy and anxiety that other more physical races might do it better – is also, perversely, evident throughout the series, even as *Twilight* seems to embody a staunchly conservative brand of heteronormativity. There is something 'unnatural' about the relentless denial that informs the series' white protagonists' relationship. Theirs is a sexuality which is not allowed to express itself in the 'normal' way: Bella's hysterical dreams and hallucinations during Edward's absence bear testimony to the crippling consequences of this enforced celibacy. When their relationship is finally consummated, the destruction of the marital bed and the bruises Bella finds on her skin, even as the white feathers of her popped virginity settle around her body, suggest a BDSM experience comparable to the bolder housewrecking scene between Buffy and Spike. The love triangle of *Twilight* is, in the crudest sense, one of necrophilia and bestiality, and further, the scene where, under the pretext of saving her life, Jacob climbs into Bella's sleeping bag while Edward watches is by no means free of kinky overtones. While Dyer's assertion that vampires cannot reproduce[42] is not borne out by the events of *Breaking Dawn*, there is something undeniably white about the unconsummated, non-sexual, deadly, slightly perverted relationship between vampire and human, just as the vampire itself crystallises many meanings of white identity itself.

Notes

1. Ken Gelder, *Reading the Vampire* (London: Routledge, 1994).

2. Bram Stoker, *Dracula* (Westminster: Constable & Co, 1897).

3. Judith Halberstam, *Skin Shows: Gothic Horror and the Technology of Monsters* (London: Duke University Press, 2006), pp. 92–3.

4. Milly Williamson, *The Lure of the Vampire: Gender, Fiction and Fandom from Bram Stoker to Buffy* (London: Wallflower, 2005), p. 20.

5. Dale Hudson, 'Vampires of Colour and the Performance of Multicultural Whiteness', in Daniel Bernardi (ed.), *The Persistence of Whiteness: Race and Contemporary Hollywood Cinema* (London: Routledge, 2008), p. 127.

6. Ibid., p. 129.

7. Gelder, *Reading the Vampire*.

8. Williamson, *The Lure of the Vampire*.

9. Halberstam, *Skin Shows*.

10. Richard Dyer, *White* (London: Routledge, 1997), p. 210.

11. Hudson, 'Vampires of Colour', p. 128.

12. Dyer, *White*, pp. 132–33.

13. Stacey Abbott, *Celluloid Vampires: Life After Death in the Modern World* (Austin: University of Texas Press, 2007).

14. Dyer, *White*.

15. Ewan Kirkland, 'Whiteness, Vampires and Humanity in Contemporary Film and Television', in Deborah Mutch (ed.), *The Modern Vampire and Human Identity* (forthcoming).

16. Ewan Kirkland, 'Dexter and Whiteness', in Richard Greene, George Reisch and Rachel Robison-Greene (eds), *Dexter and Philosophy: Mind Over Splatter* (Chicago: Open Court Publishing Company, 2011), pp. 215–6.

17. Dyer, *White*, pp. 45–6.

18. Ibid., p. 22.

19. Sean Redmond, 'The Whiteness of Stars: Looking at Kate Winslet's Unruly White Body', in Sean Redmond and Su Holmes (eds), *Stardom and Celebrity: A Reader* (London: Sage, 2007), p. 267.

20. Dyer, *White*, p. 10.

21. Ibid.

22. Gelder, *Reading the Vampire*.

23. Nicolas Michaud, 'Can a Vampire Be a Person?', in Rebecca Housel and J. Jeremy Wisnewski (eds), *Twilight and Philosophy: Vampires, Vegetarians, and the Pursuit of Immortality* (Hoboken: John Wiley & Sons, 2009), p. 40.

24. Dyer, *White*, p. 15.

25. Ibid., p. 32.

26. Shannon Sullivan, *Revealing Whiteness: The Unconscious Habits of Racial Privilege,* (Bloomington: Indiana University Press, 2006).

27. Ibid., p. 10.

28. Rebecca Housel, 'The Tao of Jacob', in Housel and Wisnewski, *Twilight and Philosophy*, p. 241.

29. Sean Redmond, 'The Science Fiction of Whiteness', *Scope: An Online Journal of Film and TV Studies* 6 (2006), http://www.scope.nottingham.ac.uk/article.php?issue=6&id=184 (accessed 6 June 2011).

30. Richard Dyer, *The Matter of Images: Essays on Representations* (London: Routledge, 1993), p. 141.

31. Dyer, *White*, p. 23.

32. George A. Dunn, 'You Look Good Enough to Eat: Love, Madness, and the Food Analogy', in Housel and Wisnewski, *Twilight and Philosophy*, p. 7.

33. Chrys Ingraham, *White Weddings: Romancing Heterosexuality in Popular Culture* (London: Routledge, 1999).

34. Dyer, *White*, p. 27.

35. Steve Garner, *Whiteness: An Introduction* (Abingdon: Routledge, 2007).

36. Dyer, *White*.

37. Ibid., p. 39.

38. Ibid., p. 12.

39. Ibid., p. 208.

40. Sean Redmond, 'The Whiteness of the *Rings*', in Daniel Bernardi (ed.), *The Persistence of Whiteness: Race and Contemporary Hollywood Cinema* (London: Routledge, 2008), pp. 91–101.

41. Dyer, *White*, p. 220.

42. Ibid., p. 215.

13

SCENT, SIBLINGS AND THE FILIAL: QUEERING *TWILIGHT*

R. Justin Hunt

When I first watched *Twilight* (2008, dir. Catherine Hardwicke), I was struck by two things, both by way of introductions:[1] Bella's smell and the Cullens' performance of family. While seemingly very different structures, their inter-relatedness in and through the bodies of Bella and Jacob create an interesting choreography of boundary marking, and boundary breaking, that provokes a sense of the queerness of *Twilight*'s characters. This chapter will argue that notions of kinship in *The Twilight Saga* are markedly queer. This queerness is exposed in and through smelly tracing of bodies which cross into and out of various social circles, thus disturbing simple identificatory boundaries. Knowing who fits where, and how those desired relationships come into practice, is a complex, and potentially queer, relationship to the body's smell.

In the first film, Bella and Edward 'meet' in their biology class and what transpires is a sensuous miscommunication of desire. Bella's desire to know Edward is thwarted by his apparent disgust at her smell. As a fan blows her hair in Edward's direction, he violently covers his mouth, appearing to retch at her scent. Her shame response – shrinking and smell-checking her clothing and body – is in opposition to what we find out later is Edward's automatic response to her scent, something he describes as 'his own personal brand of heroin'. Bella's scent, as we will see, is perhaps her most notable capacity for Othering (or, in other words, for delineating a unique identity position within an already convoluted structure of identification) in the cosmology of *The Twilight Saga*. It is in and through her scent that the boundaries between worlds, both monstrous and sexual, become blurred. I will return to the issue of scent after first considering the family structure of the Cullen clan.

Just one scene before this, Bella has been introduced by her new classmates to the Cullen 'children'.

Bella: Who are they?
Angela: The Cullens.
Jessica: They're, um, Dr and Mrs Cullen's foster kids. They moved down here from Alaska, like, a few years ago.
Angela: They kinda keep to themselves.
Jessica: Yeah 'cause they're all together, like TOGETHER together. Uh, the blonde girl, that's Rosalie, and the big dark-haired guy, Emmett, they're like a thing. I'm not even sure that's legal.
Angela: Jess, they're not actually related.
Jessica: Yeah, but they live together. It's weird ...

Jessica's aside, 'It's weird', doubly marks the Cullens as identifiably Other (in that they 'keep to themselves') but also sexually obtuse within normative heterosexual couplings. The Cullens, it would seem, perform family, badly. Their structure as a family is perverted, in the eyes of Jessica at least, because they are a family of seemingly sexually active sibling couples. As a family of vampires they are further at odds with normative structures, within the cosmology of *Twilight*, in that they are 'vegetarian', eating only animals and not humans. Further, their entry into this family is by filial choice rather than reproductive chance. Becoming a son or daughter of Dr Cullen means joining a structure of relation where, while performing normative heterosexual binaries, they are thwarting (easily) identifiable kinship structures within the social.

The pioneering work of Kath Weston in *Families We Choose: Lesbians, Gays, Kinship*[2] has already charted a course, now being ever re-tooled, to consider 'families of choice'. In her study, lesbian and gay bodies were shown to be resisting 'procreative assumptions' of family and confirming new types of affective relationships. Those bodies that do not find space within normative strictures of heterosexual couples were promoting various forms of relationality. Judith Butler's evocative response to the question of kinship, in her 'Is Kinship Always Already Heterosexual?'[3] argues for a critical engagement with kinship structures which resist seeing *any* such structure as normative. Kinship structures, for Butler, are 'forms of human dependency, which may include birth, child-rearing, relations of emotional dependency and support, generational ties, illness, dying and death'.[4] Butler argues to queer our assumptions about any such set of relational practices. To queer kinship is also to offer a queer kinship, as, in the words of Sara Ahmed, 'queer does not have a relation to exteriority to that with which it comes in contact.'[5] In other words I am not attempting to argue that *Twilight* or its characters are queer, *per se*, but that their identifications might disturb normative conventions, thus highlighting the obtuseness of normative boundary structures.

One such structure the Cullens subvert in particular is that of the sibling. Their chosen partner becomes their sibling life-partner. This subversion, while potentially always already queer, is not unique or outside of (legal) normative familial relationality. In fact, the Cullens' employment of 'in-lawing' as a mode of passing for and as family/lovers is well-known historical practice. Their subversion of the sibling structure is actually a move to thwart the ideologies of the heterosexual family.

Holly Furneaux, in her article on families of choice within the work of Dickens, opens up the Victorian family, on which so much cultural pressure has been realised as a model of the nuclear (heterosexual) family. Quoting Laurence Stone, she offers that the 'new family [carried] a much greater load of emotional and sexual commitment. It was more ... conjugal and less kin and community oriented ... more private and less public.'[6] The family, and its home, was often a site of a number of non-blood-related members acting to maintain the group. Affairs of the heart crossing generational or same-sex lines found purchase through the practice of in-lawing, whereby a brother or sister married the love object of their sibling so as to make siblings-in-law. This new sibling/partner became a legal member of the family. Without the social sanction (in-lawing) the sibling/partner could never be so proximate or intimate to the new family and the body it desires. As Furneaux argues, the queerness of this construction (and the queerness of Dickens and his rendering of these structures) is the 'possible congruity of the opposite-sex and same-sex desire *within* marriage and family'.[7] The legal/familial sanctioning of sibling-love profits an unhinging of any normative notion of 'family'. As Simon Bacon, in his chapter in this collection, offers, this performance of family 'reveals how meaningless [a] particular society's construction of identity really is'. Both Bacon and I are interested as to the resultant unravelling of upheld norms because of the Cullens' efficacious performance of 'family'. I, however, do not see the Cullens' staging any notion of perfection as a means to enlighten the ideological burden of the nuclear family, but simply profiting from a system already well (and queerly) established.

The Cullen kinship, however, is queer, not simply because it stages heterosexual couples as the incestuous brother/sister but because it requires of its participants active choices in relation to living and (un)dying, together, contra to the normative strictures of their subcultural sect. Bella's desire to kin with the (un)dead, is also queer and, as we will see, her scent marks this abject wish – destabilising boundaries between the living and the (un)dead. And, importantly, it is Bella's traceable crossing – the smells she carries back and forth – which unmask the complexly queer relations operating within Forks.

The Cullens' kinship is based on choice. Queerly, it destabilises the homogenising force of the metaphors that filiality and vampirism offer. Vampirism is often read as a move to make same, a sameness through a living death.[8] The same is also true of typical narratives of the lycan. The lycan, or werewolf, is seen as a contagious becoming-wolf that infects, replicating itself, tortuously. Werewolves in *Twilight* are not infected, but born.[9] The monstrous becoming is a generational 'gift'. Interestingly, both the pack of werewolves (born not chosen) and the clan of Cullens (chosen not born) utilise a filial system of kinship to describe and perform their sociality. The Quileute werewolves are born into a siblinghood through a blood relation to an ancient Native American past. The 'brothers', in their telepathic connections and aggressive response behaviour, stage a certain, racialised homogeneity. In fact, their pack purpose – to eradicate all vampires (save the Cullen clan) – enacts a fraternal fascism promoting clean lines of generationality within heteronormative reproductive cultures. Or, put another way, their brotherhood keeps the human bloodlines safe to reproduce normatively. The racialisation of these two similarly named yet differently enacted kinship structures is radically important, in order to consider the politics of such connections and crossings.[10]

The only body capable of addressing these filial structures, at least in the first three films in the saga, is Bella. Bella re-enters Forks as the desirous abject. Put another way: she arrives as a once-member now Other. The straight (human) boys want to be her boyfriend; the straight (human) girls want to be her friend. Jacob desires her, and his pack accepts her instantly (even if she is the 'vampire girl'). Edward desires her, but so do his family, and every other vampire she meets.

Her boundary crossing wouldn't be as remarkable if it weren't for its ability to be somatically tracked. It is scent which operates to mark her boundary crossing. When Edward brings Bella home to meet his family, already having 'outed' them in various contexts, the entire clan smells her before she enters the room. The first battle we witness is over the intoxicating smell of Bella, who cannot hide her difference within the clan because she is so odorous. Her near death in the first instalment as a result of vampire James' 'game of scent' is one of many moments when Bella's penetration of kinship structures is directly mapped onto her smell. James senses her difference from the clan by smelling her intoxicating blood. He is able to track her by her scent. The Cullens attempt to throw him off by using her clothing to lead him in the wrong direction, but this is thwarted. She cannot simply disappear into the Cullens' life because her scent obtrusively presents her body as Other.

Later, especially in the second and third films, when Bella's crossings between vampire and werewolf kinship groups are more constant, the ghostly traces of other smells linger with her. Alice remarks in film two, 'What is that godawful wet dog smell?' (*The Twilight Saga: New Moon*, 2010, dir. Wietz). Bella, having just been saved from drowning by Jacob, reeks of something other than the too-enticing blood which inspires Alice to flee when she bleeds – nearly thwarting Alice's vegetarianism. Bella's safety is compromised by her queer scent, too strong, too different, too enticing. The wolves, also, smell the vampires on her. Of course, in this way, the smell also acts as protection: the wolves' ability to smell the vampire Victoria is the only way in which they can keep Bella safe.

'The sense of smell implies a negation of corporal boundaries,' notes Marc Weiner in a paper on smell and ideology.[11] While in the context of Wagnerian narratives of desire, his analysis can help flesh out certain relationships, potentially rather queer, between smell and the body in the films, he goes on to note that 'in the act of olfactory perception, limitations of bodily and temporal identity momentarily give way, shifting the subject into a state which suggests suprapersonal communication.'[12] The haunting dialogue of Bella's scent – a siren song and calling card of past transgressions – tells the story of where she is and has been, and where she is going. These smells carry specific meanings. Weiner notes that romance accompanied by enticing fragrance is often understood as indicating incestuous relationships – relationships that blur sibling boundaries.[13] Kinship in this way smells even sweeter. Bella as sister/lover to Edward isn't simply desired by his male brother/lover body but also their sisters' and parents'. The boundaries imposed culturally by their bodies are broken down. As I have been arguing, one way in which we see this boundary dissolution is through queerly enticing scent. Or, this smell thwarts desire in the case of Bella's mixing from the clan to the pack and back again. The forbidden smells wonderful but the wonderful can be seductively offensive. Odour is attached to sexuality and, as in Weiner's reading of Wagner, racial boundary crossing. In his reading the mixing of German and Jewish bodies is at odds with nationalistic mandates. In *The Twilight Saga* the racialised tensions created between wolf and vampire, in relation to the human, become even more complicated by the marriage of Bella and Edward and their resultant child.[14]

Their marriage features an interesting moment of near in-lawing and features another important boundary crossing marked by smell. In *The Twilight Saga: Breaking Dawn – Part 1* (2011, dir. Condon) Jacob leaves his pack to join Bella and the vampires. In doing so he breaks his brotherly telepathic bond and is reduced to sensing the movements between pack and clan via his heightened werewolf sense of smell. Jacob's double boundary crossing, leaving the pack and falling in love with a vampire, creates in Butler's terms an unthinkable exception to the (normative) sexual politics of Forks. Bella interpolates Jacob into the Cullens' queer kinship when she notes that with him present the family – the nuclear family of Edward, Bella and future baby – is complete. This near in-lawing of Jacob as brother/son/lover moves him to note that the Cullens are a (real) family. Jacob is not really able to join this family (save, perhaps, in the most grotesque extension as the family 'dog') until the birth of Edward and Bella's daughter. Upon seeing her, Jacob 'imprints' (a Meyer-specific lycan process of life-partnering) onto the baby, seeing a glimpse of her and *their* future. It is at this moment, once he is able to discern his partnership as son-in-law and brother (to the vampires), that he is able to fully incorporate himself into the clan. His movement out of the pack is one from sameness to difference, from normativity to a constant disruption of social boundaries.

The structures of filiality and siblinghood deployed in these films queer for us notions of normative boundaries. Neither Bella nor Jacob are queer, *per se*, but the various social groups through which their bodies move, and the olfactory traces thereof, disturb the normative permutations of sex, desire and race within the cosmology of *Twilight*. The figure of her child offers yet another queer complexity to unpack, within the sociology of *The Twilight Saga*. Not simply its future relationship with Jacob, but its status *as* an undead future, a product of the incestuous sibling union of Bella and Edward.

Notes

1. Bella's own introduction, via voice-over, to herself and the first film is queerly interesting as well. Her first lines, 'I'd never given much thought to how I would die … But dying in the place of someone I love seems like a good way to go', identify her as already dead before the movie begins. Narratively we are watching her undead origin story. Bella is dead to the social sphere of Forks and the narrative space of *The Twilight Saga* always and already. Her desire to cast out of the living social is queerly transfixed for us in this foreshadowing to her undead transformation in *Breaking Dawn – Part 1*, when she will have died to live forever with her new family unit. Queerly, Bella's

decision to carry an (un)dead child creates a new critical space to consider the sexual politics of what Lee Edelman (*No Future: Queer Theory and the Death Drive* (London: Duke University Press, 2004)) has called reproductive futurism, a cultural obsession with the figure of the child to politically promote the futurity of cultural epistemologies. Bella's child will not 'live' as much as it will live *forever*. The future of this child is limitless. It does not carry with it the Oedipal complexities of normative reproductive futurism. In such a triangulation, the product of a heterosexual union is bound to carry and transmit history as inherited (from the law of the Father) by its birth and eventual death (so that its future children can also inherit). Instead it demarcates a rupture in the cultural narrative, as being always already undead, abject and for those reasons entirely queer. For further consideration see ibid. and Peggy Phelan, *Mourning Sex: Performing Public Memories* (London: Routledge, 1997).

2. Kath Weston, *Families We Choose: Lesbians, Gays, Kinship* (New York: Columbia University Press, 1991).
3. Judith Butler, 'Is Kinship Always Already Heterosexual?', *differences* 13/1 (2002), pp. 14–44.
4. Ibid., p. 15.
5. Sara Ahmed, *Queer Phenomenology* (London: Duke University Press, 2006), p. 4.
6. Laurence Stone in Holly Furneaux, 'Charles Dickens's Families of Choice: Elective Affinities, Sibling Substitution, and Homoerotic Desire', *Nineteenth-Century Literature* 62/2 (2007), p. 156.
7. Ibid., p. 157.
8. See, for example, William Haver, '*Homo homini lupus*', *Issues in Contemporary Culture and Aesthetics* 13–5 (Spring 2005), pp. 67–72.
9. For more relating to the functioning of these myths see Caroline Ruddell's chapter in this collection, 'The Lore of the Wild'. Her article explores in more detail the structure of the vampire and werewolf myths and how they operate within *Twilight*.
10. Ewan Kirkland's brilliant contribution in this collection, 'Racial Whiteness and *Twilight*', unpacks the complicated racial constructions that *The Twilight Saga* utilises and unmasks within contemporary American culture. His consideration of generationality (in his final section '*Twilight* and absence, denial, death') is a much more nuanced extension of thoughts I am only gesturing towards in this chapter.
11. Marc A. Weiner, 'Wagner's Nose and the Ideology of Perception', *Monatshefte* 81/1 (1989), p. 66.
12. Ibid.
13. Ibid., pp. 72–5.
14. Again, see Kirkland.

PART 5

SLASH AND BURN:
DEVIATING FANDOM AND
REWRITING THE TEXT

14

DEFANGING THE VAMPIRE: PROJECTED INTERACTIVITY AND ALL HUMAN *TWILIGHT* FAN-FIC

Brigid Cherry

The figure of the vampire in popular film and fiction has rarely been entirely monstrous. He – or indeed she, though popular culture has much more frequently portrayed a male vampire and female victim dynamic, as does *Twilight* (2008, dir. Catherine Hardwicke) – is the most human of monsters, possessing the qualities of the cultured and sophisticated gentleman and able – in the main – to pass unnoticed amongst the living. Roger Dadoun[1] may have described him as a walking phallus, fanged and predatory, but he is more likely to (also) be attractive, sensual and desirably dangerous – a Byronic figure who appeals as much as he repels. As Dracula, Bela Lugosi was a heart throb of the classic Hollywood horror film (*Dracula*, 1931, dir. Tod Browning) and indeed since Christopher Lee in Hammer's *Dracula* (1958, dir. Terence Fisher) the vampire has become increasingly erotic. Silver and Ursini have mapped the trajectory of the vampire on film,[2] recording his transition from monster to sympathetic hero. The increasingly romantic and erotic appeals associated with this trajectory of the cinematic vampire have provided substantial viewing pleasures for the female audience.[3] However, the appeal of the vampire has meant that this particular monstrous figure has transcended the confines of the horror genre and mutated into a form that threatens, in examples of paranormal romance, to become not only bloodless but purely romantic.

The popularity of paranormal romance represented by the *Twilight* novels and films, as well as other series such *The Vampire Diaries* (The CW, 2009–present) and *The Southern Vampire Mysteries* (Charlaine Harris)/*True Blood* (HBO, 2008–present), suggests a shift in the vampire genre away from Gothic horror and towards a more traditional Harlequin/Mills and Boon-style romantic fiction (a transformation that Judith Kohlenberger also explores earlier in this collection). Whilst not unproblematic – and certainly not straightforward, since at the same time horror cinema has encompassed a more violent and monstrous form of the vampire in films such as *30 Days of Night* (2007, dir. David Slade) and *Let The Right One In* (2008, dir. Thomas Alfredson) – this shift represents interesting developments in vampire audiences and fandom. In one sense, the vampire has always been an attractive and sexually appealing monster. However, the taming and domestication of the vampire that *Twilight* represents moves the vampire into the world of the everyday, making the genre more palatable for a wider – and younger – audience than that typically associated with horror, Gothic or vampire cinema.

This chapter explores this generic shift via a study of the *Twilight* fan audience, specifically focusing on fan production and the fan fiction community. The findings discussed here are part of a wider study of female fan production and feminine handicrafting.[4] In this larger study, feminine handicrafting intersects with *Twilight* fan fiction writing in a number of ways. Primarily these include the knitting and crafting of *Twilight* clothing and accessories, the dyeing of yarn in colourways inspired by fan fiction and the adoption of *Twilight* personae in the online handicrafting community. The findings discussed below do not draw on fan producerly activities in terms of knitting, dyeing and other handicrafting, but on other examples of fan fiction looked at during that study. The analysis is focused on the fan writers of the chosen examples, drawing on their fan fiction and interviews conducted with them. Two fan fiction writers are interviewed in depth for this research: kyla713 (K713) and theladyingrey (LG42), who have written various AH fics published on fanfiction.net. What makes *Twilight* such an interesting text to address in this respect is the removal of the remaining generic elements of the vampire film. In making the characters wholly human with the removal of any remaining traits of vampirism, the central relationship between Bella and Edward is reconfigured, and for some fans this intensifies the interactive relationships they develop with these characters. This consideration of projected interactivity within *Twilight* fan-fic characters highlights the communication and agency taking place within the text, the fan community and the fan fiction.

This account of *Twilight* fan fiction writing thus focuses on one key genre, this 'all human' fic (termed AH by the fans). AH is one of the most predominant forms of *Twilight* fan fiction production and this rewriting of the paranormal characters who are vampires and werewolves in the originating text as human can be analysed in order to reveal the ways in which fans take meaning and pleasure from the text. The combination of analysis of fan fiction and interviews with fan fiction writers also permits exploration of this fan community (and possibly the wider audience segment) and its interest in romance at the expense of the paranormal. Drawing on a model of projected interactivity,[5] the focus is on the way fans interact with characters in the *Twilight* text. In order to understand the complicated identity play occurring in the AH fan-fic community, such an analysis examines what these fan activities reveal about the fan identities that are present. Davisson and Booth suggest that, in order to understand the complicated identity play occurring in online fan cultures, 'one needs to conceive of the three identities that are present in the activities [of fans] – the fan, the character, the community.'[6] Fan fiction gives the writer control over these identities through their play with the character's traits, actions and environment in their own writing. In this way the fan brings the projected identity expressed in the characters in their fan fiction close to their own identity as well as aspects of the communities they belong to privilege. Exploring the ways in which fans communicate and interact with characters through the analysis of fan fiction, in combination with textual analysis and empirical studies of the fandom, contributes to a deeper understanding of fan activities in general and the *Twilight* community specifically.

The *Twilight* films offer the pleasures of romance fiction (as do the novels before them). In researching the *Twilight* fan community it is hard to distinguish between the films and the novels since the members of the communities frequently consume both and consider themselves fans of both. The fans themselves do not always distinguish between the films and the novels when they talk about *Twilight*, and their fan fiction may be based on the characters as represented in either or both media. None the less, analysis of *Twilight* fans and fan fiction writing can explore the complex negotiations of character and identification that take place across multiple platforms, these including fan fiction as well as the novels and the films and other adaptations based on them. As 'archontic literature'[7] which consciously positions itself in relation to variations of the text (and the *Twilight* films can be considered as part of the archive of the *Twilight* text, as to some extent can the later additions to the novel series), *Twilight* fan-fic 'allows, or even invites, writers to enter it, select specific items they find useful, making new artifacts using those found objects, and deposit the newly made work back into the source text's archive'.[8] The *Twilight* fans (whether readers or viewers or both) are thus actively encouraged to create texts that expand the archive.

In terms of projected interactivity, such archontic writing takes characters created elsewhere and places them in new situations or gives them new experiences, and may even rework storyworlds to suit the intentions of the fan fiction writer. Fan fiction can mirror narrative features of the original text or create entirely new narrative scenarios or worlds, and while the roster of characters usually remains relatively stable, they may be substantially rewritten in order to explore different options whilst remaining recognisable. Derecho argues that archontic writing, since it is produced by female fans who are traditionally disempowered, is able to subvert dominant ideologies.[9] Davisson and Booth's model of projected interactivity offers a potentially productive means of analysing the ways in which archontic literature enables fans to subvert (or at least play with) the meanings and subtexts of mainstream culture. Davisson and Booth base their model on James Gee's account of the relationship between characters in a video game and the player of the game, which he calls 'projective identity'.[10] Whilst identification with film characters might not be expected to resemble the interaction with virtual characters by video gamers, the ways in which fan fiction writers develop intense relationships with characters – and indeed interact with them in writing fan fiction – has clear parallels. As Davisson and Booth state: 'fans develop a relationship to the characters about which they write. This activity is an articulation of both the desires of the fans and the fan's perception of the character's desires.'[11]

In *Twilight*, for example, the fan writers frequently perceive the desires of the characters Bella and Edward as being primarily, even solely, focused on each other. This is a trope of conventional romance fiction. This contrasts with the vampire genre, where such desires might include the lust for blood, the desire to become a vampire and thus immortal or to destroy the monster, even where these are bound up with sexual desire. It is therefore hardly surprising that writers of AH fan fiction articulate and exaggerate their perceptions of the characters' romantic activities and expunge the remaining vestiges of vampirism from the text. The seemingly curious transformation of genre taking place in one of the most predominant forms of *Twilight* fan fiction in this sense seems meaningful. Identities thus encompass the fan writers' explorations of love, relationships and family, and the reworking of characters from the novels and films in terms of romance fantasies.

The concept of AH fan fiction is also interesting in that it seems at odds with the appeals of the paranormal romance, namely that a vampire is an intriguing, mysterious lover who offers a frisson of danger and is far more interesting than a human boyfriend might be. Stripping out what makes the character unique might seem at odds with the popularity of *Twilight* in general and Edward in particular. Fan fiction is of course produced for other fans, moreover for fellow fans within a specific fan community. AH *Twilight* fan fiction is an example of a specific sub-genre arising and spreading amongst a subset of fans and being disseminated quickly through social networking, internet archives of fan fiction and fan forums (particularly www.twilighted. net in this instance). *Twilight* fans themselves do not always at first realise that AH fic exists and do not necessarily go looking for it as a distinct sub-genre, but might come across it very easily when searching for *Twilight* fan fiction in general. LG42 says that: 'When I finished reading the books, I did an internet search, looking for more about the series. I discovered an AH fic called *Wide Awake*. At first I found it terribly confusing; Phil was a bad guy, Renee was dead, Edward was trying not to sleep? Once I got my head wrapped around the concept, though, I was hooked.' K713 says that 'I was one of those people who could not understand the appeal of AH fics at first when I was told [about it] after reading the books and going to fanfiction … because I was less than happy about how the series ended.' But her 'initiation' into AH resembles Bacon-Smith's account of the female *Star Trek* fan community in the days long before the internet made fan fiction accessible to anyone,[12] when word-of-mouth brought others into knowledge of slash fiction. K713 goes on to say that: 'Someone told me that AH was actually more interesting at times than AU,[13] and being someone to try anything once, I gave it a shot.' It also indicates the phenomenon of the cultural meme, whereby a particular form of fan-fic becomes the sole interest of a community. K713 says, 'Now I find it difficult at times to read AU.' There is also perhaps a pragmatic reason for the predominance of AH fic. K713 says that 'canon *Twilight* is not my strong suit, and I've never quite been able to capture the magic of the supernatural/ vampire aspect of the characters.' AH allows the fan to ground her writing in what she knows from everyday life.

As Jenkins[14] has argued, fan-fic writers push the boundaries in rewriting the text, but fan communities generate norms within which the writers work. Fan writing deliberately reworks the original text, but the community defines the extent and direction of that reworking, in this case with all-human fics that explore the relationship between Bella and Edward (predominantly) and between other combinations of characters. K713 goes on to say that:

> I think AH has become so popular because ... it's the idea of putting a familiar character or face on another character within a separate story, and placing it in alternate situations. I think that, even if I had liked the way the series wrapped, I would not have been so willing to let go of the characters still, and there is just endless possibilities as to what to do with the characters when they are human.

Within the AH community, the fans can thus develop more intense relationships with the characters they love, as well as correct what they see as the deficiencies of the text. This also allows the characters to engage with the socio-cultural and socio-political experiences of the real world.

For example, the AH fan-fics often follow the relationship trajectory of Bella and Edward falling in love and 'living happily ever after' but play out and resolve the romance plot in more satisfying ways. In the films (and novels) the consummation of Bella and Edward's relationship is drawn out until their wedding night in *Breaking Dawn* (the main reason for the labelling of *Twilight* as abstinence porn). K713's fic *All I Want For Christmas* similarly has the consummation of the relationship held off until the wedding night, but she rewrites this element of the story so that Bella and Edward get married very soon after admitting their love for each other. She also has them marrying twice in the story, firstly in chapter 3 (of 9) before his deployment overseas and then again in chapter 8 when he returns and they have a 'proper' wedding ceremony, and therefore doubling the 'pay off'. In one respect, this double wedding around a pregnancy (Bella falls pregnant immediately after the first and has their baby before Edward returns from his tour of duty and the second) mirrors the marriage to Edward and the transformation into a vampire which 'bookend' Bella's pregnancy in *Breaking Dawn – Part 1* (2011, dir. Bill Condon). Whereas in *New Moon* (2009, dir. Chris Weitz) they are separated because other vampires are a threat to her, in *All I Want For Christmas* it is Edward's military career that keeps them apart. Bella does not anxiously yearn for Edward as she does in the film because firstly, they are married quickly (which removes the long drawn-out aspects of the novel's and film's 'abstinence porn') and secondly, it is during her pregnancy (which brings anxieties of its own). The war that Edward fights is relocated from the paranormal realm (where the fight is with Victoria and her newborn vampire army) to the real world conflict (Afghanistan), thus grounding the story in the here and now of the fans' everyday experiences (or at least the socio-historical backdrop to their lives).

On a more personal level, in *All I Want For Christmas*, Bella is established at the beginning of the fic as an Iraq war widow and single mother who has to face up to her son's Christmas wish for 'a daddy'. Edward is introduced as her deceased husband's best friend from the military and has taken on something of a substitute father role in her son's life. Mikey would like Uncle Edward to be his daddy, but Bella sees him just as a friend and has sworn she will never become involved with another soldier. The story is thus much less invested in the typical romance plot of falling in love, than in the emotional upheavals of bereavement and in particular the anxieties faced by military wives. Although the story swaps narrative point of view between Bella and Edward (this fic is somewhat unusual in that it is written in the third person, whereas *Twilight* fic is commonly written in the first person, also replicating the narrative voice of the novels) it is largely told from Bella's point of view as she goes through her pregnancy and the birth of a daughter whilst apart from Edward. Bella's longing for Edward is not for consummation, as it is in the abstinence porn of the original, but for Edward's safe return from war and the normality of family life that will bring: 'Inside that plane was the missing pieces of their hearts; the wait was over.'[15]

Twilight's predominantly female fandom is an indication of the gendered aesthetic and generic appeal of the series. The romance genre is as significant, if not more so, as any vestigial anchoring in the horror/vampire genre, even to the extent of eradicating the fact that the male love interest is a vampire (as Judith Kohlenberger argues elsewhere in this collection, *Twilight* bears a resemblance to the nineteenth-century sentimental novel). This encourages the female fans' interactions with the text primarily through the projected interactivity played out in romance fan fiction. This is a significant factor in *Twilight* fandom, where much fan fiction is based on the heterosexual couple (this is not to downplay the importance of *Twilight* slash fiction, which is discussed by Bethan Jones in the following chapter of this collection). The example cited above illustrates how the fan fiction writer takes control of the relationship through her play with the characters' traits, actions and environment, here exploring the issues and concerns of American military action overseas in relation to the 'war on terror'. In this way the fan brings the projected identity of characters close to their own identity, or at the very least their experiences of the national concerns in America during the last decade (the writer is in her 30s and is a single mother). LG42 also says that: 'If the vampires are human, they have to deal with issues of mortality, maturity and professional satisfaction. I've explored issues such as living with a terminal disease, function-impairing disabilities, finding oneself, and deciding what one wants to be when one grows up.' These are all common life events that a large number of fans will either experience themselves or see others from their families or social circles experiencing.

This plays out in particular in forms of angst fiction featuring variations on Edward – namely, Geekward and Brokenward, for example. In other examples of K713's fic Edward is invariably trapped (an actor in a loveless marriage falling for his co-star Bella, for example) and isolated (a lonely ER doctor who is pushed into online chat rooms where he encounters Bella). LG412 says:

> The supernatural character I've explored the most deeply in an all-human context is Edward, so I can speak most easily to his character. As presented in the books, he can only be explained as a supernatural character. His tortured self-loathing is the product of guilt over what he has done as a vampire, and his constant self-doubt is fueled by what he sees as his monstrous nature. What's fun about making him human is finding ways to capture aspects of his personality and explain them in other ways. Why would a young man hate himself or doubt himself so much? Why would he have such hang-ups about sex?[16]

The characters for these writers have become real and express a range of human anxieties that are familiar to writers and readers alike. Furthermore, elements of characterisation that are more firmly human (and thus relatable to in the way LG42 describes) enable further interactivity with the characters. This is not to say that these fans do not like genres based in the supernatural and the paranormal. K713 says:

> Yes I do enjoy other vampire stories outside of *Twilight*, while other paranormal [sic], such as the werewolf, not so much. I've always enjoyed reading and watching vampires since I was much younger, with Anne Rice and even Bram Stoker's *Dracula*, and even as recent as *Buffy the Vampire Slayer*. It's always been a fascination of mine, however, *Twilight* really did strike something different in me that other vampire stories/series have not in the past. The characters in *Twilight*, to be honest, appeal to me less when they are werewolves (although there are the exceptions of Paul and Seth, novel and movie). The vampires are what appeals to me the most. Whether it's the vegetarians and what their lifestyle brings to the story, or the nomads and the differences their lifestyle and personalities

contribute, and then of course, the Volturi, which were fascinating to me from their introduction in *New Moon*. It's the whole society feel and the vast differences of the characters even within the same coven that kept me fascinated the most.[17]

Such fans are not romance fans per se and from this response they do in fact seem to be interested in the vampire genre and in particular ways in which such narratives explore aspects of vampire society and culture. They are not necessarily vampire or Gothic horror fans, but are attracted to the vampire, one of the reasons why they were drawn to *Twilight* originally. Similarly, LG42 says that:

> I was drawn in by the characters and relationships. The supernatural elements held no particular appeal, other than that they opened up really interesting storylines. While I have enjoyed other series with supernatural elements (*Buffy the Vampire Slayer* and *Black Dagger Brotherhood*, for example) those too drew me in with interesting, relatable characters and relationships.[18]

There is evidence in this response that elements of horror are of less importance than strong characters, a finding that also came out of research into the tastes of female horror film fans.[19] However, what is also clear from the writers' responses to the research questions is that they are interested in and identify with flawed characters, and the concept of the tortured vampire is one that offers particular pleasures. K713 says that she enjoys *Twilight* because: 'in a lot of ways it's very different from the other vampire stories and novels I've read in the past. The characters each had their own specific characteristics. And Edward is one of those tortured characters that just seems to draw people in, both in the books and the movie.' This suggests that the writer finds complex and troubled characters much more interesting than straightforward hero-types. Whilst Edward is not the decadent Byronic figure or predatory Dracula type, he represents sufficient difference from the norm as to be an ideal mysterious and tragic figure.

It is these character traits that the writers privilege and develop in their fiction. It is also what attracts them to creating their own extensions to the narrative. K713 says that 'it's some of the characters' attributes that make it so appealing and inspiring to write about as well. There is not a single character involved in the story that doesn't have a flaw that is very easy to relate to in real life.' Her comments suggest that the all-too-human traits are far more important than the fact that they might also be a vampire: 'There is something very human about each and every one of them, with or without the vampire aspect involved.' Ultimately, this leads to the eliding of the vampire characteristics totally. As a primary example of the paranormal romance, *Twilight* is already a text that loosens the generic links of the vampire to horror and the Gothic. If the paranormal romance genre offers the pleasures of romance fiction with a little more danger in the form of monstrous entities in the lead role (and this has always been true of *Dracula* to a certain extent), then when fan fiction writers are extending the text for their own pleasures it follows that a focus on the romance (as opposed to the Gothic monstrosity) would take precedence. K713 states that:

> It's very easy to take beloved characters that you couldn't get enough of in a favorite series, paranormal, fantasy, or otherwise, and set them into a story in your own mind regardless. But I really think that it was Stephenie Meyer's humanizing of these characters even within a paranormal realm, as they live within society as much as possible rather than outside it. And the fact that it's written in such a way that you can almost believe that it could have taken place somewhere if such things were real. The backbone of any AH story is pretty much there, because of the humanization of them in the first place.[20]

Furthermore, this writer is able to prolong her imaginative play with the characters without having to change them considerably from the originating text. 'All that really changes for me is the supernatural aspect behind them, because I find them so relatable as vampires and werewolves as well.'[21] This writer indicates that she can fully relate to the characters despite the fact that they have a monstrous side; it is not, though, that their monstrosity does not appeal (it clearly does, just as it might for a more overt vampire fan) but that their individual (and inherently human) personality dominates. With human characters, the writers are free to explore any dimension of the character they so choose. K713 says that 'the *Twilight* fan fiction realm has given a lot of freedom to the writer to put a familiar character or face within a story, both for the writer and the readers.' In one sense this could simply indicate that the fan fiction writer is continuing the story through narrative gaps, for example. More importantly, though, the fact that she calls them 'faces' suggests they are brought vividly to life both in her imagination and her fiction. She can draw on particular characteristics that hold an appeal for her, or that she has a strong affinity with. 'A lot of the themes and ideas I have developed through my fics have actually been through different attributes of the characters

I pulled out of the books, since characters are your main core of any story. Edward just happens to be one of the most entertaining characters to play around with, because he is so multi-layered.' If Edward is indeed a potentially polysemic character, he offers a wide range of topics and themes the fan-fic writer can draw on.

These might also be themes and ideas that could not be so well explored were the characters to remain paranormal creatures.

In LG42's fic *String Theory,* for example, her Geekward version of Edward is a PhD student trying to engage fellow student Bella in more than his usual line in embarrassing small talk, negotiating 'dates' to a Muppets movie with her disabled father along. It is written in a light, comic tone, with much play made of cultural competencies to *The Muppets Show* (Jim Henson 1976–1981). LG42 writes Bella as a fan of the Muppets and as a fan writer she is clearly familiar with the series and films herself. In the header of chapter 11 she writes: 'Stephenie Meyer owns *Twilight.* I own the entire set of *The Muppet Show* DVDs.' She also includes lyrics from Muppets songs in the fic, with Bella frequently quoting these. Bella and Edward's growing relationship thus takes place to the soundtrack of the Muppets:

> Over the course of the next hour, every time another beloved classic Muppet character shows up, Bella nudges her father, laughing and smil-ing at him. They're in their own happy bubble, where there are no life-altering disabilities or responsibilities. Just optimism and *joy.*
>
> And I'm a part of it. Every time I sneak a glance at her, it's like remem-bering all over again why it's such a gift to give. Watching her face light up with happiness … it's a gift.
>
> And about halfway through the movie, I get a present of my own. While our hands have been joined all this time, as Kermit and Miss Piggy go on a romantic walk through the streets of Paris, I feel Bella shifting and leaning closer to me. At the same time, her thumb starts tracing out little arcs on the back of my hand.[22]

LG42 says that she 'was drawn in by the romance'. And this is what dominates in her fiction. She goes on to say that: 'Bella and Edward's love was epic and all-consuming – utterly divorced from reality but a brilliant fantasy. I par-ticularly fell for Edward's character. He was tortured and alone and in need of love; he was ultimately redeemed by love.' In both *String Theory* and *Love Amongst the Ruins* her versions of Edward are indeed redeemed, and healed, by love. Although she uses Edward's point of view in *String Theory* to illustrate this redemption through love for Bella; in *Love Amongst the Ruins* she alternates between Bella and Edward's voices. Her statement that 'I related to Bella's character. I don't know what teen hasn't gone through insecurity and the fear that one won't be loved in return. It may not be heroic, but in my mind, it's very real' comes through strongly in the fic. Edward and Bella fall in love despite the odds – he has a pain management issue due to a spinal injury sustained in the car crash that killed his parents and he is being blackmailed by a manipulative Bree. However, Bella cannot stand his seeming inability to respond to her as she expects and goes through the traumas of believing he does not love her in return.

The personal, gender and political concerns touched on in fics such as *All I Want For Christmas* and as mentioned by LG42 are not necessarily straightforward in terms of personal beliefs or a feminist agenda, but the fact that the writers move the boundaries of the genre in this way reflects their responses to the original text. Their archontic writing is thus linked to the pleasures of the text and is expressed through the rewriting of characters such as human Edward. K713 states that she has 'a shameless and hopeless addiction to Robert Pattinson' and calls this her 'guilty pleasure' (a topic further explored by Francesca Haig elsewhere in this collection). This is significant for fan studies, as not only do fans' pleasurable responses become manifest in the text (rewriting the romance between Edward and Bella or Edward and other characters), but the very act of writing those characters develops the potential for fans to participate interactively with them. As already established by Henry Jenkins,[23] fans involve themselves in the creative process by remediating and rewriting the text. Fan production exists at the heart of an intertextual relationship with the originating text, but over and above this it works against the one-way communication of media production and consumption to facilitate potential social interactions between fans and fictional characters, often in an attempt to meet the fan's own needs.[24] As Anne Krustritz points out, fan writing often serves to make the relationship with the characters more intimate by turning them into real people[25] – in the case of *Twilight* AH fan-fic this is expressed at the level of literal representation as human. Furthermore, the processes of projected interactivity result in the characters becoming manifest in the interfaces between fan identity and character identity. Perhaps the last word then should go to the fan writers. As LG42 says:

I adore seeing these characters reinvented, and making them all human opens up such an array of possibilities for reimagining them. I think die-hard fans turn to fanfic for MORE. More of their favorite characters, favorite relationships, etc. AH fic allows so many different ways to explore those characters and relationships, while also giving writers and readers a way to find pieces of their own lives in the stories.

Notes

1. Roger Dadoun, 'Fetishism in the Horror Film', in James Donald (ed.), *Fantasy and the Cinema* (London: BFI, 1989).
2. James Silver and Alain Ursini, *The Vampire Film: From* Nosferatu *to* Bram Stoker's Dracula (New York: Limelight, 2004).
3. Brigid Cherry, 'Refusing to Refuse the Look: Female Viewers of the Horror Film', in Mark Jancovich (ed.), *Horror, the Film Reader* (London: Routledge, 2001), pp. 169–78.
4. See Brigid Cherry, 'Knit One, Bite One: Vampire Fandom, Fan Production and Feminine Handicrafts', in Gareth Schott and Kirstine Moffat (eds), *Fanpires: Audience Consumption of the Modern Vampire* (Washington: New Academia Press, 2011).
5. Amber Davisson and Paul Booth, 'Reconceptualizing Communication and Agency in Fan Activity: A Proposal for a Projected Interactivity Model for Fan Studies', *Texas Speech Communication Journal* 23/1 (2007), pp. 33–43.
6. Ibid., p. 41.
7. Abigail Derecho, 'Archontic Literature: A Definition, A History, and Several Theories of Fan Fiction', in Karen Hellekson and Kristina Busse (eds), *Fan Fiction and Fan Communities in the Age of the Internet* (Jefferson, NC: McFarland, 2006), p. 63.
8. Ibid., p. 65.
9. Ibid., p. 72.
10. James Gee, *What Video Games Have to Teach Us About Learning and Literacy* (New York: Palgrave Macmillan, 2003).
11. Davisson and Booth, 'Reconceptualizing Communication and Agency in Fan Activity', p. 36.
12. Camille Bacon-Smith, *Enterprising Women: Television Fandom and the Creation of Popular Myth* (Philadelphia: University of Pennsylvania Press, 1992).
13. AU, standing for Alternate Universe, is a form of fan fiction where canonical elements of the original text are changed, allowing writers to explore different settings, plot developments or character relationships.
14. Henry Jenkins, *Textual Poachers: Television Fans and Participatory Cultures* (London: Routledge, 1992).
15. Kyla713, *All I Want For Christmas*, Fanfiction.net, 15 December 2010, http://www.fanfiction.net/s/6557703/7/All_I_Want_For_Christmas (accessed 3 December 2011).
16. LG42, personal communication, 17 December 2011.
17. K713, personal communication, 16 December 2011.
18. LG42, personal communication, 17 December 2011.
19. Cherry, 'Refusing to Refuse the Look'.
20. K713, personal communication, 16 December 2011.

21. K713, *All I Want For Christmas*.

22. TheLadyInGrey42, *String Theory*, Fanfiction.net, 27 November 2011, http://www.fan-fiction.net/s/7589412/11/String_Theory (accessed 7 December 2011).

23. Jenkins, *Textual Poachers*.

24. Lincoln Geraghty, 'A Network of Support: Coping with Trauma Through *Star Trek* Fan Letters', *Journal of Popular Culture* 39/6 (2006), pp. 1002–24.

25. Anne Kustritz, 'Slashing the Romance Narrative', *Journal of American Culture* 26 (2003), p. 375.

15

NORMAL FEMALE INTEREST IN VAMPIRES AND WEREWOLVES BONKING: SLASH AND THE RECONSTRUCTION OF MEANING[1]

Bethan Jones

Academic scholarship has begun to pay more attention to slash fan fiction[2] over the last 20 or so years, but the genre has largely been theorised using a sociological or anthropological approach. Camille Bacon-Smith's[3] and Henry Jenkins'[4] studies of *Star Trek* female fandom both propose slash as a method for women to challenge traditional masculinity and replace it with a preferable version. Other studies have focused on the 'resistive' aspect of slash, with Patricia Lamb and Diana Veith arguing in *Romantic Myth, Transcendence, and* Star Trek *Zines*[5] that slash posits a loving relationship between two equals, as opposed to the inequality of the relationship between a man and a woman, by removing 'gender as a governing and determining force in the love relationship'.[6] Constance Penley, in *Feminism, Psychoanalysis, and the Study of Popular Culture*,[7] further argues that 'the slash phenomenon [was] one of the most radical and intriguing female appropriations of a popular culture product that [she] had ever seen', noting that it illustrates how 'women, and people, resist, negotiate, and adapt to their own desires this overwhelming media environment that we all inhabit'.[8]

As the majority of academic work on slash focuses on male/male pairings, slash featuring women and/or penned by lesbians has been highlighted as comparatively unstudied.[9] The explanations put forth for this are varied: that there are not enough strong female characters on television;[10] that heterosexual female writers are not turned on by writing (or reading) about female pairings;[11] or that slash enables writers to examine relationships between characters who are equals in patriarchal society.[12] Ignoring femslash however, is to ignore an important genre within 'fan-fic', which may enable scholars to further understand the ways in which erotic fan-fic, and particularly slash, provide a 'critique of the constructions of gender and sexuality found in the original works'[13] and, perhaps, offer an ideological critique of texts whose source creator has attempted to limit the sexuality of his/her characters.

It is not my intention within this chapter to re-examine previous debates on slash, such as the much-discussed question of whether slash is a legitimate decoding of its source,[14] or the discussion on whether slash is a form of romance fiction or pornography.[15] Rather, I am interested in exploring the ways in which sexuality is limited in the *Twilight* films, firstly through the imposing of hegemonic norms of masculinity, patriarchy and religion; and secondly how specific slash stories and writers in the *Twilight* fandom reconstruct these limitations.

It is also worth noting, at this point, my involvement in fandom and how this has affected my approach to this study. Much as Jenkins positions himself as an 'academic fan'[16] in his 1992 work on *Star Trek* fandom, I too consider myself an acafan in my study of slash. While not a *Twilight* fan, I am a member of various fan communities, and a fan-fic writer as well as a scholar. I have therefore attempted to achieve a balance between these positions of mutual knowledge and critical distance.[17] Slash authors have, in the past, been stigmatised by scholars, fans and convention organisers.[18] I hope to be accountable for my representations of slash and slash writers and to refrain from making judgements or sweeping generalisations about *Twilight* slash and its authors.

In this study, slash stories posted to four open *LiveJournal* communities were analysed, alongside responses received from interviews conducted with *Twilight* slash writers. Each community was selected for its focus on *Twilight* slash and/ or non-canonical pairings.[19] The founders of each *LiveJournal* group were contacted for permission to post a call for interviewees, and exchanges were then continued with those who responded. These interviews took place via electronic mail between March and October 2011. Each writer interviewed granted permission for their work to be used in this chapter and has given their informed consent to their answers being quoted.

Twilight slash encompasses both alternate universe (AU) and all human (AH) stories,[20] each of which focuses upon or diverges from the canonical text in different ways. The sheer number and range of slash fics in The *Twilight* fandom means that not all these texts can be analysed here, and therefore this study has been limited to slash focusing primarily on Bella/Alice and Jacob/Edward pairings. While this may seem like an arbitrary decision, and certainly precludes me from examining other issues that pairings such as Jasper/Seth bring to the fore,[21] this decision has been based on the critiques of the *Twilight* series' depiction of sexuality, discussion of which can be found elsewhere in this collection. Bella, Edward and Jacob, as the three members of the 'love triangle', are the characters whose depictions of sexuality are the most debated in academic literature. In examining how slash reconstructs these attitudes towards sexuality, it is therefore pertinent to focus upon these characters.

'Bizarrely moral for a vampire' – representations of sexuality in *Twilight*

It would seem that there are three distinct ways in which sexuality in the *Twilight* films is limited: firstly, through the coding of sexuality, especially female sexuality, as dangerous; secondly, through the promotion of what Lev Grossman refers to as the 'erotics of abstinence';[22] and lastly through the situating of the series in a world with a broadly Christian, specifically Mormon, subtext. These former elements are addressed throughout the course of the chapter, and as such, require no further discussion here. I therefore propose to address the Mormon subtext of the saga first.

Meyer's portrayals of sexuality and gender in the *Twilight* series can, many argue, be traced back to her Mormon religion. Averill notes that 'Edward's particular brand of monstrosity, vampirism, makes his restraint a very powerful affirmation of what Judeo-Christian patriarchy deems acceptable sexual behaviour,'[23] while Wilson has argued that the strong work ethic and traditional roles for women expounded by Mormonism, as well as its belief that humans can become divine, and love and marriage transcend death, all influence the series.[24] The relationship between Mormonism and Meyer's vampires has also been recognised by fans. The experiences that Cassie (one fan-fic writer interviewed for this study) has of the Mormon religion enable her to understand where some of Meyer's ideas concerning Bella originated:

> I think it had a lot to do with her religion or at least her unrealistic ideal of how a young woman should act. My sister married into a Mormon family, so I can see how that plays into the books. My brother in law and his family are Mormons and I happen to live with them. I live in a house

where the women (my sister and I) are expected to keep house, take care
of the kids, and do all of the cooking.[25]

Given the issues surrounding sexuality, gender and religion in *The Twilight Saga*
– explored elsewhere in this anthology – it is, perhaps, no surprise that some
fans have taken it upon themselves to '[repair] the damage done in a system
where contemporary myths are owned by corporations instead of owned by the
folk',[26] through constructing alternative narratives in their own fictions. From
depictions of patriarchal society where white, masculine heterosexuality is the
norm,[27] fans attempt to depart from the source text to construct a more equal,
accepting society in which both female and male sexuality are embraced. It is
to these fan texts that I now turn.

Jakeward: 'an intriguing thought' – *Twilight* slash reconstructing sexuality

The typical plot for a slash story, as defined by Henry Jenkins, involves 'a series
of movements from an initial partnership, through a crisis in communication
that threatens to disrupt that union, towards its reconfirmation through sexual
intimacy'.[28] This 'initial partnership' usually refers to an on-screen friendship
between the characters, with slash writers centring their stories around homosocial
bonds already established in the canonical text. In *The Twilight Saga*, however, slash
writers are faced not only with pairing two male characters who hate each other,
but in creating a homoerotic text where no mention of homosexuality is present in
the canon,[29] as Cassie explains: '*laughs* 'Slash is nonexistent in the series, even
hintings towards homosexual couples. It's sad, but true. Finding slash in the series
involves a lot of reading between the lines and misconstruing facts.'[30]

In her story *Toeing The Line*, Cassie takes on one of the tropes of *Twilight*
slash, having Jacob imprint[31] on Edward in order to progress the relationship
from that of mutual hatred to romance.

'... I imprinted', he said, the realization dawning on his face before he
looked up at his alpha. 'Didn't I?'

He didn't know how to explain the dread that filled him as Sam nod-
ded in affirmation. Imprinting was a good thing, wasn't it? It's what they
all hoped for. What they strived for, well, besides keeping La Push vampire free.

He had found the other half of his soul ... so why didn't he feel happy?
Why was anger boiling in the pit of his stomach, why was he tasting the

stinging taste of bitterness? What was he missing in the huge complex puzzle that he just couldn't remember?

He chewed on his lower lip and looked back up at the ceiling. He tried to remember, but he couldn't, his mind had blocked the identity of the person he had imprinted on. But why? Who could he have possibly imprinted on that he wouldn't want to remember ... ?

Jacob froze. His heart stilled. His mind slowed to a stop. His eyes snapped to Sam. His wide, shocked eyes. 'I ...' he started slowly, softly. 'I imprinted on a leech, didn't I?'[32]

The story progresses from Jacob's realisation that he has imprinted onto Edward, to his refusal to act on his lupine desires for him – an action that could lead to his death. Edward, aware of the repercussions of his failure to help Jacob, agrees to have sex with him and prevent full-scale war (the peace treaty between the Quileutes and the vampires exists as long as no one is killed by a vampire. Edward's refusal to sleep with Jacob would have resulted in Jacob's death, and the breaking of the treaty). Here, imprinting is treated in a very different way to Meyer's representation of it. skargasm, another fan-fic writer, comments that

> The wolves are hot-blooded creatures, but [Meyer] constrains them by imprinting – they are all waiting for their one true love. I can't remember which one it is, but he imprints on a child and from that point on he has no interest in sex with anyone else – he will wait faithfully for that child to grow up for a relationship with her. I have read arguments about the whole imprinting on a child being pedophilic [sic] (is that a word?!) but I actually think Meyer is stopping them having sex – you have to wait until your chosen one has grown up before you can have sex; you have to wait until you're married to have sex; Leah and Sam were in a relationship which was presumably sexual and she was kicked to the kerb for Emily – punishment for having sex perhaps?[33]

This is a view also enforced by academic arguments. Lydia Kokkola states that '[imprinting] can happen only once, and the "choice" of love object is often unlikely, albeit always heterosexual ... Imprinted love, the series strives to clarify, is a perfect love, unclouded by petty concerns like sexual desire.'[34] Thus Cassie's depiction of imprinting certainly reconstructs the ideas of the heterosexual eternal family and pre-mortal love[35] that are prevalent in Meyer's text. However, from being a preserve of heterosexual masculinity, where the 'imprinter' becomes what the object of his affection needs, imprinting is reconstructed as a way of allowing a homosexual relationship to occur, of examining the arguments in *The Twilight Saga*'s assertion that perfect love is unclouded by sexual desire. Jacob does not become what Edward needs him to be; rather, his imprinting is reinterpreted as a destructive force *unless* sexual intercourse is allowed to take place:

> 'Once a shifter imprints and if the imprint isn't accepted,' Quil explained softly, 'he will go into heat over the three days of the full moon, the actual full moon being the peak of the heat. This is said to attract the imprint and force acceptance, but dire consequences will befall the shifter if he doesn't ... ah, if he doesn't accept his imprint's seed ...'[36]

Catherine Tosenberger suggests that the joy of an enemy slash pairing like Jacob/Edward lies in watching the antagonists overcome their differences. She suggests that dislike is 'recast as sexual tension, and when the characters are both men, part of the pleasure is in seeing their negotiation of expectations of male aggression (rather than friendship) in terms of desire'.[37] This seems to be echoed amongst some slash writers, with Cassie noting

> I write emotionally charged fanfiction and when two people hate each other, I love dealing with that emotion and twisting it into something unexpected. I don't aim to have them falling in love, but I love bending the definition of 'love'. There are many different forms and degrees of love and I suppose I love the fiery passion behind a love that's birthed from hate. Now looking at 'there's a thin line between love and hate'; I personally believe that *love* and *hate* are the two *strongest* emotions you can feel towards a person though they are polar opposites. To hate someone, you have to at least care about them to allow the hate to affect you. I personally think it'd be much worse to have a person indifferent towards you rather than hate you, because if a person hates you, they're still thinking about you.[38]

Jenkins argues that the construction of slash 'depends on reading certain looks and gestures exchanged amongst the characters as showing some hidden emotional truths'[39] and suggests 'Fans can point to the screen and say that you can see it in their eyes, these men really care about each other.'[40] As with the *Twilight* novels, fans of *The Twilight Saga* are tasked with creating a homoerotic text where none exists in the canon. skargasm notes that she writes

Paul/Emmett narratives because, during the films, they struck her as having chemistry which could be seen as unresolved sexual tension:

> Mainly in *Eclipse*, there is a scene where they are chasing Victoria. Emmett loses his temper and jumps over the boundary into Quileute territory and Paul smacks him down into the river. The way Emmett looks, chest heaving with water dripping down his body whilst Paul is snarling at him just struck me – no idea why. Then later, during the battle scene, Emmett comes to Paul's rescue and/or vice versa and there seems to be a possessiveness there – they can hurt each other, but no one else can. Probably reading into it things that aren't there, but that's what struck me and that's where I write from.[41]

Similarly mia, a 'vidder' (a fan who engages in the fan practice of creating music videos using the footage of one or more sources) on *LiveJournal*, suggests that it is the tent scene between Edward and Jacob in *The Twilight Saga: Eclipse* (2010, dir. David Slade)[42] that makes her think there is a connection between the characters. Slash writers and vidders like mia draw on moments in the films that suggest, however obliquely, a connection between the characters. They use these moments to produce what Jenkins[43] refers to as 'constructed reality' videos, creating a new story by linking together footage from the source text rather using those shots to simply interpret an event, or provide an alternative perspective of it.

mia's video *Toeing the Line*, produced as a trailer for Cassie's *Toeing the Line* fic, draws on the plot outlined within whilst also acting as a story in its own right. Taking clips from *Twilight* (2008, dir. Catherine Hardwicke), *New Moon* (2009, Chris Weitz) and *Eclipse* (2010, dir. Dariaslade), mia's fanvid reads the characters in a radically different way to that intended by both the films and books. As has been mentioned elsewhere, heterosexuality is the norm in the saga, but by removing clips from their original context and re-editing them together, *Toeing the Line* recontextualises the images to produce a new and different narrative. As well as dealing with imprinting, however, both mia and Cassie's *Toeing the Line* and mia's corresponding vid depict a violent relationship between Jacob and Edward which, it could be argued, corresponds to the violence that occurs in Edward and Bella's consummation of their marriage. As previously mentioned, one of the ways in which sexuality is limited in *The Twilight Saga* is by its being coded as dangerous: sex with Edward results in Bella covered in bruises (*Breaking Dawn – Part 1* (2011, dir. Bill Condon)); Jacob is a predator forcing his unwanted attentions on Bella (*Eclipse*); sex leads to a pregnancy which almost kills Bella. Only in the confines of marriage (and a marriage in which Bella is no longer human, but part of the Cullens' vampire family) is sex considered acceptable. The relationship between Edward and Jacob in *Toeing the Line* is certainly dangerous – it is violent, full of conflict, and one wrong move could lead to war – but it is coded very differently to the dangerous sexuality seen in *The Twilight Saga*. Cassie subtly alters the notion of imprinting so that if the imprinter is rejected (something we never see in the saga) he will die. This means that sex, rather than destructive and undesirable when outside the appropriate contexts (of marriage and reproduction), is necessary for survival. The danger in the fic is that the desire for sex, if left unacknowledged, will have dire consequences – a direct contrast to the 'erotics of abstinence' which Grossman[44] suggests is presented in the series, where characters engage in elaborate acts of 'foreplay', but pull back before sex becomes a real possibility.

The second difference between the coding of sexuality as dangerous in *Toeing the Line* and *The Twilight Saga* is that the violence in Cassie's reimagining takes place between equals. Whereas it is made clear in *The Twilight Saga* that Edward could kill Bella if he so wished, that danger is removed in the fic, wherein the relationship develops between two characters who are as strong as each other. It has been argued elsewhere that slash enables writers to examine relationships between characters who are equals in patriarchal society,[45] but *Twilight* slash enables writers to examine relationships between characters who are equals in terms of physical strength. It could easily be argued that Jacob and Edward are far from equals even though they hold similar positions in terms of gender and patriarchy: Jacob is a working-class Native American living on a reservation; Edward is a middle-class, white male living in a large house adorned with works of art and expensive items.[46] In this way they are no more 'equals' in society than are men and women. But what Jacob has that Bella doesn't is inordinate strength, and this strength matches Edward's. What could kill Bella barely scratches Jacob, and this is used effectively in the fic to counteract the films' claim that sex is dangerous. Just as the bruises Bella sustains on her honeymoon have been reinterpreted by fans as a mark of desire (a Google search using the term 'bite me, Edward' brings up t-shirts, hooded jumpers, notebooks and temporary tattoos emblazoned with the phrase, as well as songs about Edward Cullen and blog posts regarding the desirability of a boyfriend like Edward), the violence portrayed in *Toeing the Line* is actually rewritten as a turn-on for the characters:

Instead he drew back his fist and aimed for that smirking jaw, all the while growling, 'You son of a bitch!' under his breath. But the punch never landed, because Edward's hand darted out and grabbed his fist and before he could react further, Jacob was pulled forward. He noticed Edward's smirk widened just a fraction before their lips crushed together roughly.

Jacob [sic] initial response, he realized and clung to, was not his own. His wolf had taken over, purring in pleasure at the contact with its chosen mate. The shifter kissed back, almost desperately so.[47]

The very nature of their bodies, then, draws Edward and Jacob together in ways that Edward and Bella are only able to achieve once she has been turned into a vampire. As Elven, who also writes *Twilight* fan-fic, notes: 'Edward constantly laments over the fact that he could hurt Bella. With Jacob... he doesn't have to worry about that. Edward is cold whereas Jacob is hot, when their bodies meet the combination is something attractive for both of them.'[48]

Of course, not all 'Jakeward' slash relies on imprinting to get the pair into bed, and not all Jakeward slash pairs violence with desire. *All Is Not Lost*, another fic written by Cassie, is 'the first part of a multichapter [sic] story concerning the natural progression of Edward and Jacob's relationship without using imprinting as a crutch'.[49] In this fic, Bella dies after Renesmee's birth, leaving Edward a single father. While it could be argued that *All Is Not Lost* perpetuates Meyer's argument that female sexuality is dangerous in killing Bella after the birth of her child (in the first paragraph we read the following thought from Edward: 'They were supposed to have all of eternity laid out before them, but instead the birth of their daughter had killed her – her fragile human body could not handle the strain of carrying his child, his part vampire child'), sexuality is also used as a route to healing:

> In that moment, Jacob saw a side of Edward he never thought he'd be allowed to see; he saw vulnerability shining in the vampire's eyes. Something about the way Edward looked tugged at his heart, he felt the urge to cry rise up within him and Jacob had to force it back. The vampire looked so lost, so heartbroken...
>
> He wanted to fix it, and the sudden need to pick up the pieces of Edward's broken heart and mend it was such a shock to the young shape shifter. Jacob looked away, heat rising in his face as he pushed himself off of the couch. Bella had barely be [sic] dead for two months, and he had imprinted on Renesmee... he ought not to be wanting to piece together a broken heart that was not his to piece together. He was confused and terrified, though he could not explain the terror that he felt.[50]

This portrayal is in direct contrast to that of the series. Edward regards himself as protective of Bella, but illustrates this through displays of jealousy and possessiveness (removing the battery from Bella's car; preventing her from seeing her friends). In the above extract Jacob is clearly protective of Edward, but this is illustrated through his compassion for the vampire and the desire to 'fix' it. Sex and desire in fic, then, are not necessarily equated to danger and violence.

As has been mentioned previously, Meyer sites *Twilight* in a world with a Mormon subtext, and as a result homosexuality does not feature in the series. The focus on the family is constructed as predominantly white, heterosexual and middle class, yet in *Twilight* slash the theme of same-sex families is explored. Cassie introduces this idea in *All Is Not Lost* with Renesmee referring to Jacob as 'Papa Jake'. While both Jacob and Edward are initially resistant to their feelings for each other, they come to realise how much each needs the other through Renesmee. Using her ability to project her thoughts onto others, she shows Jacob and Edward her memories of them together acting, as Cassie notes, as a family. The relationship between Renesmee and Jacob also reflects this shift from single-parent family to a family with two homosexual parents. This shift, as far as Renesmee is concerned, is a logical progression and also enables Cassie to use the canonical imprinting of Jacob on Renesmee as a starting point in her depiction of a same-sex family. This fic acts as a counterpoint to the markedly heterosexual *Twilight* series. Not only is homosexuality depicted as normal but Jacob and Edward, as gay parents, raise a child who accepts the relationship totally.

'you'll still be my friend, even though i love Alice, too?' – the role of the erotic in *Twilight* femslash

While critics argue that the *Twilight* series codes female sexuality as monstrous and deviant, in line with our era's way of thinking,[51] *Twilight* femslash subversively construes it as something conversely natural and human. *Acceptance*, by mskathy,[52] a prominent femslash writer, for example, has Bella explain 'I learned long ago that I wasn't the kind of girl who was opposed to sleeping with someone on the first date. I wasn't a slut, I just knew what I wanted sometimes and was okay with getting it,' while *Paper Moon*, by the same author, opens with Bella at a lesbian bar looking for someone to take home. While these actions may seem more stereotypically masculine, representative of the 'guy culture' in which 'women are used as pawns to prove one's sexual viability, as objects who [sic] males masturbate over',[53] they can also be used as a commentary on *Twilight*. Throughout the course of the saga, Bella is portrayed as a sexual being but is told repeatedly by Edward that sex is off-limits, and thus 'wrong'.[54] Her agency in the matter of their sexual relationship is removed and her sexuality policed by Edward, who determines when they will kiss and for how long, and when they ultimately sleep together. In femslash, however, Bella is given agency to act in the way she cannot in the series: to desire women, to kiss at will and at length and to engage in sexual intercourse that doesn't leave her battered and bruised.

Bella is largely considered by academics and fans alike to be a weak character and, tellingly, most of the writers interviewed for this project actively dislike her. Heidi, a slash writer in both the *Twilight* and *Harry Potter* fandoms, for example, argues that while Bella is a very flat character, the good thing about her is that her lack of depth allows readers to put themselves in her place: 'When I read the books initially, she had enough personality traits similar to mine that she wasn't difficult to identify with in order to get lost in the story. Stepping back from that initial reading, though, she's actually a fairly bland character, especially when attempting to write her into fan fiction.'[55]

Thus in much of the femslash examined for this chapter, Bella is rewritten as a stronger, more interesting character. mskathy's *Paper Moon* depicts Bella as joint partner in a law firm dealing with civil rights that she runs with her (non-canonical) sister and best friend. Further, meeting Alice at a lesbian bar one evening, the two begin a relationship in which sex and honesty play prominent roles.

> As we laid [sic] together, recovering from having given each other a thorough fucking, I started to wonder just how I had gotten to this place, emotionally. I could already tell I didn't want Alice to be another name on the laundry list of names Bella Swan Has [sic] Fucked (wasn't it long enough?), but I had no experience in this area. I also had no clue what Alice wanted, and that was important; you can't have a one-way relationship.[56]

Unlike the relationship between Bella and Edward in the series – a 'one-way relationship' in which Edward calls the shots – her relationship with Alice is comprised of give and take. This is made clear in the dialogue surrounding Bella's birthday, where she agrees to a party Alice wants to arrange, and Alice in turn agrees to making it a small affair because of Bella's distaste of parties.[57]

If Cassie's *All Is Not Lost* makes readers aware of *Twilight*'s focus on heterosexual families by promoting a homosexual family unit, mskathy's *Paper Moon* brings the series' subtexts of Mormonism and homophobia to the fore.

The story is situated in Salt Lake, Utah, a conservative religious state and the home of Mormonism. Bella notes frequently throughout the text that only a few people know she is gay and she does not feel comfortable expressing her sexuality in public; she refers to dating 'a few nice Mormon boys' and also reiterates her parents' worry that they had done something to raise her 'wrong'.

> As [Carlisle] pulled me into a hug, I laughed. Alice's family was the complete opposite of mine. Before he died, Charlie would get squeamish every time we discussed my future, or any potential girlfriends. I learned to just avoid topics about my love life. Renee? She had been an easier sell to the idea that I was gay, but she nagged me nearly non-stop about babies and husbands and having a full life, *blah blah blah.*[58]

As Brigid Cherry has written elsewhere in this volume, AH enables fans to correct what they see as the deficiencies of the text, as well as allowing them to engage with the socio-cultural and socio-political experiences of the real world. mskathy's voicing of 'typical' concerns from and about homosexuals reflects the attitudes faced by many gay and lesbian people in the 'real world', and acts as a commentary on the concerns fans and critics have raised with regard to *Twilight*'s attitude to homosexuality. The disregard of gay and lesbian relationships in a text as mainstream and as popular as *Twilight* can be damaging to the position of homosexuality in the world outside of the novels. Indeed, the very fact that mskathy's Bella specialises in civil rights cases suggests that the author, unlike Meyer, is aware of the issues surrounding not only homosexuality, but race and gender, coding this fic, amongst many others, as anti-*Twilight* in many respects.

mskathy also comments on the subject of same-sex relationships in *Double Date*: while Edward and Alice, and Bella and Jasper, appear to be in heterosexual relationships, each couple is also involved in a sexual and romantic relationship with the other – Edward and Jasper and Alice and Bella, as well as Bella and Edward and Alice and Jasper also being paired together in the course of the story. As Alice notes at the beginning of the fic, 'I don't think most "normal" people would have understood the relationship that Edward and I had, so I knew it was no use to explain the relationship Jasper, Bella, Edward, and I had,'[59] a comment that could also be applied to attitudes towards any non-heterosexual form of sexuality in the 'real' world. Bjorklund[60] has put forward the argument that slash furthers the feminist tenet of decreasing sexism and homophobia, and is 'a means whereby we may defy a wide variety of social conventions and taboos'.[61] This can be seen in *Double Date* through the unconventional relationship that exists between the protagonists:

> Now I had not only a beautiful friendship with Jasper, Bella, and Edward,
> I was lucky enough to have three people who loved me fiercely and would
> do anything for me.
>   The last thing holding me back from being truly happy with our relationship was that we didn't live together. Craving being around all three
> of them all the time, I wanted to fall asleep in the same bed and wake
> up to their beautiful, sparkling eyes. I even wanted to fight about the
> stupid things in life, like setting up a kitchen together with Bella, or
> where Jasper would have to park his precious Audi since Edward had two
> cars.[62]

As with *All Is Not Lost*, however, the relationship depicted here is presented
without comment or judgement: it exists, the characters are happy, and that is
all that matters. In comparison to *The Twilight Saga* (and indeed many real life
homosexual relationships) the relationship is simple and straightforward, and
judging from the comments the fic received, accepted as such by its readers.

Conclusion

Anne Kustritz warns that 'slash fiction is easy to trivialise and disregard as the
insignificant practice of a few pathological individuals, but in doing so, one
may bypass an activity with great potential'.[63] From the analysis of *Twilight*
slash and femslash stories, and the interviews with their authors in this chapter,
Kustritz's comment has hopefully been proved correct. Slash writers are in a
unique position to experiment with critiquing not only constructs of sexuality,
but also concepts of gender and religion. Writing in a patriarchal society, where
heterosexuality is the 'default', slash allows both writers and readers to examine
and subvert societal norms.

Cassie sees slash as 'more realistic, I think, where gender roles are concerned'.[64] She also notes that, unlike the series, inter-racial relationships are
more common in fan-fic. Heidi concurs, commenting that much fan-fic ignores
Twilight's chaste depictions of sexuality, but further adds that slash particularly
reconstructs sexuality more than other forms of fan-fic:

> It's just so easy to change the sexuality of the characters without them
> losing their canon traits. It makes me think that *Twilight* could have

been written in such a way that wasn't so restrictive. However, I think it depends a lot on the story. Since a lot of the writers of slash are heterosexual women, often the male characters read just like women, and I think that does a disservice to gay men and perpetuates stereotypes in the same way that *Twilight* does a disservice to women.[65]

Of course, slash is not without its problems, and extolling its virtues without analysing some of the issues raised would be to present a rather biased view of the genre. Slash relies upon the writer interpreting the canon text in a way other than that intended by the author, but for the story to be slash rather than an original creation, there must be more than a passing resemblance to the source text. In much *Twilight* slash, particularly femslash, this resemblance comes in the focus on family and children. Much like how the family occupies a large part of the source text, and representations of women and motherhood are based on Mormon values, the family in *Twilight* slash follows a similar pattern. In *Paper Moon* Esme is found in the kitchen; Alice desperately wants to have children; and Bella imagines a white wedding and house with picket fences. Similarly, in *Double Date*, Bella and Jasper have a child and the fic ends with Alice announcing she is pregnant. Even in slash, then, some societal gender norms still exist.

While slash writers are still subject to more derision from the mainstream media than those fic writers dealing with 'gen' or 'het',[66] they are, none the less, growing in number, bringing new and varied interpretations to the fore. ArcadianMaggie, a predominantly Jasper/Edward fic writer, explains her love of slash and reasons for involvement as numerous: 'You have the built in tension of cultural issues regarding homosexuality, romance without the unappealing formulaic male/female dynamic which makes many feminists' skin crawl, plus two hot guys getting it on.'[67] While this echoes debates around slash that have taken place in the academic world, Maggie's comment also illustrates the awareness these writers have of the ways in which slash can examine and reconstruct the problematic issues of the canon text.

For a series such as *Twilight*, where female sexuality is coded as largely dangerous and negative, homosexuality ignored and religious teachings played out upon the screen, slash can hold a mirror up to society and ask us to reconsider whether the text's ideas are relevant or desired. *Twilight* slash writers reconstruct ideas of religion, gender and sexuality – ideas limited by Meyer, whether on the page or on the screen – by writing characters and stories which are limited only by the writer's imagination.

Notes

1. The title for this chapter is derived from Shoshanna Green, Cynthia Jenkins and Henry Jenkins' chapter on slash, 'Normal Female Interest in Men Bonking: Selections from the *Terra Nostra Underground* and *Strange Bedfellows*', in Cheryl Harris and Alison Alexander (eds), *Theorizing Fandom: Fans, Subculture, and Identity* (Cresskill, NJ: Hampton Press, 1998).

2. Fan-fiction ('fan-fic' or 'fic') is writing by amateur fans based on a particular text, using its situations or characters in different ways (Juli Parrish, 'Inventing a universe: Reading and writing Internet fan fiction', e-thesis, University of Pittsburgh (2007); Henry Jenkins, *Textual Poachers: Television Fans and Participatory Cultures* (London: Routledge, 1992); Sheenagh Pugh, *The Democratic Genre: Fan Fiction in a Literary Context* (Bridgend: Seren Books, 2005)). Slash is a genre of fan-fic that posits a homoerotic relationship between two characters. The genre takes its name from the '/' symbol that separated the names of Kirk and Spock, the first slash pairing (Constance Penley, 'Feminism, Psychoanalysis, and the Study of Popular Culture', in Lawrence Grossberg, Cary Nelson and Paula A. Treichler (eds), *Cultural Studies* (New York: Routledge, 1992)). Slash is most commonly written about male pairings, although slash written about female/female pairings (referred to as 'femslash') also exists.

3. Camille Bacon-Smith, *Enterprising Women: Television Fandom and the Creation of Popular Myth* (Philadelphia: University of Pennsylvania Press, 1992).

4. Jenkins, *Textual Poachers*.

5. Patricia Lamb and Diana Veith, 'Romantic Myth, Transcendence, and *Star Trek* Zines', in Donald Palumbo (ed.), *Erotic Universe: Sexuality and Fantastic Literature* (New York: Greenwood Press, 1986).

6. Ibid., p. 254.

7. Penley, 'Feminism, Psychoanalysis, and the Study of Popular Culture'.

8. Ibid., p. 484.

9. Christine Scordari, 'Resistance Re-examined: Gender, Fan Practices, and Science FictionTelevision', *Popular Communication* 1 (2003), pp. 111–31.

10. Bacon-Smith, *Enterprising Women*; Green, Jenkins and Jenkins, 'Normal Female Interest in Men Bonking'.

11. Ibid.

12. Penley, 'Feminism, Psychoanalysis, and the Study of Popular Culture'; Green, Jenkins and Jenkins, 'Normal Female Interest in Men Bonking'; Mirna Cicioni, 'Male Pair-bonds and Female Desire in Fan Slash Writing', in Cheryl Harris and Alison Alexander (eds), *Theorizing Fandom: Fans, Subcultures and Identity* (Cresskill: Hampton Press, Inc., 1998).

13. Henry Jenkins, 'Fan Fiction as Critical Commentary', *Confessions of an Aca/Fan*, 27 September 2006a, http://www.henryjenkins.org/2006/09/fan_fiction_as_critical_commen.html (accessed 17 December 2010).

14. Sara Gwenllian Jones, 'The Sex Lives of Cult TV Characters', *Screen*, 43 (2002), pp. 79–90.

15. Lamb and Veith, 'Romantic Myth, Transcendence, and *Star Trek* Zines'.

16. An aca-fan or scholar-fan is an academic who identifies as a fan, as popularise by Matt Hills in *Fan cultures* (London: Routledge, 2002).

17. John Tulloch and Henry Jenkins (eds), *Science Fiction Audiences: Watching* Doctor Who and *Star Trek* (New York: Routledge, 1995).

18. Jenkins, *Textual Poachers* and 'Fan Fiction as Critical Commentary'.

19. A non-canonical pairing is a romantic pairing that is contrary to what appears in the source text. Canon pairings in *Twilight* include Edward/Bella and Alice/Jasper; while non-canon pairings include Edward/Jacob, Alice/Bella, Charlie/Esme.

20. For further discussion on how AH fic is used by fans to reconfigure the relationship between Edward and Bella, see Brigid Cherry, 'Defanging the Vampire: Projected Interactivity and All-Human Twilight Fan-fic' in this collection.

21. Issues surrounding relationships between an adult and a minor, for example, which, while touched upon in an almost paedophilic way (Natalie Wilson, *Seduced by* Twilight: *The Allure and Contradictory Messages of the Popular Saga* (Jefferson, NC: McFarland & Co., 2011), p. 58) in the series, are, on the whole, depicted in relation to societal norms in *Twilight* slash.

22. Lev Grossman, 'Stephenie Meyer: A New J. K. Rowling?', *Time Magazine*, 24 April 2008, http://www.time.com/time/magazine/article/0,9171,1734838,00.html (accessed 3 February 2011).

23. Lindsey Averill, 'Un-biting the Apple and Killing the Womb: *Genesis*, Gender and Gynocide in Stephenie Meyer's *Twilight* Series', paper presented at the 2010 Joint Conference of the National Popular Culture and American Culture Associations, St Louis, Missouri, 31 March–3 April 2010, p. 8.

24. Wilson, *Seduced by* Twilight, pp. 140–8.

25. Cassie, personal communication, 30 April 2011.

26. Jenkins, *Textual Poachers*, p. 23.

27. For further discussions on race and colonialism see Kirkland and Bacon in this collection.

28. Jenkins, *Textual Poachers*, p. 206.

29. The only references to homosexuality that we see in the *Twilight* series come in the form of homophobia, for example when Leah teases Jacob about his goodbye to Quil, saying, 'Thought you were going to make out with him' (Stephenie Meyer, *Breaking Dawn* (New York: Little, Brown, 2008), p. 265. Emphasis in original).

30. Cassie, personal communication, 11 May 2011.

31. Imprinting is the means by which the Quileute shape-shifters find their soul mates. Once someone imprints (an involuntary action), the bond between the imprinter and imprintee becomes more important than any other relationship the imprinter may have.

32. Cassie, *Toeing the Line*, Fan Fiction.net, 21 December 2010, http://www.fanfiction.net/s/6360112/1/Toeing_the_Line (accessed 19 February 2011).

33. skargasm, personal communication, 30 May 2011.

34. Lydia Kokkola, 'Virtuous Vampires and Voluptuous Vamps: Romance Conventions Reconsidered in Stephenie Meyer's *Twilight* Series', *Children's Literature in Education* 42/2 (2001), p. 6.

35. Mormon doctrine teaches that 'we' existed as spiritual beings before birth. This gave rise to what Tyler Chadwick calls the 'folk doctrine of pre-mortal coupling' ('Where

Twilight Meets Mormon Studies,' *A Motley Vision: Mormon Arts and Culture,* 2 December 2009, http://www,motleyvision.org/2009/twilight-meets-mormon-studies (accessed 19 January 2011)) where male and female spirits promise to find each other on Earth and marry for eternity.

36. Cassie, *Toeing the Line.*
37. Catherine Tosenberger, 'Homosexuality at the Online Hogwarts: Harry Potter Slash Fanfiction', *Children's Literature* 36 (2008), p. 193.
38. Cassie, personal communication, 30 April 2011.
39. Henry Jenkins, 'How to Watch a Fan-Vid', *Confessions of an Aca/Fan,* 18 September 2006b, http://henryjenkins.org/2006/09/how_to_watch_a_fanvid.html (accessed 17 October 2011).
40. Ibid.
41. skargasm, personal communication, 21 May 2011.
42. Wilson, *Seduced by* Twilight, ch. 7, for an in-depth analysis of class and race in the *Twilight* series.
43. Jenkins, 'How to Watch a Fan-Vid'.
44. Grossman, 'Stephenie Meyer: A New J. K. Rowling?'
45. Cf. Green, Jenkins and Jenkins, 'Normal Female Interest in Men Bonking'; Cicioni, 'Male Pair-bonds and Female Desire in Fan Slash Writing'.
46. mia also comments that she blames the interactions of the actors behind the scenes for her reading of homosexual connections between the characters (*Toeing the Line* Trailer, *LiveJournal,* 27 February 2011, http://mia-dcwut-09.livejournal.com/90230.html (26 October 2011)). While I do not have the space to cover real-person slash in this chapter, it does exist as a genre of fan-fic in *Twilight* fandom, and events such as Robert Pattinson kissing Taylor Lautner at the 2011 MTV Movie Awards result in the production of more real-person slash as well as cementing fans' readings of a homoerotic subtext in the films. For further discussion of real-person slash, see Nia Edwards-Behi, 'That's not my Judesie!': *Sherlock Holmes* (2009) and Real-Person Fanfiction', *Erotic Adaptations: A One-Day Symposium,* De Montfort University, Leicester, 26 January 2011.
47. Cassie, *Toeing the Line.*
48. Elven, personal communication, 10 May 2011.
49. Cassie, *All Is Not Lost,* Fanfiction.net, 12 May 2011, http://www.fanfiction.net/s/6985279/1/All_Is_Not_Lost (accessed 19 February 2011).
50. Ibid.
51. Wilson, *Seduced by* Twilight, p. 114.
52. mskathy, *Acceptance,* Fanfiction.net, 2 September 2009, http://www.fanfiction.net/s/5350277/1/Acceptance (accessed 19 February 2011).
53. Ibid., p. 85.
54. See, for example, Rana's chapter in this volume.
55. Heidi, personal communication, 16 May 2011.
56. mskathy, *Paper Moon,* Fanfiction.net, 10 July 2008, http://www.fanfiction.net/s/4743181/1/Paper_Moon (accessed 19 February 2011).
57. Bella's dislike of parties is evident in the canonical text as well, illustrating how fan-fic uses the canon as a springboard – retaining some elements and discarding others.

58. mskathy, *Paper Moon*.

59. mskathy, *Double Date*, Fanfiction.net, 3 January 2009, http://www.fanfiction.net/s/4768223/1/Double_Date (accessed 19 August 2011).

60. Edi Bjorklund, 'Thinking About Slash/Thinking About Women', *Nome* 11 (1988), pp. 30–9.

61. Ibid., p. 38.

62. mskathy, *Double Date*.

63. Anne Kustritz, 'Slashing the Romance Narrative', *Journal of American Culture* 26 (2003), p. 383.

64. Cassie, personal communication, 26 May 2011.

65. Heidi, personal communication, 27 May 2011.

66. 'Het' is short for heterosexual pairings, and is used to describe stories which contain heterosexual depictions of romantic or sexual relationships. 'Gen' is a shortened form of 'general' in which romance and sex are consigned to the background, if written about at all.

67. ArcadianMaggie, personal communication, 23 May 2011.

ABOUT THE CONTRIBUTORS

Mark Richard Adams is working towards his PhD at Brunel University, where he is researching issues surrounding fandom and resistance in regards to the revived series of *Doctor Who* and the fan-producers involved in its production. He has presented at several academic conferences on subjects including the relationship between public service broadcasting and commercial interests, the historical development of the authorship and queer monsters in the works of Clive Barker. The last of these three will feature in a forthcoming publication. Mark is one of the assistant editors of *Intensities: The Journal of Cult Media*. He has lectured in film and television, specifically speaking on *Doctor Who*, televisuality and the BBC. Mark's main research interests are fandom, audiences, queer theory and cult horror.

Simon Bacon is an independent scholar based in Poznan, Poland. He is currently leading a research project on 'Monsters and the Monstrous' for the independent research network Inter-Disiciplinary.Net. He is also the chief editor of the academic journal *Monsters and the Monstrous* and is co-editing a book on *Undead Memory: Vampires and Human Memory in Popular Culture*.

Brigid Cherry is a research fellow in communication, culture and creative arts at St Mary's University College, Twickenham, UK. Her research is focused on cult media and fan cultures, and she has recently published work on *Doctor Who* fans' responses to the return of the series and to changes in actor and production personnel, supernatural fan fiction, and cosplay and fan identity in the steampunk community. She has also written on Gothic TV, the female vampire in *Daughters of Darkness*, and *Doctor Who*'s Martha as an apostolic figure. She is currently working on a major project on fan handicrafting, and has published material on vampire knitting and *Doctor Who* handicrafting. Her film guidebook on *Horror* was published by Routledge in 2009, she is co-editor of *Twenty-First-Century Gothic* published in 2011, and had an edited collection on *True Blood* published by I.B.Tauris in 2012.

Wickham Clayton's completed PhD thesis for Roehampton University is on the aesthetics of the *Friday the 13th* film franchise. His contributions to collections include to *Tainted Love: Screening Sexual Perversities*, edited by Donna Peberdy and Darren Kerr (I.B. Tauris, 2012). Wickham is a published film critic and has also presented at multiple academic conferences in the UK, largely focusing on the form and structure of a wide range of texts within American cinema. Wickham is currently acting as a contributing co-editor, with Bethan Jones, for a special issue of the online journal *Intensities* focusing on transmedial adaptive relationships between film/television and board games. He is also contributing editor of a forthcoming collection utilising formalist analysis on Hollywood slasher films entitled 'From Hell's Heart, I Stab at Thee': Style and Form in the Hollywood Slasher. Wickham has developed two undergraduate Introduction to Film courses for Danville Community College in Virginia, USA, and designed the Silver Screen spring film series for Galaxy Cinema in Cary, North Carolina, USA beginning in 2007. Wickham's primary research interests are aesthetics, genre and the films of Woody Allen.

Nia Edwards-Behi is a PhD candidate at Aberystwyth University, where she is researching issues of changing taste formations through an analysis of the marketing and reception of four controversial films from the 1970s and their recent remakes. She contributes teaching to undergraduate modules on the horror genre, contemporary Hollywood and British cinema. She has recently presented conference papers on *The Twilight Saga*, *Sherlock Holmes*, *Straw Dogs* and Walter Benjamin. Forthcoming publications include a chapter on Dario Argento's *Tenebre*, and an edited collection on adaptations of *Sherlock Holmes*, with Mareike Jenner and Stephanie Jones. In addition to her academic pursuits, Nia is assistant director of the Abertoir Horror Festival, Wales' only festival to celebrate the horror genre, which takes place annually at the Aberystwyth Arts Centre.

Francesca Haig is an author and academic. She gained her PhD from the University of Melbourne, and is Senior Lecturer and Programme Leader in Creative Writing at the University of Chester. Her published articles address subjects ranging from pseudoscience to Shakespeare, but her principal research area is Holocaust fiction. She recently edited a special issue of the journal *Modernism/Modernity* (20/1) on Holocaust representations since 1975. Haig's novel, *The Fire Sermon* (the first in a trilogy) will be published in 2015 by Harper Voyager (UK) and Simon & Schuster (US). Her first poetry collection, *Bodies of Water* (Five Islands Press, 2006) was highly commended in the Anne Elder Award for the best first book of poetry in Australia. Her poetry has also been published in various national and international journals and anthologies, including *Motherlode*:

Australian Women's Poetry, 1986–2008 (Glebe, New South Wales, Puncher & Wattman, 2009). In 2010 she was awarded a Hawthornden Fellowship.

Sarah Harman is a PhD candidate at Brunel University's Screen Media Research Centre and has presented papers at international multidisciplinary conferences on the subject of femininity and film. She is assistant editor of *Intensities: The Journal of Cult Media,* and contributing co-editor of a journal special issue for *Sexualities* on *Fifty Shades of Grey.* She is also a member of the Onscenity Research Network and was co-organiser of the 2012 Sexual Cultures conference held at Brunel. Her research interests include feminism, gender, sexuality, adaptations, film, television and pornography.

R. Justin Hunt is a lecturer in Dance and Performance Studies at the University of Lincoln. He is also a producer and performer based in London and works across the intersection of queer studies and performance. He received his BA from Emerson College and his MA from the Tisch School of the Arts, New York University. He completed his PhD in 2012 at the University of Roehampton. Justin is currently working on a book project entitled *Looking for Sex in the Archive.*

Mark Jancovich is Professor of Film and Television Studies at the University of East Anglia, UK. He is the author of several books including *Horror* (London: Batsford, 1992) and *Rational Fears: American Horror in the 1950s* (Manchester: Manchester University Press, 1996). He is also the editor of several collections including *Horror, The Film Reader* (London and New York: Routledge, 2001); *Defining Cult Movies: The Cultural Politics of Oppositional Taste* (with Antonio Lazaro-Reboll, Julian Stringer and Andrew Willis, Manchester: Manchester University Press, 2003); and *Film and Comic Books* (with Ian Gordon and Matt McAllister, Jackson, Mississippi: University Press of Mississippi, 2007). He was also the founder of *Scope: An Online Journal of Film Studies*; is series editor (with Eric Schaefer) of the Manchester University Press book series, Inside Popular Film; and is series editor (with Charles Acland) of the Berg/Continuum book series, Film Genres. He is currently writing a history of horror in the 1940s.

Bethan Jones is a PhD candidate at Cardiff University's School of Journalism, Media and Cultural Studies. Her thesis, which adopts Stuart Hall's model of encoding/decoding to examine how viewers engage with television fiction and its portrayal of gender, is tentatively titled 'The G Woman and the Fowl One: Fandom's Rewriting of Gender in *The X-Files*'. Bethan has written about gender in *Buffy the Vampire Slayer* and *The Twilight Saga;* fanmixes as fan-adopted paratexts; *Harry Potter* and social media; and erotic adaptations of *The X-Files.* Her work has been published in the *Journal of Creative Writing, Transformative Works and Cultures* and Deborah Mutch's collection, *The Modern Vampire and Human Identity.* Her research interests include participatory culture, gender, fandom, cult TV and fan activism.

Ewan Kirkland teaches film and screen studies at the University of Brighton. His research interests include videogames, children's culture and representations of gender, race and sexuality in the media. Publications in this area include articles on masculinity in horror videogames, heterosexuality in romantic comedy cinema, and whiteness in popular television. Other work includes articles on *The Powerpuff Girls*, *Battlestar Galactica*, *Buffy the Vampire Slayer*, *Dexter*, *Little Big Planet*, *Dora the Explorer* and the videogame series *Silent Hill*. In 2010 Ewan co-organised the first of a series of international conferences on images of whiteness, at Mansfield College, Oxford. He is currently researching constructions of monogamy and heteronormativity in science fiction cinema.

Judith Kohlenberger studied English and American Studies, specialising in American Cultural Studies, at the University of Vienna, Austria, and currently holds a PhD Fellowship at the Austrian Academy of Sciences. Her diploma thesis on contemporary American cinema was awarded the annual Fulbright Prize in American Studies and the 2010 Academic Excellence Award by the Austrian Federal Ministry of Science. She is currently working on her PhD thesis, which explores legitimatory discourses of science in American popular culture. Her research interests include European Romanticism and Gothic fiction, cultural and literary theory, gender studies as well as hemispheric approaches to the Americas.

Ruth O'Donnell gained her PhD in Media Arts from Royal Holloway, University of London in 2012. The subject of her doctoral dissertation was the star persona of Tom Cruise. In addition to dark romance, her research interests include star studies, psychoanalysis and representations of masculinity in Hollywood film.

Marion Rana is Chief Editor of *interjuli* (www.interjuli.de), a scholarly magazine on international research in children's literature. She studied British and American Studies, Pedagogy and Political Science at the Johannes Gutenberg University in Mainz, Germany and the University of Chichester in the UK. She has recently completed her PhD thesis, entitled 'Disruptive Desire: Sexuality in Young Adult Literature'. Her most recent publications deal with (national and cultural) Othering and Otherness in the *Harry Potter* series, the *Twilight* films as ambiguous tales of sexuality and sexual awakening, and the eroticisation of sexual and domestic violence in *Twilight* and *Vampire Diaries*.

Caroline Ruddell is Lecturer in Film and TV Studies at Brunel University. She has published on witchcraft in television, anime, Rotoshop and the representation of identity on-screen. Caroline is currently researching the Gothic and fairytale in popular film and television, and split personality on-screen. She is reviews editor for the Sage publication *Animation: An Interdisciplinary Journal* and sits on various editorial boards.

Natalie Wilson teaches Literature and Women's Studies at Cal State University San Marcos. Her areas of specialization include feminist theory, popular culture, women's literature, militarism, pedagogy, and activism. Natalie has written *Seduced by Twilight*, a book examining the *Twilight* cultural phenomenon from a feminist perspective, and co-edited *Theorizing Twilight*, both published by McFarland Press in 2011.

INDEX